# The June 1967
# Arab-Israeli War

# The June 1967 Arab-Israeli War
# Miscalculation or Conspiracy?

edited by Elias Sam'o

with a foreword by Eqbal Ahmad

Medina University Press International
Wilmette, Illinois 60091
1971

Published by Medina University Press International
908 Ashland Avenue
Wilmette, Illinois 60091

Manufactured in the U.S.A.

Elias Sam'o is Assistant Professor of Political Science
at Central Michigan University

# Contents

*v*

# FOREWORD

When Dr. Elias Sam'o invited me to introduce his anthology to the public, I hesitated despite my respect for his keen grasp and balanced views on the Arab-Israeli conflict. Since the War of June 1967 several anthologies had already appeared in English. I wondered if another anthology could be substantially different enough from its predecessors to justify publication. Hence I wished to see the manuscript before committing myself to writing a foreword. It impressed me as an unusual anthology for reasons of its compactness, the objectiveness which appears to have guided the editor's selections, and the assumptions which have determined the structure of the book. In addition, the editor's two original contributions, instead of summing up the selected documents, are fresh analyses which put the preceding material in a newer perspective and bring us up to date with the latest development in a seemingly unresolvable political tragedy.

This, to my knowledge, is the first anthology by an Arab scholar which includes a Zionist-Israeli view on the conflict. This is an important fact for it reflects the changing attitudes and the growing maturity of the Arabs' desire to understand Israeli positions and policies. Even more significant is the fact that Dr. Sam'o, whose people have been widely portrayed as being driven only by the emotions of hate and revenge, has not caricatured the Israelis by giving us an extreme or strident Israeli position. He does not present to us even the majority Israeli position, which is that of the Zionist government and which would not accept withdrawal from territories occupied in 1967 and a modicum of justice to the Palestinians as a price of peace with its neighbours. Instead he has selected Simcha Flapan, a dissenting leader in Mapam, editor of *New Outlook*, and one of the few Israeli personalities who concede the genuineness of at least some of the Arab's grievances, and regard actual rather than rhetorical mutuality of concessions as being a necessary condition for peace. I believe that this choice reflects the growing Arab desire to hear the voice of reason and reconciliation from Israelis and the Jewish people.

One hopes that instead of caricaturing Arab opinion by concentrating on the most strident of Arab rhetoricians, the Israelis also would seek to understand the anguish of the Arabs , particularly of the Palestinians, and their quest for justice and restoration of lost rights. A solution to this tragic debacle between a kindred people would come only when the Jewish and Arab communities in Palestine would begin to seek their cultural and political expression in a relationship of mutual respect and creative cooperation. For this reason one wishes that instead of entering into the endless controversy over who was responsible for the June War, Simha Flapan had taken seriously Isaac Deutscher's courageous critique of Israelis as well as Arabs and discussed the "binationalist" and peace seeking trends he mentions toward the end of his article.

The structure of this anthology accurately reflects the realities of the Arab-Israeli conflict. Apologists of imperialism have tended to portray it as a clash of two competing nationlisms. Yet no one denies that the significance and special risks of the Arab-Israeli confrontation owe to the fact that from the beginning it has been a central focus of international power struggle. Correctly then, the book presents views from the West, U.S.S.R., Israel, the Arab World, and the United Nations - the five main players in the development and continuation of a conflict which has cost the Palestinian people their homeland and produced three wars in two decades.

A Palestinian voice is conspicuous by its absence in this volume. That too reflects the realities of power in the Middle East, and accurately expresses the situation of the Palestinian people whose existence as a nationality Israeli leaders and governments have consistently refused to recognize. In the cruel game whose rules, or lack of them, Dr. Elias Sam'o has outlined with insight and accuracy, only the Palestinians have been mere pawns. Dispossessed, displaced, and discriminated against in Israel, in Jordan, and in the occupied territories, they are without the power to force themselves as players in the game that decides their destiny, and denies their right to live as free men in a land that was their home for centuries.

Dr. Elias Sam'o's essay portraying the reversal of Nasser's situation suggests that by reason of their backwardness and disunity the Arabs in general have been subsidiary actors and victims if not exactly the pawns in this conflict. The significance of Abdel Nasser lay in the fact that by virtue of his personality and through bold, sometimes reckless, diplomacy he won for the Arabs the illusion of being full participants in the developments that affected their lives. The war in June destroyed much of that illusion. Consequently a period of introspection, agitation and growing instability is to be expected in the Arab World.

For reasons of the intelligence that has guided the selection of the articles and documents, for its structure which reflects the realities of the Arab-Israeli debacle, for the moderation and humanity which defines the editor's quest for understanding and a meaningful international dialogue on the subject, this anthology would be of particular use to students seeking an introduction to the Arab-Israeli War of June 1967 and its sequel.

Adlai Stevenson Institute of International Affairs              Eqbal Ahmad
Chicago, Illinois

# Introduction

Perhaps the most important event which took place in the Middle East in recent history, and certainly since the creation of the state of Israel, was the June 1967 War. It was not the first war between the Arabs and the Israelis, and very likely not the last; nevertheless, it has already had far-reaching consequences for the parties involved in the conflict and for those with major interests in the region.

First, the June 1967 War has resulted in the occupation, for the first time since the creation of the state of Israel, in 1948, of a substantial non-Palestinian Arab territory by the Israelis—an area which is approximately three times the size of Israel.

Second, whereas before the June 1967 War Israel was viewed by many Arab states as a source of irritation and discomfort, since then it has become more of a threat and a challenge to its neighbors. It is a threat not only because it is militarily superior but also because it has effectively occupied Arab territories with the intention of keeping a substantial amount of these territories permanently. The challenge stems from the fact that the Israelis have created a modern state which the Arabs envy and seek to emulate. The June War has made it clear that the Arab states, in order to deal effectively with Israel, must have to modernize their own societies. From the Arab perspective, if the Israelis can do it, so can the Arabs. This simple but elusive formula is what frustrates many Arabs today.

Third, Israel's swift and decisive victory and its ability to effectively control Arab territories and the people residing in them have forced many Arab states not only to reconcile themselves to the reality of Israel but also to realize that it has become a major power in the region. This realization has divided the Arab states on the question of peace with Israel. While some states—for example, Egypt and Jordan—have stated that under certain conditions they would accept a peaceful settlement with Israel, others—notably Syria, Iraq, and Algeria—have rejected any formula for peace that does not include the return of the Palestinians to their homeland.

Fourth, the Arabs' defeat, coupled with the destruction or the capture of most of their weapons, has placed them in a position of desperate need for new, sophisticated weaponry to restore their shattered pride and sense of security. Their dependence on the Soviet Union for military hardware and political support has limited their options in international politics.

Fifth, the Àrabs realize now that United States commitment to the existence and well-being of Israel is beyond question. Thus, for the Arabs, the antagonist is not the "little" state of Israel but the most powerful state in the world—the United States.

For the Israelis, the consequences of the war and the lessons they learned are significant. First, their swift and decisive victory on the battlefield has not brought them peace and security. If anything, the last Arab defeat has raised the national consciousness of the Arab masses and has brought about a greater feeling of determination to recover their losses.

Second, Israel's further occupation of Arab territories and control of a large number of Arab people have raised intense debate in Israeli society with regard to the future of these people and their territories. It has also created a fear among some Israelis that their society, subjected to external pressure for compromise and internal dissention, might be moving toward militarism.

Third, the Israelis have realized, due to super-power involvement and competition in the region, that their military superiority not only is incapable of providing them with adequate security but also has limited their options *vis-a-vis* their adversaries.

These are some of the major consequences of the June 1967 War. As for the super powers who participated in the conflict by proxy, there has been a major change in their roles and a deepening of their involvement in the conflict. The roles played by the United States and the Soviet Union during the first Arab-Israeli war in 1948 were minor, and during the Suez War, in 1956, they found themselves on the same side. However, in the 1967 crisis they were not only on opposite sides, each supporting an adversary in the conflict, but there developed the possibility of a super-power collision, which neither side wanted but none was sure of preventing. Thus, it can be said that the two super powers have recognized that both have vital interests in the Middle East and major stakes in the outcome of the conflict.

Though these are significant changes resulting from the June War, it is too early to assess the full impact on the political, social, and economic institutions of the involved countries. Many of the books which have been published about the Arab-Israeli conflict in general and the June War in particular present a biased point of view, either pro-Israeli or pro-Arab. This book, which is a collection of previously published articles by specialists on the Arab-Israeli conflict, an original article by the editor and a co-authored one, present not only the views of the two parties to the conflict—Arabs and Israelis—but also Western, Soviet, and United Nations views.

The purpose of this book is threefold. First, the Arab-Israeli conflict, having been present for several decades, will continue to be the focal point in Middle Eastern politics and a major international conflict for some time. The contributors analyze, from different perspectives, the general origins as well as the specific causes of the June War. They also speculate on the future of the conflict and present various alternatives for its peaceful settlement.

Second, this book brings into focus the views and roles of the parties directly involved in the conflict—the Arabs and Israelis—as well as those of the parties indirectly involved—the United States, the Soviet Union, and the United Nations.

Third, my article raises, on the theoretical level, the possibility of a tripartite collusion between the United States, the Soviet Union, and Israel.

Finally, the last essay in the book traces some of the major developments in the conflict which have occurred since the June War.

The book is divided into six parts. Part One, entitled "An Arab View," contains an article by Hisham Sharabi, Professor of Government at Georgetown Universtiy. In this article, "Prelude to War: The Crisis of May—June 1967," Professor Sharabi traces the development of the main events taking place in the Middle East leading to the outbreak of hostilities. He notes, "In May and June, 1967, the U.A.R. was not prepared to go to war." Therefore, President Nasser, having achieved a diplomatic victory, was seeking a way to avoid war. Conversely, the author further notes, "Israel's real intention was not to 'damp' the crisis or 'defuse' it. The problem for Israel's leaders was to choose the appropriate moment to strike." For the Israelis, the anticipated rewards of military action against the Arabs exceeded those which would be incurred from diplomatic negotiations. The author attributes Israel's behavior during the crisis to the basic assumptions underlying its policy toward the Arabs. He notes that Israel's policy toward the Arabs is "predicated on the belief that the all-consuming passion of one's enemy is to destroy it; only his realization of Israel's invincibility and of his own vulnerability prevents him from doing so." The author concludes his article with an analysis of the causes behind the Arabs' failure.

Part Two, entitled "Western Views," comprises three articles written by Western scholars which represent three prevalent views on the Arab-Israeli conflict with particular emphasis on the June 1967 War. The first, written by Charles W. Yost, former United States Ambassador to the United Nations, to Laos, to Syria, and to Morocco, is a neutral and objective view that recognizes a degree of justice in the positions of both sides in the conflict. The author sets the factual background by reconstructing and recounting the events which culminated in the outbreak of war on June 5, 1967, between the Arabs and the Israelis. His main thesis is that neither the Arabs nor the Israelis plotted, planned, or intended to start a war in the spring of 1967. "It seems," he suggests, "more likely that they blundered into it."

The second article presents a pro-Israeli view. The author, C. B. Marshall, formerly Professor at the School of Advanced International Studies at the Johns Hopkins University, defends Israeli policies, citing the need for Israeli security and national survival against a menacing threat of Arab aggression. The core of the problem, according to Marshall, is the Arabs' refusal to concede Israel's right to exist. In the face of the Arabs' refusal to recognize this right and their determination to destroy the state, the author notes that the Israelis had no choice but to take actions to prevent the Arabs from destroying them.

Unlike the previous and the following authors, who blame both the Arabs and the Israelis for precipitating the war, Marshall pins the blame on the Arabs and their sponsors, the Russians. His only reservation about Israel's policies preceding the war is that "perhaps Israel aggravated the probability of war by too long mitigating defiance with deference." As for the Arabs, whom the author refers to as intransigents and Russian clients, they are the ones to blame for the outbreak of hostilities because they have for too long defied and refused to recognize Israel. The immediate blame for the outbreak of the war, according to Marshall, should be placed on Nasser for his actions during the weeks preceding the beginning of hostilities.

The third article, an interview with the late Isaac Deutscher, presents a view sympathetic to the Arabs. Deutscher considers the creation of the state of Israel in 1948 by European Jews to have constituted an injustice to the Palestinian people. He does not, however, question the right of Israel to exist as a sovereign state. Conceding this point, he is, nevertheless, critical of both Israel's refusal to rectify the injustices its creation has inflicted upon the Palestinian people and Israel's aggressive and expansionist policy.

Isaac Deutscher, specialist on Marxist and Soviet affairs, literary critic, political commentator, and economist, holds that all the parties involved— the Arabs, the Israelis, the Americans, and the Russians—are collectively responsible for precipitating a war which, according to him, "aggravated all the old issues and created new, more dangerous ones." The author considers the war a part of American imperialistic offensive over vast areas of Asia and Africa.

The Russians, according to Deutscher, were " bunglers,," and their policy was "muddleheaded." He blames them for having excited the fears of the Arabs, encouraging them to make risky moves. He further notes that the Arabs "cannot go on denying Israel's right to exist" and indulging in "bloodthirsty rhetoric" about "wiping Israel off the map." He is also critical of Nasser's declaration to blockade the Straits of Tiran, which "was a provocative move though practically of very limited significance." The author is particularly critical of Israel's "doctrine" *vis-a-vis* the Arabs which "holds that Israeli security lies in periodic warfare which every few years must reduce the Arab states to impotence." On the contrary, the author contends that Israel's desire for security through victorious wars has achieved the reverse.

Part Three, entitled "An Israeli View," consists of a long article written by Simcha Flapan, one of the editors of and frequent contributor to the Israeli periodical *New Outlook*. In this article, entitled "The Arab-Israeli War of 1967: A Reply to Isaac Deutscher," the author's primary goal is to refute Deutscher's arguments about the causes of the June 1967 War.

After complimenting Deutscher for having "a sharp observing eye, a clear exposition, and a passionate dedication to the cause of socialism," the author accuses him of "oversimplifications which obscure certain rather important aspects of the problem." He further notes that Deutscher, "when speaking of Israel . . . abandons all pretensions to objectivity and displays a vehement bitterness and disgust," and "his partisanship is simply revolting." Having said this, the author sets out to show that Deutscher's analysis of Israel's relations with the United States, as well as his study of the war, are inaccurate.

Contrary to Deutscher's assertion that Israel, in its war against the Arabs, was playing the role of an agent of American imperialism, the author notes that the U.S. changed its position during the development of the crisis "from open support of Israel and hostility to the Egyptian and Syrian governments to complete neutrality and the desire to reach an agreement with Nasser." In fact, the author continues, "if the United States sought to exploit the Israel-Arab conflict to serve imperialist policies, its real ally remains Arab feudalism, reaction, and capitalism, with which the U.S. shares $6 billion of petroleum revenue each year."

According to Flapan, it was Nasser, not Israel or the U.S. who triggered the crisis because his government was faced with domestic difficulties as well as with difficulties throughout the Arab world. Having taken measures unacceptable to Israel, Nasser "proved incapable of controlling the situation and ending the crisis by any political compromise whatsoever."

In conclusion, the author notes that, "even after its great victory, Israel remains a minority within the Arab world—that is to say, the weaker side whose existence is definitely not assured; while the Arab world, not withstanding its momentary setback, has its whole future ahead of it."

Part Four, entitled "Soviet Views," contains two selections. The first is a speech by Aleksei Kosygin, Chairman of the Council of Ministers of the Union of Soviet Socialist Republics, delivered on June 19, 1967, to the United Nations General Assembly during its Fifth Emergency Special Session. Following some introductory remarks concerning the urgency of preventing an outbreak of hostilities in the Middle East which could lead to a nuclear confrontation, the Soviet premier traces the development of the June 1967 crisis: "The facts irrefutably prove that Israel bears responsibility for unleashing the war, for its victims and for its consequences." He blames the Israeli "ruling circles" who have "conducted a policy of conquests and territorial expansion at the expense of the lands of neighbouring Arab States," as well as "certain imperialist circles." The premier holds Israel and those who stand behind it responsible for the dangerous situation in the Middle East. Then he warns Israel: "Attempts to consolidate the fruits of aggression will in the long run backfire against Israel and its people." He continues, "the Soviet Union will undertake all measures within its power . . . to bring about the elimination of the consequences of [Israeli] aggression."

The second selection, entitled "The Soviets; The Puppet," is an article attributed to a high Soviet Official. Unlike Premier Kosygin, who blames

Israel for precipitating the crisis, this official is very critical of President Nasser and his decisions to remove UNEF from Egypt and blockade the Gulf of Aqaba. The Soviet official further stresses that Nasser "committed the error" of believing that he had more time for diplomatic maneuvers than he actually had. Nasser, according to the author, also "made a major mistake in neglecting the military side of the crisis. It did not even occur to him to put his airfields in a state of alert." After the war broke out, the author continues, "the Egyptians mistakenly believed they could take the first punch thrown by the Israelis in ground fighting."

The Israeli victory, the author notes, has been very costly to Soviet prestige among the Arabs, but "there is only one great power that can help the Arabs recover from the disaster—the Soviet Union." As to how to recover from the disaster, his advice to the Arabs is "to launch a surprise air attack one day on the vulnerable territory of tiny Israel."

Part Five, entitled "The United Nations View," consists of the report of the Secretary General on "The Withdrawal of the United Nations Emergency Force." During the course of the May-June, 1967, crisis few individuals came under as much criticism as did U Thant for agreeing to withdraw UNEF from Egypt. The Secretary General's objective in presenting his report is, in his words, "to establish an authentic, factual record of actions and their causes." He further notes: "The emphasis here, therefore, will be upon facts. The report is intended to be neither a polemic nor an apologia. Its sole purpose is to present a factually accurate picture of what happended and why." He traces the developments which lead to the creation and the subsequent withdrawal of the force. He disagrees with the contention that the maintenance of UNEF in the area against the will of the government of the United Arab Republic could have solved the conflict or prevented its consequences. He notes that the consent and the active cooperation of the Egyptian government was essential for the creation as well as the effective operation of the force. To have told the Egyptian government that it could not unilaterally remove the force would have meant penalizing a government which had cooperated "with the international community . . . in the interest of peace." He stresses the point that "Israel in the exercise of its sovereign right did not give its consent to the stationing of UNEF on its territory and Egypt did not forego its sovereign right to withdraw its consent at any time."

Part Six, entitled "Interpretations," includes two articles. The first, entitled "The June 1967 War: Miscalculation or Conspiracy?" is written by the editor. This article is essentially an exercise in unconventional but conceptual thinking with regard to the developments leading to the June 1967 War. The May—June, 1967, crisis is divided into two periods. Using the game theory as a framework, the first period, which ended on May 22, 1967, was a zero-sum game played primarily by two players: Egypt and Israel. The second period, which began with Nasser's speech on May 22, 1967, declaring the closure of the Gulf of Aqaba to Israeli shipping was a non-zero-sum game played by three players: the United States, the Soviet Union, and Israel. In this game Nasser ceased to be a player and became a part of the pay-off. After analyzing the setting within which the crisis took place and the various interests of the United States, the Soviet Union, and Israel in the region, it seemed that defeating Nasser and, in the process, humiliating him with a decisive Israeli blow was in the interest of all three players. Thus, conceptually the crisis of May—June, 1967, produced a non-zero-sum game played by the three players in which cooperation among them would have maximized their gains. The cooperation could have been explicit or implicit.

The second article, entitled "Resolution 242 and Beyond," is written by the editor and Cyrus Elahi, both assistant professors of Political Science at Central Michigan University. The authors trace and analyze some of the major developments in the conflict since the June War. They analyze Security Council Resolution 242 which, it was hoped, "was to provide a general framework for a peaceful settlement of the conflict." Following an exploration of the various interpretations given to the "withdrawal clause" in the resolution, the authors note that "for Resolution 242 to be relevant and consistent as the basis for a viable settlement of the Arab-Israeli conflict, the withdrawal clause would have to mean total withdrawal." However, Israel rejects this "total withdrawal" and insists on the "partial withdrawal" interpretation. This rejection has given rise to three debates which the authors analyze. The first debate is taking place inside Israel; the second is between Israel and the United States; and the third is taking place in the United States between those who support the Israeli position and those who support the Rogers Plan. The authors conclude: "Until the Israelis agree to abandon their expansionist policies and begin to comply with international exhortation—based not on the illusion of omnipotence, but on what is feasible—the conflict will continue; for, the maximum offers of one side are less than the minimum demands of the other."

What is made clear in these selections is that there is no agreement among the authors as to the causes of the June, 1967 War. Each side tries to hold the other responsible for the outbreak of hostilities, while, in fact, all the parties in the conflict share the blame in varying degrees. The only major consensus among these authors, however, is that nobody won the war; for even Israel, having won a decisive victory on the battlefield, faces greater difficulties today, internally and externally, than it did before the war.


I would like to extend my deep appreciation to all those who helped in making this project possible. I am especially grateful to Dr. Eqbal Ahmad for writing the foreword, my colleague, Dr. Cyrus Elahi, and to Miss Hisako Shimura and Professor Ibrahim Abu-Lughod for their encouragement, constructive criticism, and advice. I am also grateful to Miss Bethalee Smith for typing part of the manuscript. The editor appreciates the kindness of all the writers and the publishers who have given permission to reproduce their material in this book.

Mt. Pleasant, Michigan                                      Elias Sam'o
July, 1971

# Part One

# An Arab View

# Prelude to War: The Crisis of May-June, 1967*

Hisham Sharabi

In early May, 1967, certain indications led many observers to believe that Israel was preparing for massive military action against Syria. Retaliatory action had been carried out against Syria a month earlier, on April 7, when Israeli air strikes were made only a few miles from Damascus. On November 13, 1966, massive action had been taken against the Jordanian village of Es Samu, in which a number of Jordanian civilians and soldiers were killed and a large part of the village was leveled. The cause of these attacks, according to official Israeli statements, was increasing Arab guerrilla activity on the Israeli side of the armistice line.

The crisis took shape as intelligence reports began to come in about Israeli troop deployment along the Syrian-Israeli border. On May 8, two Syrian intelligence officers arrived in Cairo and informed President Nasser of an impending Israeli attack against Damascus. Information concerning troop movements was corroborated by Lebanese sources. By May 10, according to Eric Rouleau, *Le Monde's* Cairo correspondent, President Nasser had become convinced that Israel was in fact making preparations to attack Damascus and overthrow the Ba'th regime. His view was confirmed when the Russians

*From Hisham Sharabi, "Prelude to War: The Crisis of May-June, 1967," in *The Arab-Israeli Confrontation of June, 1967*,. ed. Ibrahim Abu-Lughod (Evanston Ill.: Northwestern University Press, 1970), pp. 49-65, by permission of the publisher.

*3*

informed him that the Israelis had timed a swift strike at the Syrian regime for the end of May "in order to crush it and then carry the fighting over into the territory of the U.A.R." In Tel Aviv, Israeli leaders, including General Rabin, spoke publicly of attacking Damascus and demanded the immediate cessation of guerilla activity. The *New York Times* correspondent in Tel Aviv reported on May 12 that Israeli authorities had already decided that the use of force against Syria "may be the only way to curtail increasing terrorism." President Nasser believed, according to Rouleau, that the Israeli attack would take place within the next few days, on or about May 17.

In retrospect, it is ironic to note how Israel's actions in May, 1967, served to intensify precisely those conditions which they were supposed to alleviate. Israel was determined to put an end to the nascent Palestinian guerrilla movement. The Israeli leaders had begun to realize that the Palestinian Arabs were engaged in a serious effort at organizing themselves as an independent force and that a Palestinian revolutionary movement was afoot. El Fatah, the Palestinian liberation movement, now appeared as more than a mere handful of "infiltrators" and "terrorists." Israel, by persistently attributing resistance activity to Syrians, Egyptians, and Jordanians, had succeeded in obscuring the real nature of this activity as an autonomous Palestinian revolutionary movement. Israel's policy has been to refuse to acknowledge the existence of the Palestinian Arabs, referring to them simply as "the Arab refugees." This has enabled Israel to fight the guerrillas by means of retaliatory action against its neighbors in accordance with its basic strategic principle of always waging war on Arab soil, never on its own.

It is probably in large part because of the new dimension which the Palestinian guerrilla movement represented (as an *internal* movement of resistance it violated the fundamental principles upon which the concept of Israeli "defense" was based) that the reaction to increasing activity by El Fatah was so strong in early 1967. Israel's theory of punitive retaliation underwent radical transformation both in structure and goal. It was no longer sufficient to "teach its neighbors a lesson"; it was now necessary for Israel to impose its explicit will on them. Thus the retaliatory raid gave way to military strikes aimed at repressing or overthrowing recalcitrant and undesirable regimes. With this new policy Israel could kill two birds with one stone: it could destroy the Palestinian resistance movement in embryo and maintain "peace" and "stability" in the surrounding regimes. In May, 1967, the crisis gathered momentum as a direct result of Israel's intention to do something about the Ba'th regime in Damascus. This marked not only an escalation of Israel's political and military aggressiveness but also a self-conscious expansion of its role in the broader context of a United States Soviet confrontation in the Middle East.

Seen in this light, the situation in May looked ominous, even by Middle Eastern standards. For Israel's immediate neighbors it appeared that unless something were done they might have to submit to a new kind of threat from Israel. Their first obligation, however, with regard to Syria was to suppress the Palestinian movement in their midst.

Israel's new attitude implied another and equally serious warning. The U.S.S.R., as well as the other "progressive" states, was convinced that the overthrow of the Ba'th regime would seriously upset the balance of forces in the Arab world in favor of Zionism and its allies, the "conservative" regimes and colonialism. There was a general consensus among all revolutionary elements in the Arab world that the American-Israeli offensive in the area would have to be arrested. Syria was not the real issue but rather the symbol and immediate cause of the confrontation.

As in past years when collectively threatened, the Arabs turned to the U.A.R. and Gamal Abdul Nasser for guidance and leadership. In the U.A.R. events followed rapidly. The armed forces were put under a state of emergency on May 16; later the same day the commander of the United Nations Emergency Force (UNEF) in Sinai was handed a letter from General Fawzi, the chief of the Egyptian Armed Forces, asking him "to withdraw all U.N. troops immediately" from the Egyptian-Israeli border and from Sharm el-Sheikh. On May 18, U Thant gave orders to UNEF to withdraw from the U.A.R. He said he had serious misgivings about this move but could not refuse the U.A.R. "without putting into question the sovereign authority of the government of the United Arab Republic within its own territory." Foreign Minister Mahmoud Riad explained the same day to the representatives of the nations with troops in UNEF that the emergency force had completed its tasks and was no longer needed in the Gaza Strip and the U.A.R.

On the following day, May 19, Israel conveyed to the Western powers that it would fight any move to close Aqaba and cut off shipping. It maintained that former president Eisenhower had agreed that such an event would entitle Israel to rectify the situation with U.N. support. On May 22, in a speech given at air-force headquarters in Sinai, President Nasser announced the closure of the Straits of Tiran to all ships flying the Israeli flag or carrying strategic materials to Israel.

> We are now face to face with Israel, and if they want to try their luck without Britain and France we await them. The Israeli flag will not pass through the Gulf of Aqaba, and our sovereignty over the entrance to the Gulf is not negotiable. If Israel wants to threaten us with war, they are welcome.

On May 30 Jordan (followed later by Iraq) concluded a mutual-defense pact with the U.A.R.

It was probably at this point, or perhaps a day or two earlier, that the Egyptian president decided that the Israeli threat to Syria had abated sufficiently to allow him to de-escalate Egyptian military pressure. At a press conference on May 30, attended by representatives of the world's major newspapers and news agencies, he declared that the U.A.R. did not want war but that if attacked it would have to repel aggression. He suggested that the Palestine Mixed Armistice Commission be revived to supervise the phased withdrawal of Egyptian and Israeli forces from the armistice lines and offered to take the question of the Straits of Tiran to the International Court of Justice for adjudication. In an interview on June 3 with Anthony Nutting he emphasized that so far as the U.A.R. was concerned the Middle East crisis had eased and no further escalation was planned. He was reported to have given the impression that he shared the Soviet and French view that war should definitely be avoided. At the time that Nasser, and behind him the U.S.S.R., was seeking a way to avoid war. Israel had apparently opted for war.

In Amman on June 4, King Hussein warned Britain and the United States that they stood to lose their friends in the Arab world "forever" if they fell into the "Zionist trap." In Tel Aviv the appointment of Moshe Dayan as defense minister was welcomed by the Israeli army with the expectation that they would see more action. In Washington on June 4, a warm Sunday afternoon, the atmosphere was alive with rumors of an impending explosion in the Middle East.

In Tel Aviv, as well as in Washington, sufficient intelligence had been available to show with certainty that a pre-emptive strike by Israel would result in a swift Israeli victory which within days would bring about the collapse not only of the Ba'th regime in Damascus but also of Nasser in the U.A.R. When Israeli planes attacked shortly after sunrise on Monday, June 5, a new chapter was being written in the political life of the Arab world.

Looking back at Egyptian military and diplomatic moves in May and early June, one is struck by their overwhelmingly deterrent character. Note, for instance, the theatrical aspect of Egyptian troop movements through the main streets of Cairo in the middle of the day. An almost festive mood was generated by blatant broadcasts reporting every move of Egyptian troops in Sinai. From the beginning of the crisis the U.A.R. was making signals to dissuade Israel from going through with its threats against Damascus. The U.A.R. was addressing not only Israel but also the United States.

In May and June of 1967, the U.A.R. was not prepared to go to war. Some 50,000 Egyptian troops were committed to Yemen, including some of the best-trained soldiers. President Nasser had no illusions as to the military capability of the Arab world. Earlier at Port Said he had put it plainly:

> I am not in a position to go to war; I tell you this frankly, and it is not shameful to say it publicly. To go to war without having the sufficient means would be to lead the country and the people to disaster.

Nasser had read the report put out by the Institute for Strategic Studies in 1965 and probably agreed with its conclusions. In armor the Israelis could expect to knock out at least two Arab tanks for every one of their own, and in the air the "kill ratio" was two or three Arab planes to one Israeli plane.

The Israelis said they would regard the closing of the Gulf of Aqaba to Israeli shipping as an act of war. From the Egyptian standpoint this act was not considered to be irrevocable, nor was it thought to be an act that would inevitably lead to war. Nasser's judgment was that he enjoyed room to maneuver without getting too close to the brink. The problem of sovereignty over the gulf was far from settled by American assurances to Israel in 1957. At a news conference on July 16, 1957, Secretary of State John Foster Dulles had acknowledged the questionable status of the gulf.

> There is and always has been a difference of opinion about the international status of the Gulf of Aqaba. The Arab countries believe that the six-mile limit applies rather than the three-mile limit; and that, since the position of Israel on the Gulf is not fixed by any permanent boundary decision, Israel does not have the right to claim a voice in the access to the Gulf; and that, if the countries which do have permanent boundaries to the Gulf, namely, Egypt, Jordan, and Saudi Arabia, agree to close the Gulf, they think that they have the right to do it. There is a certain amount of plausibility from the standpoint of international law, perhaps, to those claims. This is not the view of the United States.

On May 24, 1967, President Nasser outlined to U Thant in Cairo the following points: the Straits of Tiran should be recognized as Egyptian territorial waters; Israel should fully accept the provision of the 1949 armistice agreement; the U.N. should be responsible for policing all frontiers and demarcation lines; and Israel should strictly observe the demilitarized zones. Nasser's intention was not to restore the *status quo ante bellum* obtained before the Israeli attack of 1956, but that of 1948. As his hand seemed to grow stronger, Nasser thought more and more in terms of the totality of the Palestine problem. In a speech to the Pan-Arab Workers Federation on May 26, he declared that "the Arabs insist on their rights and are determined to regain the rights of the Palestinian people;" on May 29, he told the members of the Egyptian National Assembly that "the question today is not of Aqaba nor is it the Tiran Straits or the United Nations Emergency Force. It is the rights of the people of Palestine."

President Nasser had achieved a diplomatic victory and was ready to negotiate a political settlement. It is not certain whether the Israeli leaders (or the White House for that matter) fully appreciated this element in the crisis. Now, perhaps for the first time since 1948, the Arab side was in a position to tackle a political settlement of the Palestine problem. The Egyptian president, spokesman for all the Arabs, was at this point capable not only of entering into negotiations but also of contemplating concessions hitherto unthinkable. The central problem was, of course, connected with the rights of the Palestinians. Nasser publicly made it clear that all other problems (including passage through the Suez Canal) were ancillary to the acknowledgment of the rights of the Palestinian Arabs.

As late as June 4, Charles Yost, United States special envoy to Cairo, observed, "There does not seem to have been any intention in Cairo to initiate a war." In an interview two days earlier (broadcast in part in the United States on the evening of June 4), President Nasser told British M.P. Christopher Mayhew that if the Israelis do not attack, "we will leave them alone. We have no intention of attacking Israel." The U.A.R. sent firm assurances to the United States to this effect and maintained a dialogue with Washington until the hour of the Israeli attack. During this week, agreement was reached on a proposed visit by U.A.R. Vice-President Zakaria Mohieddin to Washington and a subsequent return visit by Vice-President Hubert Humphrey.

According to Eric Rouleau, the *Le Monde* correspondent in Cairo, all the U.A.R. required to withdraw its troops from the frontiers was a public declaration by Israel renouncing its intention to attack Syria. It is probably true that both Washington and Tel Aviv were aware of this fact, but neither seemed willing to leave the U.A.R. with a strong hand. It is now obvious that for Israel the real problem was not one of security: a country which has demonstrated that it can dominate its neighbors militarily could not have entertained serious fears about its security. It seems certain that the Israeli leaders had full knowledge of the U.A.R. military condition (certainly the White House had) and Israel's military superiority was indisputable. It is also probable that the report submitted in late May to President Johnson by Pentagon analysts contained a forecast very close to the events which actually took place the week of June 5.

In this light, the events of the preceding days of crisis had favored Israeli interests. Indeed, the situation was slowly building up in a way that was giving Israel increasing freedom of action. In retrospect it is evident that Israel's real intention was not to "damp" the crisis or to "defuse" it. The problem for Israel's leaders was to choose the appropriate moment to strike. This decision was tied to certain preconditions. What were these preconditions? One, certainly, was a favorable world opinion siding with a "beleaguered little country" defending itself against numerically superior forces. On the diplomatic level, another was a disunited and neutralized United Nations. United States backing, or at least tacit approval of Israel's policy, was an essential precondition.

Did the United States give the green light to Israel? Was there American-Israeli collusion? After the outbreak of war, was there American assistance, or a promise of assistance in case things went wrong? Of course, definite answers to these questions cannot be given now and will have to await revelations which only time will make possible.

It is not surprising that President Nasser's signaled promises—withdrawal of troops, adjudication of the Aqaba question, political settlement of outstanding issues—were ignored. From Israel's standpoint, the anticipated rewards of military action certainly exceeded those of diplomatic negotiations. Israel acted, not spontaneously in fear or in anger, but calmly, in the light of careful calculations based on extensive intelligence and highly sophisticated analysis of the over-all political and military situation. For the Arabs, the cost was enormous: a crushing military defeat, with some 20,000 soldiers killed; over 500,000 new refugees, including 120,000 Syrians and 250,000 Egyptians; and occupation of the entire area from the Suez Canal to the Jordan River, as well as the Syrian Golan Heights, some thirty miles from Damascus.

How did the war start? Ambassador Yost expressed the view of many observers when he stated, "No government plotted or intended to start the war." The war was the product of circumstances beyond the control of any of the parties involved. But what were the conditions under which the situation went out of control? Why did Israel spurn a political settlement when this was possible? How can we explain Israel's overnight transformation from a supposedly threatened, helpless country to a conquering military power?

The answers to these questions are to be sought not in the crisis itself but in an analysis of Israel's over-all strategy.

Israel, like the United States, bases its strategy on the principle of total preparedness, on the theory of total force. It is a policy predicated on the belief that the all-consuming passion of a country's enemy is to destroy it; only the enemy's realization of Israel's invincibility and of its own vulnerability prevents it from doing so. Hence the overriding concern of this policy is to determine the costs required to maintain military superiority and to preserve a correct estimate of the enemy's awareness of and responses to this military position.

Israel can have only an aggressive policy, not just because of strategic considerations (small territory, long borders, population size, etc.), but also because it is rooted in a movement of colonization. It acts with the knowledge that in the eyes of its adversaries it is not a "state" but a usurper of conquered land. Its relationship with its adversary is thus based solely on force -a relationship which precludes any objective grounds of legitimation that might allow for bargaining in terms of a mutually acceptable "maximum." Settlement for Israel has to be enforced. In its view, the adversary should have only one position from which to bargain, that of the conquered. Precisely because of the lack of any binding legitimacy, the adversary has to be kept in a condition of constant and effective threat. This position necessitates an offensive posture not only in war but also in peace; a domination diplomacy becomes the condition of every nonmilitary approach. What are the aims of this diplomacy? They are, simply, to keep the adversary constantly on the receiving end, where he will always be eager to receive but always incapable of determining the price of what he receives. This is the substitute for legitimation which sets the relation between conqueror and conquered on a level where enforced equilibrium provides for the conqueror the promise of progressively increasing stability.

A distinctive characteristic of Zionist strategy is that it is directed not at resolving conflict but at protracting it. The resolution of conflict would necessarily require concessions and the relinquishing of gains forcibly acquired; it threatens not only to stifle an expansive orientation but also to undermine Israeli strategy at its inception. Thus a primary tactic of Zionist diplomacy is to bring about those conditions which would temporarily suspend conflict but which would introduce no radical change in the *status quo*. By disengagement, by creating distance and blocking or channeling contact, a *modus vivendi* is created out of a violently accomplished fact, and the conditions for an equilibrium which in time would bring about a sense of mutual benefit are set up. For the conquered the payoff is necessarily assessed in relative terms; hence, every little gain would represent a bonus and an incentive to acquiesce.

To Israel, attitudes of compromise on the Arab side (beginning with the Geneva Protocol of 1949) have always been a source of embarrassment and have always been spurned. President Habib Bourgiba's conciliatory position regarding the Arab-Israeli conflict, far from bringing relief to Tel Aviv, provoked profound discomfort in Israel's leadership circles. A compromising attitude on the part of Israel would require a radical transformation in its diplomatic-military thinking and a shift from offensive to conciliatory strategy. Israel is not yet prepared to make such a shift. It is probably correct to say that Israel needs some fifty years of friction and tension to enable it to build itself economically and establish strong and stable institutions capable of bringing about conditions of permanent equilibrium. Thus, from the standpoint of Israel's dominating diplomacy, the final resolution of conflict is possible only when the tactics of protracted conflict reach their limit and become irrelevant. This goal cannot be achieved until a position of domination has been reached and continuing conflict is no longer required to sustain equilibrium.

This diplomatic-military strategy must assign high priority to the policy of territorial expansion. Expansionism is an expression of a policy of force, but it is also a reaction to a "yielding environment." As Arthur Koestler (a former Zionist) put it, "A yielding environment acts as a vacuum, a constant incentive for further expansion." It may be necessary to add that beyond a certain point it would be disadvantageous for Israel to expand. What is the limit of Israeli expansion? Its final determination will depend mainly on the outcome of the diplomatic-military conflict; but the general outline of the territorial extent of the Jewish state has been adumbrated by various spokesmen since 1919. One of the more recent statements was made by the Israeli prime minister following the war of 1967 (as quoted by Rouleau in *Le Monde*):

> We are not disposed to give up one inch of our territory; negotiations must begin from the recognition of the existing territorial *status quo*. Palestine was cut up in the course of the First World War by the

Sykes-Picot Agreement; it was divided a second time by the creation of Transjordan by Churchill; and it was divided a third time in 1948. We cannot accept a fourth amputation. . . . No more than 20,000 kilometers are left of old Palestine. It is our hope that in the next few decades millions of Jews will be able to emigrate from Russia, Europe, and the United States.

The Suez Canal in the U.A.R., the Litani River in Lebanon, the Jabel Druz in Syria, and eastern boundaries of Jordan are the frontiers of a greater Israel which would be acceptable to all Israelis, from Gahal to the Zionist faction of the Communist Party. Israel's optimum policy would aim to surround itself with a ring of weak and subservient states-a Maronite state, a Druze state, a "Palestinian state," a Kurdish state,—extending from the Persian Gulf to the Mediterranean, and to enforce a *Pax Judaica* over the entire region.

A cardinal principle of the hard strategy which is at the basis of all Israeli political and military thinking is the necessity always to carry "defensive" war outside Israel's boundaries and never to allow its boundaries to be penetrated. (Guerrilla warfare and a "people's war of liberation," since they are not subject to this principle, are threats which require a different strategy.) Thus defensive war is necessarily preventive war. Israel cannot allow itself to give up the incentive to preempt territory, for it equates its security with its capacity at all times to anticipate and thwart the enemy's power of pre-emption. An important corollary of this strategic thinking is related to the problem of boundaries. So long as the objective possibilities for pursuing a hard strategy exist, Israel will seek to adjust its boundaries through territorial expansion. It has no other choice, given the external conditions of surrounding Arab weakness. Next to military preparedness, the question of boundaries constitutes the most important element of Israeli diplomatic-military strategy.

Under what conditions, in terms of this hard strategy, would Israel consider itself compelled to engage in all-out "defensive" (preventive) war? Precisely when the fundamental principles on which its hard strategy is based are violated: for example, when the U.A.R. (or any other neighboring Arab state) acquires new weapons which might upset Israel's position of unconditional viability; when its real or "distant" boundaries are seriously threatened as they were by Egyptian action in the Straits of Tiran; or when a nationalist revolutionary government takes over in Jordan or Lebanon. In the future Israel may also feel it necessary to launch a "defensive" war against its neighbors in order to put an end to Palestinian guerrilla activity. During periods of peace Israel has depended on circumscribed retaliatory expeditions following punitive threats as a primary weapon of limited action. In this situation the threat is to be regarded as a diplomatic weapon, decisive in the process of bargaining. Diplomacy, as a system of threats (and promises), gives way to retaliation or war only when it fails or when it breaks down. Short of military action, the threat of war, "punitive" or "defensive," is the crucial element dominating the course of conflict.

What makes the Israeli threat convincing and therefore effective? Or, viewed from the Arab standpoint, what makes the Israeli threat credible? To carry out a threat one must have the means at one's disposal and the will to use those means. If a threat is to be credible, a sufficient proportion of threats made must be carried out-enough that the party threatened will take all threats seriously. The efficacy of threats then lies in their power to elicit or at least greatly influence the performance of the threatened party in the desired manner.

Israel's strategic position focuses on four different levels: the first is concerned with Jordan, Syria, Lebanon, and Iraq; the second, with the Arab states in general, including those of North Africa; the third, with the U.A.R.; and the fourth, with the Palestinian Arabs. The latter two may be regarded as decisive, at least for the foreseeable future.

Israel's relation to the Palestinians is that of an occupying power to a conquered people. Dispossessed and in disarray, the Palestinians have lost all viability as a people. But out of total negation there has arisen a resistance which has now taken the form of organized total revolution. (In contrast, Arab opposition to Israel in North Africa and Arabia is still only potentially effective and in its present state stands at the opposite pole to the urgent actuality of Palestinian resistance.) Israel's position vis-a-vis Jordan, Syria, Lebanon, and Iraq is one of strength with the potential for domination. Only with respect to the U.A.R. is Israel's superiority conditional, placing the two states in a relationship of conditional viability toward one another. It is this mutually conditional viability which tends to make the Arab-Israeli conflict (on the formal military and diplomatic levels) primarily an Egyptian-Israeli conflict. The only real military threat to Israel is the U.A.R. Similarly, no decisive political action can be undertaken by Israel with respect to any other Arab state without the U.A.R.'s participation or tacit consent.

It is worth noting here that there exists a factor which could radically transform Israel's position with regard to the U.A.R. and its other Arab neighbors, but not necessarily with regard to the Palestinian guerrilla fighters. If Israel were to acquire an effective rocket system (for example, the MD680) together with a nuclear tactical weapons system, it would become unconditionally viable, and at the same time its neighbors, including the U.A.R., would be reduced to virtual impotence.

What would be the political consequences of such a situation? The acquisition of a similar weapons system by the U.A.R. would restore the balance of arms but would create a new situation-though still in Israel's favor. The neutralization of the conflict militarily would set it permanently against a strictly political background. Under these conditions the *fait accompli* becomes the core of the *status quo* and with time solidifies into permanent structures. It is at this point that Israel's hard strategy reaches its final limit and is transformed into a conciliatory strategy. The need for protracted conflict would no longer obtain.

Self-criticism after the Arab defeat tended to begin with the premise that in order to confront Israel the Arabs must acquire an advanced scientific and technological culture. The theoretical validity of this principle is obvious, but it lacks practical relevance to immediate problems. The situation of conflict is a concrete historical situation to which any desideratum, whether of mental attitude or of technological proficiency, is related only theoretically and in an abstract way. What is decisive to the outcome of conflict, particularly to a political-military conflict having immediate bearing on the fate of millions of people, is not *potential* power but rather available *actualized* power. Certainly, to be effective, especially in war, one has to modernize and acquire the requisite technological know-how, but can the Arabs modernize while they are locked in unequal combat? Can they, when their freedom of social and political action is threatened daily, plan even for modernization?

The Arabs' shortcomings are near at hand and can be seen plainly without much recourse to theoretical analysis. On the technical level the Arabs suffered in the June War from such things as miscalculation, faulty intelligence, inability to convey messages, and inadequate communication. Necessity may still bring to bear the required funds and energies to insure needed reforms. Response here is not to a desired goal that one sets up but to vital necessity. There is a qualitative difference in action animated by the will to survive and mere incentive to reform. The revolutionary element is set into motion by the first; the second comes in its train. In the end what is *available* in will, energy, and material resources is decisive for revolutionary change. Thus, what is concretely accomplished, and that alone, will determine Arab viability in the continuing conflict.

Three interrelated aspects of Arab diplomacy have contributed to the success of Israel's hard strategy. First, the Arab side, by the nature of its position, has had restricted or limited freedom of action on both diplomatic and military levels. This is plainly illustrated by the decisions and events of the critical days preceding the Israeli attacks on the U.A.R., Jordan, and Syria in June, 1967. The Arabs, incapable of devising a unified strategy , were incapable of carrying out a rational military plan. Because they could not admit the principle of compromise in the diplomatic field, they were always forced into a position of inflexibility and retreat before the highly mobile diplomacy of their adversary.

The Arab side denied itself the advantage of the political and diplomatic offensive by placing itself in a position where it could not make fundamental concessions. Israel, basing its policy on a hard strategy which also precluded basic concessions, was able to use Arab inflexibility to appear always willing to reach a reasonable settlement. The same structural limitation which has prevented the Arabs from seizing the political and diplomatic initiative has prevented them from seizing the military intiative. In the May—June crisis,

President Nasser's hand was from the very beginning greatly weakened by his adversary's knowledge that the U.A.R. was not likely to make a pre-emptive strike.

Arab diplomacy has always given Israel's hard strategy optimum advantages in both war and peace. In peace it has contributed to Israel's capacity to sustain the stable disequilibrium which has always worked in its favor, for it has served to consolidate the *fait accompli*. And in war it has enabled Israel to engage in "punitive" and "defensive" strikes which have hitherto allowed Israel to expand territorially and to establish the effective system of retaliatory threats that have safeguarded its gains.

Secondly, one must consider the inescapably "irrational." or at least only partly rational, character of the decisions and choices of Arab diplomacy. What we call the Arab side does not in reality constitute a single entity; it has no coordinated organizational arrangements, no unified political or military structure, no adequate communications and information systems. Inherent in Arab agreements is a multiplicity of conflicting decisions, desires, intentions; formal collective agreements lack substantive content and as a result have little practical import. Israel's dependence on this fragmentation of Arab will, and on its corresponding practical ineffectiveness, figures significantly in Israeli strategic thinking and action.

Finally, the Arab position is bound to a "radical" view of the Palestine question; this is at once a source of great strength and of great weakness. Arab opinion, official as well as popular, is founded on right as the basis of all claims to Palestine. From this perspective it is difficult to separate the ancillary problems from the central problem of right. Zionism, on the other hand, takes as its starting point the opposite position. It assumes a given *status quo* and ignores all historical perspectives. For the Arabs, all military effort ultimately aims at "restoring Arab rights in Palestine." In the Israeli perspective, this is equated with driving the Israelis into the sea. All Israeli effort, both military and political, seeks to preserve, consolidate, and expand the Zionist presence. It necessarily turns away from fundamental claims and focuses on the singular problem at hand. It knows that its cause is tactically best served by concentrating on individual problems—boundary adjustments, transit rights, shipping, hydraulic claims.

The May—June crisis thus signified different things to Arabs and Israelis. It was (as President Nasser put it) not the Gulf of Aqaba, the Suez Canal, or any other limited problem which was behind the crisis but the "right of the Palestinian Arabs to their land and homes." For the Israelis this was not the issue; in the logic of Israel's hard strategy all this belonged, as the question of Jerusalem does now, to the non-negotiable category of the conflict. What from the Arab standpoint constitutes the heart of the matter, for the Israelis constitutes the settled. and non-negotiable aspect of it. Their position on "right to land and home" has forced the Arab states to view problems ultimately in terms of fundamental human rights. While as a principle of political orientation this has greatly restricted Arab maneuverability, it has also preserved intact the Arab claim to Palestine. On the psychological level, and on the level of legality, this constitutes a major source of strength for the Arab side.

One minor point remains to be disposed of.American writers now and then advise the Arabs that they should submit to the facts of life and reconcile themselves to the existence of the Zionist state, "however unjust its creation appears to them," and that they would do well "not to threaten and harass . . . [Israel or] . . . arouse among their people false hopes about its dissolution." Arab writers have noted with irony that such advice comes from people whose country, to safeguard its security and prosperity, has seen fit to engage in wars thousands of miles away from its coasts. The war against Zionism, these writers say, far from aiming to preserve "security and prosperity" aims to pervent a new and vicious type of colonialism from enslaving the Arabs at home; furthermore, they point out, Arabs are defending themselves, not in some distant land, but on their own invaded soil.

# Part Two
# Western Views

# The Arab-Israeli War: How It Began*

Charles W. Yost

The Six-Day War in the Middle East grew out of the sterile confrontation to which the peoples of the region had committed themselves over the past twenty years. Each party had frequently proclaimed its intention to go to war under certain circumstances. It seems unlikely, however, that either of them plotted and planned war for 1967. It seems more likely that they blundered into it.

Both sides might on many occasions have moved to end their confrontation by compromise, but neither side showed the slightest willingness to do this. The Israelis, feeling themselves beleaguered by fifty million hostile neighbors and acutely conscious of the recent fate of six million Jews in Europe, believed any significant concession would merely whet insatiable Arab appetites and start Israel down the slippery slope to extinction. The Arabs, looking upon the establishment of Israel as the latest in a series of imperialist occupations of their homeland, of which the presence of a million Palestinian refugees was a constant reminder, found it emotionally and politically impossible to accept Israel as a permanent fact of life and to forgo harassing it and conspiring against it.

This common intolerance and mutual harassment had brought on war in 1956. It is pertinent to note that General Dayan, in the *Diary of the Sinai Campaign,* published in 1966, wrote that the three major objects of that

*From Charles W. Yost, "The Arab-Israeli War: How It Began," *Foreign Affairs,* XLVI, no. 2 (January, 1968), 304-20, by permission of the publisher.

campaign from the Israeli point of view were "freedom of shipping for Israeli vessels in the Gulf of Aqaba; an end to the Feydayen terrorism; and a neutralization of the threat of attack on Israel by the joint Egypt-Syria-Jordan military command." With slight variations, these were the issues that brought on war again eleven years later.

Through the latter part of 1966, so-called El Fatah incursions into Israel—sometimes carried out by Palestinian refugees, sometimes moving through Jordan or Lebanon, but for the most part mounted in Syria—grew in number and intensity. In October two particularly serious incidents in which several Israelis were killed caused Israel to appeal, as it often had before, to the U.N. Security Council. Six of its members proposed a relatively mild resolution calling on Syria to take stronger measures to prevent such incidents. This was, however, as on previous occasions, vetoed by the Soviet Union in the supposed interests of its Arab friends.

A new and more radical Syrian government had come to power by *coup d'etat* earlier that year. It enthusiastically supported the claims and machinations of the so-called Palestine Liberation Army, which mobilized and inflamed the refugees and carried out some of the raids. The Syrian prime minister declared in a press conference in October: "We are not sentinels over Israel's security and are not the leash that restrains the revolution of the displaced and persecuted Palestinian people." Early in November, morever, a "defense agreement" was concluded between Syria and the United Arab Republic, involving a joint military command and other measures of "coordination and integration" between the two countries.

It had long been Israel's practice, whenever it judged that Arab raids had reached an intolerable level, to retaliate massively. It did so on November 13, against Es Samu in Jordan, where, according to U.N. observers, eighteen Jordanian soldiers and civilians were killed and fifty-four wounded. The fact that moderate Jordan rather than extremist Syria was the target of retaliation seemed ill judged to most of the world but was excused by Israel on grounds that there had recently been thirteen acts of sabotage committed on Israeli territory from Jordanian bases. Be that as it may, the reaction to this disproportionate and misplaced retaliation were considerable, both in the Middle East and throughout the world.

The U.N. Security Council, by a vote of fourteen to zero with one abstention (New Zealand), censured Israel "for this large-scale military action in violation of the U.N. Charter and of the General Armistice Agreement between Israel and Jordan." It warned Israel "that actions of military reprisal cannot be tolerated and that, if they are repeated, the Security Council will have to consider further and more effective steps as envisaged in the Charter to ensure against the repetition of such acts."

Perhaps more important in its effect on subsequent events, the Jordanian prime minister in a press conference charged the U.A.R. and Syria, which had been denouncing King Hussein's government, with failing to bear their share of the confrontation with Israel. He accused the U.A.R. of failing to supply promised air cover and urged that Egyptian troops be withdrawn from Yemen and sent to Sinai on Israel's southern flank. The U.A.R. commander in chief of the Arab Command replied publicly with similar recriminations, but the charges must have struck home to a regime so peculiarly sensitive to face and prestige.

From January to April, 1967, the Syrian-Israeli frontier was agitated by an ascending series of clashes, ranging from potshots at tractors plowing to exchanges of fire between tanks, artillery, and aircraft. These clashes were primarily caused by the refusal of both sides, at different times, to permit the U.N. Mixed Armistice Commission even to mark the armistice line at disputed points and by the insistence of both parties on farming and patrolling disputed areas.

On April 7, 1967, one of these clashes escalated into what in retrospect appears to have been the prelude to the Six-Day War. An exchange of fire between tanks gave rise to intervention first by Israeli and then by Syrian aircraft. By the end of the day Israeli planes appeared over the outskirts of Damascus, and six Syrian planes were shot down.

The most serious aspect of this affair was that for the second time in six months Arab forces suffered a very bloody nose at the hands of Israel without the "unified Arab Command" in Cairo lifting a finger. President Nasser, who aspired to be leader of the Arab world and who had formally established a military apparatus at least for the containment of Israel, had sat quietly by while first his rival and then his ally had been conspicuously and roundly chastised. Neither the rival nor the ally hesitated publicly or privately to point out this dereliction. Nasser could of course reply, and perhaps did, that the El Fatah raids were excessive and untimely, that the Arabs must not be provoked into fighting.before they were ready, and that the U.N. Emergency Force, standing between his army and Israel, blocked its coming to the rescue of his Arab allies. These excuses, however genuine and well founded they may have been, were quite clearly wearing thin in the eyes of the Arabs after the April 7 affair. Those knowing President Nasser's temperament could hardly have felt any assurance that he would hold aloof a third time.

Yet the respite was brief. A month later, on May 11, the U.N. Secretary General declared at a press luncheon:

"I must say that, in the last few days, the El Fatah type of incidents have increased, unfortunately. Those incidents have occurred in the vicinity of the Lebanese and Syrian lines and are very deplorable, especially because, by their nature, they seem to indicate that the individuals who committed them have had more specialized training than has usually been evidenced in El Fatah incidents in the past. That type of activity is insidious, is contrary to the letter and spirit of the Armistice Agreements and menaces the peace of the area."

On the same day, May 11, Israeli Prime Minister Eshkol was saying in a public speech in Tel Aviv that his government regarded this wave of sabotage and infiltration gravely. "In view of the fourteen incidents of the past month alone," he said, "we may have to adopt measures no less drastic than those of April 7." In a radio interview two days later he declared: "It is quite clear to the Israeli Government that the focal point of the terrorists is in Syria, but we have laid down the principle that we shall choose the time, the place and the means to counter the aggressor." Eshkol went on to say that he intended to make Israeli defense forces powerful enough to deter aggression, to repel it, and to strike a decisive blow within enemy territory.

It would appear that a senior Israeli military officer also made a public comment on or about May 12, the exact text of which it has not been possible to find but which, whether or not correctly understood, significantly contributed to Arab apprehensions. President Nasser referred to it in a speech on May 23, saying, "On May 12 a very important statement was made. . . . The statement said that the Israeli commanders have announced they would carry out military operations against Syria in order to occupy Damascus and overthrow the Syrian Government."

These Israeli exercises in verbal escalation provoked far more serious repercussions than they were no doubt intended to do and, far from sobering the exuberant Syrians and their allies, raised probably genuine fears in Damascus, Cairo, and Moscow to a level which brought about the fatal decisions and events of the following week. The secretary general, disturbed that his statement of May 11 on the El Fatah raids might stimulate Israeli military action, announced on May 13 that that statement "cannot be interpreted as condoning resort to force by any party."

On the same day the Syrian foreign ministry summoned ambassadors from countries which were members of the Security Council and told them that a plot against Syria was being concocted by "imperialist and Zionist quarters." The ministry described "the prearranged aggressive role Israel is preparing to play within the framework of this plot," which, it declared, "began with the abortive April 7 aggression" and was revealed by "statements of Zionist Chief of Staff Rabin."

Another component in the accumulating mass of explosive elements was mentioned by President Nasser in the famous speech of June 9, in which he offered to resign. He declared at that time:

> We all know how the crisis began in the first half of last May. There was a plan by the enemy to invade Syria, and the statements by his politicians and his military commanders declared that frankly. The evidence was ample. The sources of our Syrian brothers and our own reliable information were categorical on this. Even our friends in the Soviet Union told the parliamentary delegation which was visiting Moscow last month that there was a a calculated intention.

There seems little doubt that the Soviets did transmit warnings along these lines to the Syrian and Egyptian governments. Eastern European sources have justified these warnings on the grounds that the Israeli government itself advised Soviet representatives that, if the El Fatah raids continued, it would take drastic punitive action against Syria. This was, of course, no more than they were saying publicly, but the Israelis may have hoped that direct notice to the Soviets might induce them to persuade their Syrian friends to stop the raids.

Indeed there is evidence that Israeli officials were at this time disseminating their warnings rather widely. The *New York Times* correspondent in Tel Aviv, James Feron, reported on May 12:

> Some Israeli leaders have decided that the use of force against Syria may be the only way to curtail increasing terrorism. Any such Israeli reaction to continued infiltration would be of considerable strength but of short duration and limited in area. This has become apparent in talks with highly qualified and informed Israelis who have spoken in recent days against a background of mounting border violence.

However, these private warnings, coupled with the provocative pronouncements of Eshkol and others, would seem to have backfired by convincing the Soviets, Syrians, and Egyptians that a major retaliatory strike against Syria was fixed and imminent. In a speech to the United Nations on June 19, Premier Kosygin declared: "In those days, the Soviet Government, and, I believe, others too, began receiving information to the effect that the Israeli Government had timed for the end of May a swift strike at Syria in order to crush it and then carry the fighting over into the territory of the United Arab Republic."

On the other hand, the Israelis state that on May 12 the director general of the Israeli foreign ministry, on May 19 the foreign minister and on May 29 the prime minister each invited Soviet Ambassador Chuvakhin, who had accused Israel of massing forces on the Syrian border, to visit the area and see for himself, but that in each case he refused to do so. Furthermore, in his report to the Security Council on May 19, Secretary General Thant referred to allegations about troop movements and concentrations on the Israeli side of the Syrian border but concluded: "Reports from UNTSO observers have confirmed the absence of troop concentrations and significant troop movements on both sides of the line." U.S. representatives in Israel at the time also saw no evidence of the alleged troop concentrations. Moreover, on May 15 the Israeli government, observing that Egyptian forces were crossing the Suez Canal into Sinai in considerable strength, instructed its representative at the U.N. Ambassador Rafael, to request the secretary general to assure Cairo on its behalf that it had no intention of initiating any military action. The secretary general immediately complied with the request.

Nevertheless, it should also be noted that in the May 19 report referred to above, the secretary general remarked:

> Intemperate and bellicose utterances . . . are unfortunately more or less routine on both sides of the lines in the Near East. In recent weeks, however, reports emanating from Israel have attributed to some high officials in that state statements so threatening as to be particularly inflammatory in the sense that they could only heighten emotions and thereby increase tensions on the other side of the lines.

Press accounts of these statements also seemed so inflammatory to U.S. State Department officials that they expressed concern to Israeli authorities.

The situation in mid-May was therefore the following: The aggravation of the El Fatah raids originating in Syria would seem to have brought the Israeli government to the decision, announced publicly in general terms by responsible officials and confided in more specific terms to journalists and perhaps to foreign diplomats including the Soviets, to retaliate sharply and substantially if the raids continued. There is no solid evidence, however, that they intended anything so massive as a drive on Damascus. Nevertheless, this prospect had in both Moscow and Cairo an impact which the Israelis probably did not fully anticipate or correctly assess.

The Soviets had particular reason for not wishing to see the Syrian government humiliated, defeated, and perhaps overthrown. The increasingly radical Syrian governments which had assumed power during the previous eighteen months, though they were far from being communist (the Communist party was and still is banned), had come to rely more and more on Soviet military and economic aid, to permit increasing numbers of Soviet advisors to be stationed in the country, all in all to offer the most promising field for Soviet penetration and influence to be found anywhere in the Middle East. The particular Soviet concern for Syria was dramatically shown at the end of the Six-Day War, when the prospect that Israeli forces might then drive to Damascus caused the Soviets suddenly to join in a demand, which they had up to that point stubbornly opposed, that U.N. observers police the cease-fire. It may well have been that by mid-May they genuinely feared massive Israeli retaliation which might have toppled the Syrian government and that they therefore spurred the Egyptians on to vigorous counteraction, the full repercussions of which they did not foresee. In fear of "losing" Syria they overreached themselves and urged the Arabs to take action which resulted in much more disastrous losses for their side.

Nasser, for his part, saddled with responsibility for the unified Arab Command, which was supposed to protect all the Arab states from Israel, jealous of his already damaged position as would-be leader of the Arab world, having been ridiculed by his allies and rivals for his failure to stir at the time of the Es Samu and April 7 affairs, categorically assured by Syrians and Soviets that Israel was about to attack Syria, for which public statements by Israeli leaders seemed to give warrant, may well have felt that he could no longer stand aside without fatal loss to his prestige and authority.

Israeli public statements between May 11 and 13, therefore, regardless of how they may have been intended, may well have been the spark that ignited the long accumulating tinder. On May 14 the Egyptian chief of staff flew to Damascus and, according to the Syrian official spokesman, discussed with Syrian officials "important matters concerning joint defense against Israel." On May 16 the Cairo radio announced that the United Arab Republic had declared a state of emergency for its armed forces because of "the tense situation on the Syrian-Israeli armistic lines, Israel's large military concentrations, its threats and its open demands for an attack on Damascus." On that same day, according to the Cairo radio, Foreign Minister Riad received the Soviet, Syrian, and Iraqi ambassadors in separate audiences, and Minister of War Badran received the Soviet Ambassador, accompanied by his military attaché. The fourth act of tragedy was about to begin.

At 2200 hours local time that evening, May 16, General Rikhye, commander of the U.N. Emergency Force in Sinai, was handed the following letter from General Fawzi, chief of staff of the Egyptian armed forces:

> To your information, I gave my instructions to all U.A.R. Armed Forces to be ready for action against Israel the moment it might carry out an aggressive action against any Arab country. Due to these instructions our troops are already concentrated in Sinai on our eastern borders. For the sake of complete security of all U.N. troops which install O.P.s along our border, I request that you issue your orders to withdraw all these troops immediately. I have given my instructions to our Commander of the eastern zone concerning this subject. Inform back the fulfillment of this request."

Secretary General Thant received General Rikhye's report at 1730 hours New York time that same evening and an hour and a quarter later (at1845 hours), at his urgent request, received the U.A.R. representative to the U.N. Ambassador El Kony, to whom he presented the following views: (1) General Rikhye could not take orders from anyone but the secretary general; (2) if General Fawzi was asking for temporary withdrawal of UNEF from the line, this was unacceptable because UNEF "cannot be asked to stand aside in order to enable the two sides to resume fighting"; (3) if General Fawzi was asking for a general withdrawal of UNEF from Gaza and Sinai, the request should have been addressed by the U.A.R. government to the secretary general; (4) the U.A.R. government had the right "to withdraw the consent which it gave in 1956 for the stationing of UNEF on the territory of the U.A.R."; (5) if the U.A.R. government addressed such a request to the secretary general, he "would order the withdrawal of all UNEF troops from Gaza and Sinai, simultaneously informing the General Assembly of what he was doing and why"; (6) a U.A.R. request for a temporary withdrawal of UNEF from the line would be considered by the secretary general "as tantamount to a request for the complete withdrawal of UNEF from Gaza and Sinai, since this would reduce UNEF to ineffectiveness."

Early the next morning, May 17, Egyptian troops began to move into and beyond some UNEF positions along the armistice line. At noon GMT that day General Fawzi conveyed to General Rikhye a request that the Jugoslav detachments of UNEF (which occupied the main portion of the Sinai armistice line) be withdrawn within twenty-four hours, adding, however, that the UNEF commander might take "twenty-four hours or so" to withdraw the UNEF detachment from Sharm el Sheikh (which commands the Straits of Tiran but is far distance from the armistice line).

Space permits only the briefest summary of the events which followed in rapid succession. On the afternoon of May 17, the secretary general consulted in New York with representatives of countries providing contingents to UNEF (Brazil, Canada, Denmark, India, Jugoslavia, Norway, and Sweden). According to his subsequent report to the General Assembly, two of them expressed serious doubts about complying with "a peremptory request" for withdrawal and suggested reference to the Assembly, whereas two others maintained the United Arab Republic had the right to request withdrawal at any time and that request would have to be respected regardless of what the Assembly might say. Later that afternoon, the secretary general presented to the U.A.R. representative an aide-memoire reiterating the points he had made the previous evening and concluding that, if Egyptian troop movements up to the line were maintained, he would "have no choice but to order the withdrawal of UNEF from Gaza and Sinai as expeditiously as possible."

The next morning, May 18, Foreign Minister Riad informed representatives in Cairo of nations with troops in UNEF that "UNEF had terminated its tasks in the U.A.R. and in the Gaza Strip and must depart from the above territory forthwith." At noon New York time the secretary general received a formal request from the Egyptian foreign minister to the same effect. That afternoon the secretary general met with the UNEF Advisory Committee, where he encountered the same divergence of views as at the meeting the previous day; the members finally acquiesced in his belief that, in the absence of any proposal to convene the Assembly, he "had no alternative other than to comply with the U.A.R.'s demand." He did so that same evening by a message to Foreign Minister Riad and by instructions to the UNEF commander.

The immediate reaction of Israel also deserves mention. On the morning of May 18, the secretary general received the Israeli representative, who presented his government's view "that the UNEF withdrawal should not be achieved by a unilateral U.A.R. request alone and asserted Israel's right to a voice in the matter." However, when the secretary general raised the possibility of stationing UNEF on the Israeli side of the line, the representative replied that this would be "entirely unacceptable to his government," thus reaffirming the position in regard to UNEF which Israel had taken ever since the establishment of the force in 1956.

The intent and rationale of the decisions made in Cairo during those critical days in mid-May are still shrouded in obscurity, while those made in response in New York are still bedeviled by controversy. What seems reasonably clear is that, as so often is the case in the prelude to war, the control of events slipped from everyone's hands and limited decisions, hastily taken, had sweeping consequences no one desired.

No doubt the Egyptian government decided sometime between May 13 and 16 that, in view of its assessment of the threat to Syria, it must move some of its armed forces up to the Sinai armistice line in order either to deter Israel or to come to Syria's assistance if deterrence failed. Reliable Arab sources maintain that: (1) the U.A.R. government, as late as May 16, had no intention to request the withdrawal of UNEF; (2) it desired merely the removal of several UNEF posts along the Sinai line which would inhibit the contemplated redeployment of Egyptian forces; (3) it saw no incompatibility of this redeployment with the continuance of UNEF in its other positions, *including* Sharm el Sheikh; (4) the implementation of the redeployment was left to the military leaders, who failed to consult the civilian authorities— including the president—about either the scope of the redeployment they intended to carry out or the demand addressed to General Rikhye on May 16; (5) when the secretary general confronted the U.A.R. government with the choice of either reversing the redeployment, to which its military leaders had publicly committed it, or requesting the withdrawal of UNEF, the government felt obliged to choose the latter; (6) furthermore, when the U.A.R. government unexpectedly found its forces once more in possession of Sharm el Sheikh, it felt it could not fail to exercise, as it had from 1954 to 1956, its "belligerent right" to forbid the passage of Israeli vessels and "war material" through the strait.

As to the decisions taken in New York, the U.N. authorities maintain that: (1) the indicated redeployment of U.A.R. forces *was* incompatible with the continuance of UNEF since it deprived UNEF of its essential function as a buffer between Egyptian and Israeli forces; (2) UNEF had hitherto been able to function effectively only because of an informal U.A.R. agreement that its forces would be held 2000 meters back from the armistice line in Sinai (Israeli forces patrolled right up to the line); (3) once confrontation between the two forces was reestablished, conflict between them was, in the existing state of tension, very probable, and UNEF units scattered among them would be wholly unable to prevent it; (4) two of the troop-contributing states, India and Jugoslavia, had made clear their intention to withdraw their contingents whatever the secretary general decided, and others were likely to follow suit, with the probable result that UNEF would disintegrate in a disordered and ignominious fashion; (5) the U.A.R. government had the legal right both to move its troops where it wished in its own territory and to insist on the withdrawal of UNEF at any time, just as Israel had the right to refuse UNEF admittance; (6) if the U.N. contested that right, peacekeeping would become "occupation," and other governments would not in the future admit U.N. peacekeeping forces to their territories; (7) reference of the Egyptian request to the Security Council or the Assembly would merely have produced, as subsequent events proved, a prolonged debate during which UNEF would have either disintegrated or been helplessly involved in war.

No conclusive judgment can be pronounced on these two lines of argument. What does seem apparent is that both the U.A.R. and the U.N., like Israel a few days before, acted precipitately and with little resort to diplomacy. If the Egyptian account is accurate, temporization on the part of U.N. might conceivably have led to some modification in U.A.R. military dispositions which had not been authorized by the U.A.R. government. It seems doubtful, however, that in the prevailing state of emotion dispositions once taken, even without full authorization, could have been reversed. By May 17, the crisis had already acquired a momentum which seemed inexorably to sweep all parties toward and over the brink.

Nevertheless, we can hardly fail to note parenthetically the serious shortcomings of a peacekeeping procedure whereby, as in this case, a U.N. force can be ordered out of a critical area at the very moment when the danger of war, which it is stationed there to prevent, becomes most acute. The fault, however, lies not with the U.N. but with the great powers, whose rivalries ever since 1945 have blocked the application of the enforcement procedures provided by chapter 7 of the Charter, under which a U.N. military force could be, for example, interposed between two prospective combatants, regardless of the objections of either or both. In the absence of great-power willingness to permit the Security Council to apply compulsion of that type, the U.N. has been obliged for many years to rely on a much more fragile form of peacekeeping, whereunder a U.N. force, whatever may have been the arrangements under which it entered the territory of a state, can in practice remain there only so long as its government consents. Such was the situation in Sinai before May 16.

To return to the concluding events of that month: On May 22 President Nasser announced his intention to reinstitute the blockade against Israel in the Straits of Tiran. This was the final, fatal step. It is not certain whether it was contemplated, in whatever advance planning did take place, that Sharm el Sheikh would be reoccupied and the blockade reimposed or whether the military exceeded their orders and one step led to another in dizzy and unpremeditated succession. There can hardly have been any doubt at any time, however, about the grave risks involved in restoring the blockade. It seems probable that the Russians were consulted about the redeployment of Egyptian forces and perhaps the subsequent request for the withdrawal of UNEF. Reliable Soviet sources have claimed, however, that they were not informed in advance of the reimposition of the blockade, implying that they would have objected had they known.

In any case, the reaction in Israel and elswhere was immediate. On May 23, Prime Minister Eshkol declared in parliament: "The Knesset knows that any interference with freedom of shipping in the Gulf and in the Straits constitutes a flagrant violation of international law. . . . It constitutes an act of aggression against Israel." On the same day President Johnson declared in Washington: "The United States considers the Gulf to be an international waterway and feels that a blockade of Israeli shipping is illegal and potentially disastrous to the cause of peace. The right of free, innocent passage of the international waterway is a vital interest of the international community."

Efforts were made to persuade President Nasser to revoke, suspend, or moderate the blockade, but, the action once taken, he did not feel politically free to reverse it even had he so desired. Equally unavailing were the efforts made to forestall a unilateral Israeli response by organizing a group of maritime powers to issue a declaration reaffirming the right of free passage through the straits and, presumably, if passage continued to be denied, to take effective multilateral action to reopen it. Very few maritime powers showed any interst in participating in a confrontation with Nasser and the Arab world; nor did members of the U.S. Congress who were consulted manifest any enthusiasm for risking another conflict in addition to Viet Nam. However, the exploratory dialogue between the U.S. and the U.A.R. continued until the outbreak of war; as late as June 4, an agreement was announced that U.A.R. Vice-President Mohieddin would visit Washington within the next few days and Vice-President Humphrey would later return the visit.

In the meantime, however, the crisis had assumed proportions far beyond an argument over maritime rights. The advance of the Egyptian forces to the armistice line, the ouster of UNEF, and the reimposition of the blockade were received with enormous enthusiasm throughout the Arab world. All the pent-up emotions which had been accumulating for twenty years, and which were continually refreshed by armed clashes, inflammatory propaganda, and the presence of a million refugees, erupted in paeans of triumph from Baghdad to Marrakesh.

Nasser's prestige, which had been falling for some time, rebounded overnight. Expressions of solidarity poured in. Iraq, Algeria, Kuwait, and Sudan promised troops. In a startling reversal of long-standing hostility, King Hussein of Jordan appeared in Cairo on May 30 and concluded a mutual defense pact with the U.A.R. which a few days later was extended to Iraq. The armed forces of Egypt, Jordan, and Syria were more and more concentrated around Israel's frontiers, and it seemed very likely that they would soon be reinforced by other Arab states.

This Arab euphoria, moreover, led also to verbal exaltation which could not have been without its effect on Israel. For instance, the Syrian chief of state, Dr. Al-Atasi, said in a speech on May 22:

Arab Palestinians who were expelled from their homeland now realize that armed struggle is the only way to regain their homeland. . . . The state of gangs [Israel] will not benefit by blaming others for inciting fedayeen activities. The cause of these activities is the aggressive Zionist existence itself. Let Israel know that the Palestinian fedayeen activities will continue until they liberate their homeland.

In a speech addressed on June 1 to troops departing for the "front lines" in Jordan, President Arif of Iraq declared:

It was treason and politics that brought about the creation of Israel. Brethren and sons, this is the day of the battle to revenge your martyred brethren who fell in 1948. It is the day to wash away the stigma. We shall, God willing, meet in Tel Aviv and Haifa.

Yet even at this late date, despite all these verbal pyrotechnics and concentrations of force, there does not seem to have been any intention in Cairo to initiate a war. British MP Christopher Mayhew, interviewing Nasser on June 2, asked, "And if they do not attack, will you leave them alone?" The President replied, "Yes we will leave them alone. We have no intention of attacking Israel." Similar assurances were repeatedly given the United States by the highest Egyptian authorities.

There seems little reason to doubt them. Nasser had up to that point achieved a spectacular victory. Arab unity seemed closer to reality than it had ever been. Israel had suffered a serious setback in prestige, power, and security. The mood in Cairo was an odd mixture of exaltation and fatalism—exaltation over what had been achieved, fatalism before the inescapable realization that Israel might prefer war to a political defeat of this magnitude. With the clear understanding that Israel might attack at any time, there was no overweening confidence as to the outcome but a determination to defend, whatever the costs, the intoxicating gains which had been won. Whether this determination might have been overcome by negotiation over a period of time—for example, by the vice-presidents' visiting Cairo and Washington—cannot be known for certain. In view of the support which the Soviet Union was providing its Arab friends, this seems unlikely.

In any case the Israeli government obviously decided that it could not wait. All the factors which had induced it to go to war in 1956—a multiplication of raids into its territory, a substantial build-up of Egyptian and other hostile forces on its borders, the blockade of the strait—had reappeared in even more aggravated form.. Efforts of the U.N. and the U.S. to relieve them by international action seemed unavailing. On May 30, Foreign Minister Eban said in a press conference in Jerusalem:

Less than two weeks ago a change took place in the security balance in this region. The two most spectacular signs of this change were the illegal attempt to blockade the international passageway at the Strait of Tiran and the Gulf of Aqaba and the abnormal build-up of Egyptian troops on the Israeli frontier. The Government and people of Israel intend to insure that these two changes are rescinded, and in the shortest possible time.

Six days later Israel struck with this end in view; twelve days later it had achieved its objective, and much more beside.

It is not difficult to identify in retrospect the ventures and responses on both sides which over preceding months and weeks, compounding the hatreds that had been allowed to fester for twenty years, led almost inevitably to war.

First were the El Fatah raids, organized from Syria, involving the "Palestine Liberation Army," subjecting peaceful Israeli villages to recurrent jeopardy and terror, building up through the months from October to May, unpunished, and, because of the Soviet veto, even uncensured by the U.N. Security Council. Remembering the history of the previous twelve years, it is difficult to see how any Arab or Soviet leader could have failed to realize that this murderous campaign would eventually bring forth a murderous response.

Second were the Israeli "massive retaliations" at Es Samu in November and in the air over Syria and Jordan in April, designed to punish and deter but disproportionate in size, visibility, and political impact, causing also the death of innocent people, condemned by the Security Council in the strongest terms in November, as similar disproportionate retaliations had been repeatedly condemned in the past. It is difficult to see how any Israeli leader could have failed to foresee that such repeated massive reprisals would eventually place the leader of the Arab coalition in a position where he would have to respond.

Third were the public and private statements by high Israeli authorities in mid-May which indicated the probability of even more drastic retaliation against Syria in the near future if the El Fatah raids continued. These statements, even though designed, no doubt, to deter the raids, almost certainly convinced the Syrian and U.A.R. governments that such retaliation was definitely projected and may well have persuaded them and the Soviets that the Syrian regime itself was in jeopardy.

Fourth was the decision by the U.A.R. government, presumably encouraged by the Soviets and the Syrians, to move its armed forces up to the Sinai armistice line, thus re-establishing at a moment of acute tension the direct Egyptian-Israeli military confrontation which had been the major immediate cause of the 1956 war. Under the circumstances, this redeployment of Egyptian forces was critical, whether or not it was originally intended to be accompanied by a demand that UNEF be withdrawn.

Fifth, and finally, was the decision of the U.A.R. government, finding itself whether by intent or accident once more in command of the Straits of Tiran, to exercise its "belligerent rights" by reimposing the blockade, thus reproducing the third of elements which had brought on the 1956 war. The likely consequences of this step were indeed foreseen but, in the climate of fear, passion, and "national honor" which by then prevailed, were faced with fatalism and desperation.

It remains the thesis of this article that no government plotted or intended to start a war in the Middle East in the spring of 1967. Syria mounted raids against Israel as it had been doing for years, but more intensively and effectively; Israel retaliated disproportionately as it often had done before, but in more rapid succession and in a way that seemed to threaten the existence of the Arab government; Nasser felt his responsibilities and ambitions in the Arab world did not permit him to stand aside again in such a contingency and took hasty and ill-calculated measures, which made major conflict, already probable, practically certain. All concerned over-reacted outrageously. Yet there is no evidence—quite the contrary—that Nasser, the Israeli government, or even the Syrian government wanted and sought a major war at this juncture. The fault of all of them, and of the great powers and the United Nations, lay not so much in their actions or omissions in May and June, 1967, as in their failure, indeed their common blunt refusal, to face the facts of life in the Middle East during the twenty years before that date.

There will be no peace there, no security for the inhabitants or for the great powers involved there, until the Arabs recognize that Israel, however unjust its creation appears to them, is a fact of life; that it has as much right to exist as they have; that to threaten and harass it, to arouse among their people false hopes about its dissolution, is actually as much a threat to Arab as to Israeli security; and that the two equally have more to gain than lose by peaceful coexistence. On the other hand, there will also be no peace in the Middle East until the Israelis recognize that the condition of their long-term survival as a nation is reconciliation with their much more numerous Arab neighbors, that survival cannot indefinitely be preserved by military force or territorial expansion, that displays of inflexibility and arrogance are not effective modes of international intercourse, and that in particular there will be no security for Israel until, whatever the political and financial cost, the million or more Palestinian refugees have been compensated, resettled, and restored to dignity.

# Reflections On The Middle East*

Charles Burton Marshall

A report on the Middle East issued a few years ago by the Senate Committee on Foreign Relations summed up the situation in apt words: "The area remains obdurately a most disorderly part of the world; geographically, racially, culturally, economically, and above all, politically, there is a profound inconsistency about the area. For every rule there is an exception, for every premise a contradiction." Shortly after arrival at his Cairo post in late May, a debutant American Ambassador publicly appraised the Middle East situation at the moment as closer to normal than to crisis. It was a connoisseur's judgment. An amateur would find such a distinction as difficult as detecting the subtleties of different vintages from the same vineyard. In international affairs the overworked but indispensable word *crisis* denotes a problem loaded with immediate potential for war or threatening the hold of one or more regimes on authority—most probably both, because war and the tenure of regimes are almost invariably connected. In a measure distinctive among the world's regions, the Middle East is marked by crisis protracted to normality. Accordingly, it offers considerable opportunities for contemplation of crisis management, which, in our overelaborative age, is a term of art for the age-old business of trying to stay out of trouble while striving to have one's way.

My thoughts here are merely a distant observer's musings on this topic in connection with the war which followed so soon upon the ambassador's reassurances. They do not purport to narrate or to analyze fully the happenings referred to. They are glosses on a few aspects, offered with some

*From Charles Burton Marshall, "Reflections on the Middle East," *Orbis*, XI, no. 2 (1967), 343-59, by permission of the publisher.

sense of presumption, because I am surely no expert on the Middle East. Cumulatively, I have spent about thirty days there, mostly sightseeing in and around the capitals of six of the lands concerned. Except in gross dimensions, moreover, the concatenation preceding the war remains a matter of guesswork. Because the losers' files will probably not be sifted by the winners' analysts, the contributory events may never be comprehended in depth and precision matching what is known of some aspects of the onset of the two world wars, for example. The Soviet Union will be mum or dissimulating. The Israelis will probably keep a great many secrets to themselves. It is not, however, a case of nothing being available. The governments concerned have made voluminous public utterances. The verbal processes at the United Nations alone produced huge amounts of relevant wordage, but wringing solid information from all of this is like getting gold from seawater. With what information can be gleaned, one must try to comprehend how the flare-up was sparked—how diverse versions of crisis management maintained in the Arab states concerned, in Israel, in the Soviet Union, and in the United States interacted to produce a war.

Brevity in discussing relevant attitudes among the Arab societies is not easy. The special potency of Arab rhetoric is a factor. I recall a Jordanian psychiatrist's explanation to me a few years ago. The Arabs, mostly needy, find words the least expensive substitute for alcohol, which is denied to them by religious precept. Like any intoxicant, the hyperbole in which their tongue is rich tends to unleash credulity. Any rousing speech may bring on a jag. The fact of having a common language across the Arab zone is also relevant. Successful political personalities may project themselves by mass media to the other lands, so that the jag may overlap boundaries.

Such reaction produces an impression of community and nationhood. The Arab states' regional organization is the world's most elaborate and pervasive one. There is much talk of Arab brotherhood based on traditions from a great Arab past of a millennium or so ago, when Arab order and unity prevailed from the Atlantic shores to the Persian Gulf, and Arab power dominated the Mediterranean and the Indian Ocean and extended to Bengal. In practice, the dozen or so Arab states are recurrently at loggerheads. Arab nationhood is an expression rather than a reality. Brotherliness between one regime and another is often in a Cain-and-Abel motif. The League of Arab States, however imposing in concept, is a feeble reality. Its solemn prinicples are mostly flouted. In concrete as opposed to abstract considerations, the Arab lands reflect a diversity of interests related to differing economic resources and stakes, divergent historic experiences, and contrasting relationships to outside powers.

Despite actual divisions, the idea of unification as the only rightful frame of political authority for Arabdom persists as a reproach to the legitimacy of existing Arab regimes. The result is a paradox bordering on contradiction. Arab regimes in general feel compelled to pay tribute to ideas tending to discredit their own rightful existence, but Arab regimes go on trying to maintain separate existences counter to the ideal they vaunt. The urge for unity, which none can renounce, engenders an intermittent jostle for dominance and survival. The combinations vary from stage to stage. Only a real expert, if anyone at all, could describe with assurance the pattern of interlocking contentions at any moment. In recent times cleavages have been marked between Arab regimes espousing versions of socialist progressivism and revolution and enjoying the Soviet Union's sponsorship, and other Arab regimes of a more traditional mold, opposed to the Soviet Union's purposes. These opposing groups have themselves been riven by secondary animosities.

The fact of Israel's existence—with a population culturally and religiously differentiated from the Arabs and a position bisecting the Arab range—gallingly epitomizes Arab frustration. Israel has been estabished and aggrandized in the face of Arab hostility and despite a huge Arab advantage in numbers. The emotion of pride requires attributing this result to factors of outside assistance. Israel's existence is thus seen as artificial, spurious, obtrusive, and aggressive, a lingering effect of foreign power exercised within what is rightfully an Arab domain. The U.N.'s approval of Israel's origin does not allay but accentuates the affront. Israel's independence must not be acknowledged. War, conceptual if not actual, must be maintained against Israel. The Arab regimes' conviction on this score varies from velleity to militance. For many of them, however, the issue involves survival. Any gesture of formal accommodation of Israel's existence would precipitate rebellion. In substantial numbers, in extreme poverty, and in apathy relieved only by hatred for what has overtaken them, the Palestinian Arabs who fled or were dispossessed in the violence incident to Israel's emergence two decades ago have lingered on in the environs. With a militant organization and a subsidized force, they dispose a potential for raids and sabotage against Israel and for undercutting Arab governments which might otherwise be inclined to come to terms with Israel.

In sum, opposition to Israel's existence and the proposition that Israel's presence in the Arab midst is an aggressive one requiring ultimate elimination are the two ideas in which Arab unity has been able to manifest itself. Thus Arabdom's most notable failure has provided the basis of Arab unity's one enduring success. Whatever there is of reality in Arab unity has hinged on maintaining the myth of Israel's nonexistence. Yet ambivalence has persisted because of reluctance to come to grips in the ever vaunted war and because of the double advantage in claiming noncombatant immunities along with belligerent privileges. The activist Arabs' course of contrived ambiguity played out in the spring of 1967, and war suddenly became unequivocal.

Israel's ever imminent difficulty has risen, obviously, from the fact of having control of territory in dispute with all its neighbors adjoining and beyond. It is not merely a question of legitimate location of boundaries, any dimension whatever, the basic fact of existence for an independent Israel is repugnant to them in varying degrees. The Israeli response to this circumstance and the attendant dangers has been affected by contrasting views of the country's relationship to the world at large.

One attitude is identified, though not exclusively, with Palestinian-born senior Israelis and with the upcoming generation. It is an inward-oriented view and might be described as the Canaanite attitude. The present state is regarded is a re-embodiment of the kingdoms of 933-722 and 168-63 B.C. The two millennia of the dispersion are dismissed as a parenthesis in history. This view accords with Machiavelli's precept: "That deliverance is of no avail that does not depend upon yourself; those only are reliable, certain, and durable that depend on yourself and your valor." Any hint of clientage to outside forces is shunned. The notion of Israel as a product of the United Nations—of Israel's national existence as stemming from a General Assembly resolution—is regarded as a formalistic absurdity. As the core fact in Israel's revived existence, a determining number of Jews fought for it and brought force to bear decisively. Their will to persevere has accounted for Israel's subsequent survival amid numerically superior enemies. Israel's future will be contingent on the same factor.

The other attitude looks outward. It regards a balance of exterior forces as the main circumstance essential to Israel's emergence. In view of Israel's statistically precarious situation, it stresses similar considerations for the present and future. The attitude is maintained largely among those from abroad, who have come to Israel as a refuge. It is especially concerned for the situation of Jewish kinsmen remaining in other lands. It manifests habits acquired in getting along in minority positions amid divergent environments. It puts stress on finesse, temporizing, abatement, deference, avoidance of confrontation. It emphasizes in particular a need for gingerly conduct of relations with the Soviet Union as abettor of Israel's more activist Arab adversaries.

This latter approach prevailed within the Israeli government until a figurative last minute before the June, 1967, fighting. Israel was attempting both to deter immediate enemies and to reassure their sponsor. It was seeking both to intimidate and to placate. As Plautus long ago observed, "To blow and to swallow at the same time is not easy." No lesson recurs more often in the conduct of high policy, but none is more difficult in application. Policy-makers are wont ever to eat their cake and have it. It is external reality which says, if I may have indulgence to switch cliches,to fish or cut bait. If Israel perhaps aggravated the probability of war by too long mitigating defiance with deference, a result was the engendering among its enemies of the climate of overconfidence essential to pervasive tactical surprise and thus to the quick success achieved once Israel had made up its mind.

My assumptions about the men running the Soviet Union's policies are entirely conventional. No Kremlinologist, I have no talent for calibrating the ratio of their devotion to national strategic considerations to their ideological commitment. Like a playwright who owns a theater, they work at both pursuits at once as mutually serviceable rather than competing purposes. On the basis of either, they would have reasons for ambitious concern in the Middle East. Parts of the region are loaded with petroleum. Control of the flow thereof would provide great leverage over European economies. Part of the Middle East forms a flank to Southern Europe. The region lies athwart air connections between Western Europe and the Orient. Affecting accesses to the waterways of the Mediterranean, the Black Sea and the Indian Ocean, the area bears on the Soviet Union's maritime connections with the outer world and interposes between Europe and the lands of greater Asia and remoter Africa.

Presumably, the Soviet rulers have had no intention of attempting immediate or overt dominion in the region. Their relevant ambitions are linked to a wider purpose of eliminating United States power as a factor in Europe—specifically, of eroding the North Atlantic Treaty Organization. An eclipse of NATO would entail riddance of the United States as a maritime factor in the Mediterranean. The Soviet Union would fill in behind it. As a corollary, Soviet power would dominate the waterway between the Mediterranean and the Indian Ocean. Domination of the latter, the third greatest of the oceans and the only one whose periphery belongs largely to so-called Third-World countries  susceptible to revolutionary manipulation, would present huge opportunities.

The role aspired to in the Middle East would be akin to that of Great Britain in Queen Victoria's Golden Age. Lord Palmerston, detailing British policy a century ago, disavowed coveting any part of the area"any more than any rational man with an estate in the north of England and a resident in the south would have wished to possess the inns of the North Road. All he could want would have been that the inn should be well kept, always accessible, and furnishing him, when he came, with mutton chops and post horses." In like fashion, the method does not call for the Soviet Union to possess the region. The prerogatives sought would be those of a regional arbiter exercising paramount influence among a diversity of client states, which would cultivate Soviet assistance in restraining pushy neighbors.

Such a design does not involve a timetable or master plan. Though not immediate, it is not apparitional. It has guided Soviet conduct in the area, but the Soviet Union has essayed circumspection in applying it. The Soviet Union must take care to avoid a direct challenge to the paramount naval and nuclear power disposed by the United States. It must work through surrogates, making avail of its communist doctrine regarding "national liberation wars." According to this doctrine any developments among the emerging and less developed states tending to serve the Soviet Union's advantage are asserted to have legitimacy under history's laws, and any opposing tendency is supposed to be illicit. The Soviet Union has been wont to invoke relevant shibboleths on behalf of its clients in the Middle East and against their adversaries. One is led to question whether the Soviet Union has been party to its clients' often reaffirmed intention to annihilate Israel.

Walter Lippmann, for one, professed to see such a design behind Soviet policies antecedent to the June war. Without knowing for sure, I should doubt the estimate.

The Soviet Union has endorsed Israel's right to existence and has armed the sworn enemies of that right. It has voiced support of Israel's access to the Suez Canal and abetted the barrier. Soviet delegates at the Havana Tricontinental Conference, in early 1966, endorsed proposals for the extinction of Israel. Soviet spokesmen subsequently negated the idea. The record could be lengthened. In my view, what the ambiguities and switches demonstrate is an attempt at manipulative policy. While hypothetically the Soviet Union might not grieve over Israel's disappearance, within the limitations of circumstance and for the time being the presumptive Soviet purpose has been to work Israel into being a suitor for protection, much as Iran has been pressed toward clientage by vicarious means in the form of a build-up of Egyptian naval power in environing waters.

Manipulative policies usually have the defect of being overly clever. Sponsors characteristically magnify their control. It is all too easy to take assumptions for fact and to count liabilities as assets. In this instance, Soviet policy-makers presumably overestimated their leverage on Arab clients. They certainly must have been misled into equating quality with quantity in appraising military assets accruing from their assistance. It is not hard to imagine how, because such errors recur within our own experience. I recall an illustrative example. A few years ago in an Asian country a visiting congressman told me of prodigies achieved by a U.S. military assistance program there. He dismissed my doubts by citing confidences from the brigadier general who headed the military aid mission. Next time I saw the congressman's misinformant, he conceded that he and I knew better but added that, because he was loath to jeopardize his chance for second star through any feedback to the Pentagon, he had reported progress and nothing else. The Kremlin, as well as the U.S., must have been bemused by progress reports. The events in the spring of 1967 forced a realistic accounting.

What of American attitudes relevant to the Middle East? The material stakes of the United States in the area relate to earning from petroleum properties, a significant source of foreign exchange. They relate to airways and maritime routes. The area has a highly important bearing on the security and livelihood of allies in Europe. In these respects, U.S. interests are obverse to those of the Soviet Union. The area is inherently vexatious to American preconceptions. American approaches to foreign affairs incline to be rationalistic. Rationalism in relation to Middle Eastern problems is reflected in three news items at hand as I write—one concerning a proposition to convert the new Jerusalem into another Danzig, one about reconciling Arabs to Israel's existence by subsidizing a huge irrigation scheme so as to enrich the stakes at issue, a third concerning an idea of ending national jurisdiction over all the rest of the world's maritime narrows and canals so as to set a moral example for Egypt to dispossess itself of the Suez.

Rationalism values symmetry and balance in policy. It holds all problems solvable. Rationalism assumes conflict to be aberrant. It banks on inherent harmony of interest among human groups—a harmony not always obvious and dominant, but assumed ever to be latent and susceptible of being brought into play in all situations by patient indulgence. It attributes a transforming efficacy to negotiations. Rationalism correlates community with communication. It disjoins consent and coercion in the manner of the president, who is wont to quote the eighteenth verse of the first chapter of Isaiah without noting the linkage with the twentieth verse. Rationalism puts a great value on what is called understanding. Understanding, however, is ambiguous. Such peoples as Pakistanis and Indians, or Poles and Germans, understand each other quite well, but not as sweethearts understand each other. The same is probably true of Israelis and Arabs. Conceptually, however, rationalism merges understanding as comprehension with understanding as empathy. Rationalistic approaches also involve a high degree of self-projection. An illustrative recollection from some years back concerns advice blurted by a United States representative at the United Nations to contentious Arab and Israeli representatives—that they should settle their differences in a truly Christian spirit. Rationalism, as Michael Oakeshott has put it, tries to live every day as if it were the first. It is impatient with history's obduracy. It relegates cultural and ethnic differences to secondary or even tertiary standing in human affairs. It is impatient with the idea that differences rooted in episodes of antiquity told in the twenty-first chapter of Genesis may not be susceptible of prompt solution. Rationalism goes hand in hand with functionalism—the idea of solving differences by shunting them aside and turning instead to concrete common endeavors.

The United States position regarding the Middle East is basically affected by a decision two decades ago to join with other powers in sponsoring a state of Israel in Palestine in succession to Britain's mandate. To attribute the creation of Israel to that action may be an exagggeration, but the deed was at least a gesture of authentication whereby Israel was brought into the society of states. Within limits imposed by that reality, the United States has sought to exemplify evenhandedness, but that precept is not enough to mollify Arab intransigents, who see in it the impartiality which would mediate between a householder and a housebreaker. The point applies to the part the United States played in the 1950 tripartite declaration supporting the territorial *status quo* within the region. Other powers, including the Soviet Union, acted as midwives for Israel. Other powers were involved also in the 1950 declaration. The United States, however, is the one with a fleet dominant in the Mediterranean, the one whose maritime and nuclear strength casts it as the strategic stabilizer. It is also the principal source of outside contribution to help Israel to a measure of economic success far byond its Arab neighbors. When unreconciled Arabs look outward to account for Israel's endurance in the face of their hostility, the United States inevitably and singularly springs to mind.

One particular United States commitment, involving a curiosity of sorts, is relevant. It relates to the United States maritime position. It was articulated in the denouement of the 1956 war. Israel had launched that war mainly to ensure itself maritime access to the south and east. Britain and France colluded in it to ensure their stakes in the Suez Canal. The United States took a position insisting upon unconditional withdrawal from foreign territory occupied in consequence of an attack made in the face of United Nations disapproval. Among other land parcels, this precept required Israel to give up promontories and islets commanding access to the Gulf of Aqaba, Israel's channel to the south and east. A congeries of national forces under United Nations aegis took over, but without any stipulations guaranteeing the access desired by Israel. As a consolation, the U.S. secretary of state pledged Israel unspecified support of free access to the Gulf of Aqaba—subject to a waiver in event of a ruling by The International Court of Justice denying international status to the waters concerned. Whatever its contractual significance, the pledge probably added nothing to what the interests of the United States as a maritime power would entail, but its terms, rather than expressing a motif of evenhandedness, aligned the United States with Israel's interests in the matter. What is curious is that the pledge virtually slipped from official recollection—probably because of Secretary of State Dulles' penchant for carrying his office in his brief case. Though it was referred to in former President Eisenhower's last book of White House memoirs, *Waging Peace* and in Herman Finer's *Dulles Over Suez*, its existence has been overlooked in innumerable diplomatic histories and commentaries and ignored on many occasions of testimony. The Deparment of State appears, at least figuratively, to have lacked a file copy, but Israel's Foreign Office had a well-preserved original.

In the autumn of 1966 measures got under way for rehabilitating the Soviet Union's main chosen instrument in the Middle East—namely, President Gamal Abdel Nasser's regime in Egypt, which was having trouble on the home front related to economic sluggishness, a baffling and wasting stalemate in its Yemen intervention, and a general frustration of aims to promote Egyptian ascendancy in fusing Arab unity and socialist revolution. The events thus set in train found the United States deeply involved elsewhere. No part of the horizon gave high promise. America's rationalistic assumptions about general affairs were under serious test at home, where a nation deeply committed to maintaining order over the world was showing no conspicuous talent in the rudiments of keeping order in its streets. A conception of modulated employment of force faced heavy going in Southeast Asia. In the predicament, to use Abraham Lincoln's phrase, of "an ox jumped halfway over the fence," U.S. policy confronted a cheerless choice of pulling back, redoubling exertions, or protracting the unsatisfactory level of effort—none of them certain of result or free of risk. It is easy to cite U.S. preoccupation with Vietnam as the circumstance enabling or tempting the Soviet Union and its Arab clients to attempt what they attempted. Devoted critics of the American venture in Vietnam have so argued, but not convincingly. The Soviet Union's ambitions and Egypt's activism have long antedated United States involvement in Vietnam. In any event, no one in authority in the U.S. government wished for yet another set of exigencies to crop up.

Egypt's restorative entailed a heating up of the old quarrel with Israel. Nasser's apparent purpose—and behind him, the Soviet Union's—was to lay hold of an issue with which to force even the Arab regimes in opposition either to go under or to switch over, along with their military resources substantially supplied by the Soviet Union's strategic adversaries. Borne by success, Egypt would be in a position to regain the initiative in Yemen and to win out in the competition to dominate in South Arabia in the wake of British withdrawal scheduled for early 1968. The initial step was a pact for mutual defense and military collaboration between Egypt and Syria, the latter also a Soviet client whose relationship to Egypt in recent years had flitted among union, hostility, rivalry, and collaboration. Simultaneously, commando raids from Syria into Israel by units of the Palestine Liberation Army were stepped up. In diplomatic privacy, Israel's prime minister, Levi Eshkol—who was originally from the Ukraine, where his relatives still live, and who personified the cautious, Ukraine, exterior-oriented approach—informed the Soviet Union of mounting domestic pressures against temporizing with the raids and of the necessity of making early reprisal. He was warned not to retaliate against Syria. Meanwhile the raids were being explained away as beyond the Syrian government's restraining power. Israel complained to the United Nations Security Council. There the Soviet Union vetoed a watered-down resolution urging Syria to take more effective measures to prevent raids. Thereafter the Syrian government avowed an indulgent, hands-off attitude toward the raids. In a communique issued during a state visit to Paris, the Soviet prime minister included a reference to nondiscrimination against the Soviet Union's Jews and to their freedom of movement to Israel—points with tacit implications not likely to be lost on Eshkol. Making do with second best—a case of clobbering Peter to repay Paul—an Israeli force made a retaliatory raid against a Jordanian village. This was coupled with warning that Syria's turn might be next. The action drew reproof from the Security Council. More important, it added to troubles at home for the Jordanian monarchy, which was under a powerful propaganda assault led by Egypt and Syria for its avowed opposition to Soviet purposes and for its policy toward Israel of formal hostility mitigated with tacit passivity. At the end of 1966 the Jordanian regime was being pressed heavily from within and without.

The new year brought more of the same—mounting infiltration, aborted sessions of the Syrian-Israeli mixed armistice commission, various Arab demands for annihilation of Israel, and repeated Israeli warnings of dire consequences for abettors and perpetrators of raids. By turns, these Israeli warnings named Syria or only hinted at its identity—a slight sign of trepidation. In mid-April Syria began openly to twit Egypt for reluctance to implement the joint military pact. In late April the Soviet Union openly demanded Israel's desistance from any hostile acts against Syria. A significant development, little noted, came on April 30. The Egyptian-supported regime in Yemen issued decrees extending from three to twelve miles its claim of jurisdiction over waters marginal to the mainland and appurtenant islands and claiming the continental shelf to sounding of 200 meters. Linked to the prospective British withdrawal from South Arabia and, by corollary, from Perim Island, these decrees prefigured a design to ban Israeli shipping from the Bab el Mandeb, the strait at the southern end of the Red Sea.

The pace and intensity of warnings and preparatory military moves continued rising until mid-May. According to subsequent Egyptian accounts, the Soviet Union at that juncture passed along purported intelligence indicating an Israeli mobilization against Syria. The two Arab allies thereupon announced the allerting of armed forces to "complete readiness for war." So as to permit deployments to effect its military undertakings with Syria, Egypt demanded retraction of the United Nations Emergency Force, which over a tedious decade had separated Egypt both from its adversary and from the necessity of dealing with that adversary. The United Nations Secretary General, U Thant, explained the impossibility of a piecemeal withdrawal. Egypt responded accordingly. The entire force was withdrawn and disbanded.

The Secretary General's action merits a parenthetical comment. No event of the spring was discussed more vehemently or less cogently. Some critics blamed him for acquiescing at all. Some blamed him for promptness. American, British, and Canadian sources called him irresponsible, supin, culpable, reckless, muddled, and so on, through a long invidious list—all for merely doing what he had to do. The condemnatory extravagance was uncalled for as the surfeit of encomiums six months before, when—in an episode remindful of Byron's lady who "whispering she'd ne'er consent, consented"—he had ended a charade of reluctance about re-election. A memorandum by his predecessor was cited in reproach of U Thant's compliant withdrawal of the United Nations force. The memorandum had no official status. Citing it as authoritative was like giving force of law to a diary entry. Ten years before, Dag Hammarskjold had written the memorandum as a personal interpretation to give guidance to a journalist who was undertaking a book about United Nations peacekeeping and who, in Hammarskjold's view, was too much inclined to take relevant juridic documents at face value—which, in the judgement of many, would be the only proper way to handle them. The Hammarskjold memorandum drew mainly on understandings recollected from negotiatory discussions. According to its allegations the force, once interposed with Egypt's consent, was removable only upon Egypt's and the General Assembly's concurrent determinations of the completion of its mission. Thus, by its premises, the

sovereignty of both Egypt and of governments contributing force components had been impinged upon—Eygpt's, by yielding autonomy-respecting
forces on its territory; the contributors, by yielding control of their own
forces. These were large assumptions to rest on a base as fragile as unofficial
recollections. In point of fact, three of the original ten contributory
governments had meanwhile recalled their forces; two others had cut to
merely nominal participation; and, at the moment of the Secretary General's
action, two more of the main contributory governments, sympathetic to
Egypt's cause, were opting out.

There was less to the United Nations Emergency Force than met the eye.
What was important, however, was not the impaling of a supposition by an
event but that the withdrawal made way for Egyptian forces to resume the
promontories and islets from which to blockade the Gulf of Aqaba—a move
logically consistent with formal hostilities maintained against Israel and with
a long-standing ban on Israeli shipping in the Suez Canal. After five days
bustling with mobilizations, maximum alerts, deployments, and the rallying
of more Arab States to the new alliance, President Nasser on May 23, in a
speech filled with threats of dire vengeance in event of Israeli resistance,
announced a blockade against all Israeli shipping and Israel-bound strategic
cargoes under whatever flag. Israel's prime minister denounced the move as
aggression. In Moscow, Britain's foreign minister found Soviet officials
"completely satisfied" with the new situatuion. Reportedly, however, the
Soviet authorities, fearful lest the situation should get out of hand, were also
cautioning Nasser to restrain his vaunting. On May 26 he spoke again, and
somewhat less bellicosely. Spokesmen around him began rationalizing the
blockade as a step toward a legal test as prefigured in Secretary of State
Dulles' memorandum on access to the Gulf of Aqaba and hinted at possible
flexibility in application. Gossip focused on the chance of working
something out—possibly an easing of restriction in return for a gift of
grain—during the Egyptian vice-president's Washington visit, then planned for
early June.

On the issues as now emerged, the United States was cast unequivocally
with Israel. Pressure was mounting for the president to do something. Some
of the most bitter critics of executive prerogative as applied in Vietnam
completely reversed constitutional precepts and demanded U.S. confrontation with the Arabs at whatever risk of involvement with their Soviet patron.
Many voices invoked plighted national obligations to Israel without defining
them. Amateur admirals devised strategies completely inapposite to the
waters concerned. Fortunately—especially for Israel, as matters turned
out—the president ignored the chatter. On a quick visit, the Israeli foreign
minister found him sympathetic but in no mood to be hurried into new
hostilities. Before testing the blockade, the United States would take care to
line up diplomatic support among other maritime nations—an endeavor
which elicited a few proffers of moral protest but none of material
commitment. Israel chartered a ship in the environs and rushed a crew

around Africa to man it for an early test of the issue with Egypt—a gesture soon to be foreclosed by other events.

As the month closed, Israel was under stress as its mainly civilian forces stood to arms in response to Arab troop concentrations. Its spokesmen had only a promise of abstract support from outside against the blockade. On the night of May 28 the Soviet ambassador, delivering his government's accusatory protest against Israel's military preparations, found the Israeli prime minister deferential to the extent of inviting the ambassador's inspection of Israeli military dispositions and offering to fly to Moscow at once to explain. The next day new declarations were issued from the Syrian president arriving in Moscow, the prime minister at Damascus, and Nasser in Cairo warning of dire results in store for a resistant Israel. The Soviet Union again voiced support of Nasser. Jordan's king, swept along by popular pressure, signed on as an ally in Cairo. Soviet policy-makers could congratulate themselves for having managed a crisis to the very edge of a great success. The Egyptian bandwagon was rolling. Arab governments were climbing aboard. Israel was now boxed in. Official pronouncements there of being on the brink of war and of fighting alone if necessary could be dismissed as the bravado of desperate men. Moscow's Arab clients were also in a self-congratulatory mood and, in presumption of assured success, relaxed a bit.

Egypt's assertion of blockading the Gulf of Aqaba has been cited as the precipitant of the war which soon took the Arab countries by surprise. The action provided a respectable excuse but probably was not causative. Only one Israeli flagship had entered those waters in two years. At any rate, the loopholes in Nasser's asserted ban on strategic goods might have proved sufficiently commodious. The basis asserted on April 30 for eventually closing the Bab el Mandeb, a thousand miles to the south, was probably even more portentous for Israel's interests. Jordan's adherence to the alliance has also been cited as the triggering event. It is doubtful whether it made a determining difference in Israel's military situation. It is probably erroneous to attribute the decision for war to any one factor.

The Israeli foreign minister's return from Washington on May 27 prompted a crtitical reappraisal within the Israeli cabinet. Israel's whole approach in managing the crisis was called in question. The effort both to mollify the Soviet Union and to deter its clients obviously was not working. Israel could not afford production losses entailed in having its mainly civilian forces stand to arms indefinitely. It dared not suspend the armed vigil in view of the strength mobilized around its borders. What future was therein being impelled to call up forces whenever the now more or less coordinated Arab states should decide to turn military pressure on as a convenience for policy? What future was there in trying to cope with hostile neighbors and their sponsors in Moscow on a basis of asserted unilateral belligerent rights? Implications of the Soviet Union's augmenting weight in the region were canvassed. The cabinet decided in favor of military action to undercut the military foundations of the designs entertained by the Soviet Union and its clients. In the taking of that decision one Israeli attitude submerged, and the contrasting one became ascendant. The decision was premised on an assumption that Israel must act for itself rather than wait for others. The importance of exterior balances was not, however, discounted. The decision involved an estimate, which would prove correct, that the Soviet Union, facing the implications of U. S. concern in the area along with its nuclear and naval resources, would stand aside from the combat. The action decided on was executed with the intrepidity of men who know they cannot afford defeat. The immediate result is now well known. Perhaps the most extraordinary thing about the decision and the ensuing war was the Arabs' and the Russsians' failure to foresee them—a case of governments taken in by their own plans.

Whether the success achieved will prove durable for Israel remains problematic. Israel won more ground than it could wish to hold. It has found no way of relinquishing ground by negotiation, and it has refused this time to yield to the proposition that it must surrender a perimeter not regarded as legitimate by its neighbors in order to resume a perimeter which they also hold illegitimate. The great increase of alienated peoples under its jurisdiction may well make it more vulnerable to unconventional attack. Its neighbors remain unreconciled to its existence. Their pride is more deeply wounded than ever. Perhaps none of the regimes could survive a gesture of accommodation. The Arab intransigents appear even more in clientage to the Soviet Union than before their debacle. Hopes are uttered for moderation or even reform of the Soviet Union's conduct in consequence of lessons learned. Though such an upshot is theoretically conceivable, it should be remembered that views of reality are hugely difficult to cast aside, and any regime must be tenacious of its *raison d'etre*. It is doubtful whether the Soviet Union, even if it wishes, could afford to renounce sponsorship of a revolutionary future.

There may well be room, however, for at least a show of elasticity on immediate issues. In the opportunities offered in Yemen and magnified by the prospect of British withdrawal from South Arabia, the Soviet Union has an alternative avenue toward securing a purchase on the relevant waterways. Without disadvantage to its interests and purposes, the Soviet Union can probably afford to undertake now a role of fostering Arab accommodation toward Israel. In any case, some gesture of this sort would scarcely result in alienating the Arab intransigents, who would have no other place to turn for patronage. Such a gesture, even if it fails to change the situation materially, would earn the Soviet Union credits for good intent among those ever watching for hopeful portents. The unlikely event of success, on the other hand, might forward the Soviet aim of cultivating Israel as a client.

A time when Israel can relax into what would be, by rationalist assumptions, a normal environment is not in sight, because the Middle East will probably remain as obdurate as ever. Yet changes will occur. One change in prospect pertains to the Suez Canal. Lord Palmerston had a point, a century ago, in doubting the wisdom of creating the canal, since its existence would focus too much importance and anxiety on an area too much inclined to instability. Ernest Renan, welcoming Ferdinand de Lesseps to the Academy in 1885, cited Jesus' words, "I come not to bring peace but a sword," and went on prophetically:

> This saying must frequently have crossed your mind. Now that you have cut through it, the isthmus has become a defile, that is to say a battlefield. The Bosporus by itself has been enough to keep the civilized world embarrassed up to the present, but now you have created a second and much more serious embarrassment. Not merely does the canal connect two inland seas, but it serves as a communicating passage to the oceans of the globe. In case of maritime war it will be of supreme importance, and everyone will be striving at top speed to occupy it. You have thus marked out a great battlefield for the future.

The closure enforced by Egypt as a result of the June fighting will force consideration of the question whether so vital a waterway must be left subject to whims of local ambition. The answer probably does not lie in any grandiose scheme for internationalization. It rises from circumstances imposed by the closure itself. The world's commerce is adjusting. It must learn to get along very well without the canal by using the Cape route. With a decline in international concern for the canal, Egypt's leverage will diminish. Also, Israel may then be left more and more to fend for itself. The attitude that prevailed in early June is prophetic for Israel.

# On The Israeli-Arab War*

Interview with Isaac Deutscher

**As an introduction, could you sum up your general view of the Arab-Israeli War?**

The war and the "miracle" of Israel's victory have, in my view, solved none of the problems that confront Israel and the Arab states. They have, on the contrary, aggravated all the old issues and created new, more dangerous ones. They have not increased Israel's security, but rendered it more vulnerable than it had been. I am convinced that the latest, all-too-easy triumph of Israeli arms will be seen one day, in a not very remote future, to have been a disaster in the first instance for Israel itself.

Let us consider the international background of the events. We have to relate this war to the world-wide power struggle and ideological conflicts which form its context. In these last years American imperialism and the forces associated with it and supported by it have been engaged in a tremendous political, ideological, economic, and military offensive over a vast area of Asia and Africa, while the forces opposed to them, the Soviet Union in the first instance, have barely held their ground or have been in retreat. This trend emerges from a long series of occurrences: the Ghanaian upheaval, in which Nkrumah's government was overthrown; the growth of reaction in various Afro-Asian countries; the bloody triumph of anti-Communism in Indonesia, which was a huge victory for counterrevolution in Asia; the escalation of the American war in Vietnam; and the "marginal" right-wing military coup in Greece. The Arab-Israeli War

*From "Interview with Isaac Deutscher: On the Israeli—Arab War," *New Left Review*, No. 44 (July-August, 1967), pp. 30-45, by permission of the publisher.

was not an isolated affair; it belongs to this category of events. The countertrend has manifested itself in revolutionary ferment in various parts of India, the radicalization of the political mood in Arab countries, the effective struggle of the National Front of Liberation in Vietnam, and the world-wide growth of opposition to American intervention. The advance of American imperialism and of Afro-Asian counter revolution has not gone unopposed, but its success everywhere outside Vietnam has been evident.

In the Middle East the American forward push has been of relatively recent date. During the Suez War, the United States still adopted an "anticolonialist" stance. It acted, in seeming accord with the Soviet Union, to bring about British and French withdrawal. The logic of American policy was still the same as in the late 1940s, when the State of Israel was in the making. As long as the American ruling class was interested primarily in squeezing out the old colonial powers from Africa and Asia, the White House was a mainstay of "anitcolonialism." But, having contributed to the debacle of the old empires, the United States took fright at the "power vacuum" that might be filled by native revolutionary forces or the Soviet Union or a combination of both. Yankee anticolonialism faded out, and America "stepped in." In the Middle East this happened during the period between the Suez crisis and the last Israeli war. The American landings in Lebanon in 1958 were designed to stem a high tide of revolution in that area, especially in Iraq. Since then the United States, no doubt relying to some extent on Soviet "moderation," has avoided open and direct military involvement in the Middle East and maintained a posture of detachment. This does not make the American presence any less real.

## How would you situate Israel's policy in this perspective?

The Israelis have, of course, acted on their own motives and not merely to suit the convenience of American policy. That the great mass of Israelis believe themselves to be menaced by Arab hostility need not be doubted. That some "bloodthirsty" Arab declarations about "wiping Israel off the map" made Israeli flesh creep is evident. Haunted by the memories of the Jewish tragedy in Europe, the Israelis feel isolated and encircled by the "teeming" millions of a hostile Arab world. Nothing was easier for their own propagandists, aided by Arab verbal threats, than to play up the fear of another "final solution" threating the Jews, this time in Asia. Conjuring up Biblical myths and all the ancient religious-national symbols of Jewish history, the propagandists whipped up that frenzy of belligerence, arrogance, and fanaticism, of which the Israelis gave such startling displays as they rushed to Sinai and the Wailing Wall and to Jordan and the walls of Jericho. Behind the frenzy and arrogance there lay Israel's suppressed sense of guilt toward the Arabs, the feeling that the Arabs would never forget or forgive the blows Israel had inflicted on them: the seizure of their land, the fate of a million or more refugees, and repeated military defeats and humiliations.

Driven half-mad by fear of Arab revenge, the Israelis have, in their overwhelming majority, accepted the "doctrine" behind their government's policy, the "doctrine" that holds that Israel's security lies in periodic warfare which every few years must reduce the Arab states to impotence.

Yet whatever their own motives and fears, the Israelis are not independent agents. The factors of Israel's dependence were to some extent "built in" in its history over two decades. All Israeli governments have staked Israel's existence on the "Western orientation." This alone would have sufficed to turn Israel into a Western outpost in the Middle East, and so to involve it in the great conflict between imperialism, (or neocolonialism) and the Arab peoples struggling for their emancipation. Other factors have been at play as well. Israel's economy has depended for its tenuous balance and growth on foreign Zionist financial aid, especially on American donations. These donations have been a curse in disguise for the new state. They have enabled the government to manage its balance of payments in a way in which no country in the world can do without engaging in any trade with its neighbours. It has distorted Israel's economic structure by encouraging the growth of a large, unproductive sector and a standard of living which is not related to the country's own productivity and earnings. Israel has in effect lived well above its means. Over many years nearly half of Israel's food was imported from the West. As the American administration exempts from taxation the earnings and profits earmarked as donations for Israel, Washington has held its hand on the purses on which Israel's economy depends. Washington could at any time hit Israel by refusing the tax exemption (even though this would lose it the Jewish vote in elections). The threat of such a sanction, never uttered but always present and occasionally hinted at, has been enough to align Israeli policy firmly with the United States.

Years ago, when I visited Israel, a high Israeli official listed to me the factories that they could not build because of American objections—among them steel mills and plants producing agricultural machinery. On the other hand, there was a list of virtually useless factories turning out fantastic amounts of plastic kitchen utensils, toys, and so on. Nor could any Israeli administration ever feel free to consider seriously Israel's vital, long-term need for trade and close economic ties with its Arab neighbours or for improving economic relations with the U.S.S.R. and Eastern Europe.

Economic dependence has affected Israel's domestic policy and "cultural atmosphere" in other ways as well. The American donor is the most important foreign investor operating in the Holy Land. A wealthy American Jew, a "worldly businessman" among his gentile associates and friends in New York, Philadelphia, or Detroit, he is at heart proud to be a member of the Chosen People, and in Israel exercises his influence in favour of religious obscurantism and reaction. A fervent believer in free enterprise, he views with a hostile eye even the mild "socialism" of the Histardrut and the kibbutzim and has done his bit in taming it. Above all, he has helped the rabbis to maintain their stranglehold on legislation and much of the education and so to keep alive the spirit of racial-talmudic exclusiveness and superiority. All this has fed and inflamed the antagonism toward the Arabs.

The cold war imparted great momentum to the reactionary trends and exacerbated the Arab-Jewish conflict. Israel was firmly committed to anti-Communism. True, Stalin's policy in his last years, outbreaks of anti-Semitism in the U.S.S.R., anti-Jewish motifs in the trials of Slansky, Rajk, and Kostov, and Soviet encouragement of even the most irrational forms of Arab nationalism all bore their share of responsibility for Israel's attitude. Yet it should not be forgotten that Stalin had been Israel's godfather; that it was with Czechoslovak munitions, supplied on Stalin's orders, that the Jews had fought the British occupation army—and the Arabs—in 1947 and 1948; and that the Soviet envoy was the first to vote for the recognition of the State of Israel by the United Nations. It may be argued that Stalin's change of attitude toward Israel was itself a reaction to Israel's alignment with the West. And in the post-Stalin era the Israeli governments have persisted in this alignment.

Irreconcilable hostility to Arab aspirations for emancipation from the West thus became the axiom of Israeli policy—hence, Israel's role in 1956, in the Suez War. Israel's Social Democratic ministers, no less than Western colonialists, have embraced a *raison d'etat* which sees its highest wisdom in keeping the Arabs backward and divided and playing their reactionary Hashemite and other feudal elements against the Republican, national-revolutionary forces. In early 1967, when it seemed that a republican uprising or *coup* might overthrow King Hussein, Mr. Eshkol's government made no bones about it that, in case of a "Nasserite coup" in Amman, Israeli troops would march into Jordan. The prelude to the events of June, 1967, was provided by Israel's adoption of a menacing attitude toward Syria's new regime, which it denounced as "Nasserite" or even "ultra-Nasserite" (for Syria's government appeared to be a shade more anti-imperialist and radical than Egypt's).

Did Israel, in fact, plan to attack Syria some time in May, as Soviet intelligence services believed and as Moscow warned Nasser? We do not know. It was as a result of this warning, and with Soviet encouragement that Nasser ordered mobilization and concentration of troops on the Sinai frontier. If Israel had such a plan, Nasser's move may have delayed the attack on Syria by a few weeks. If Israel had no such plan, its behaviour gave to its anti-Syrian threats the kind of plausibility that Arab threats had in Israeli eyes. In any case, Israel's rulers were quite confident that their aggressiveness *vis-a-vis* either Syria or Egypt would meet with Western sympathy and bring them reward. This calculation underlay their decision to strike the preemptive blow on June 5. They were absolutely sure of American and to some extent British moral, political, and economic support. They knew that, no matter how far they went in attacking the Arabs, they could count on American diplomatic protection or, at the very least, on American official indulgence. And they were not mistaken. The White House and the Pentagon could not fail to appreciate men who, for their own reasons, were out to put down the Arab enemies of American neocolonialism. General Dayan acted as a kind of Marshal Ky for the Middle East and appeared to be doing his job with startling speed, efficiency, and ruthlessness. He was, and is, a much cheaper and far less embarrassing ally than Ky.

## Could we now turn to the Arab side of the picture and their behaviour on the eve of the crisis?

The Arab behaviour, especially Nasser's divided mind and hesitation on the eve of hostilities, present indeed a striking contrast to Israel's determination and uninhibited aggressiveness. Having, with Soviet encouragement, moved his troops to the Sinai frontier, and even put his Russian-made missiles in position, Nasser then, without consulting Moscow, proclaimed the blockade of the Straits of Tiran. This was a provocative move, though practically of very limited significance. The Western powers did not consider it important enough to try to "test" the blockade. It provided Nasser with a prestige gain and enabled him to claim that he had wrested from Israel the last fruit of their 1956 victory. (Before the Suez War Israeli ships could not pass through these straights). The Israelis played up the blockade as a mortal danger to their economy which it was not; and they replied by mobilizing their forces and moving them to the frontiers.

Soviet propaganda still continued to encourage the Arabs in public. However, a conference of Middle Eastern Communist parties held in May (its resolutions were summarized in *Pravda*) was strangely reticent about the crisis and allusively critical of Nasser. What was more important were curious diplomatic manoeuvres behind the scenes. On May 26 in the dead of night (at 2:30 A.M.), the Soviet Ambassador woke up Nasser to give him a grave warning that the Egyptian army must not be the first to open fire. Nasser complied. The compliance was so thorough that he not only refrained from starting hostilities but took no precautions whatsoever against the possibility of an Israeli attack; he left his airfields undefended and his planes grounded and uncamouflaged. He did not even bother to mine the Straits of Tiran or to place a few guns on the shores (as the Israelis found out to their surprise when they arrived there).

All this suggests hopeless bungling on Nasser's part and on the part of the Egyptian command. But the real bunglers sat in the Kremlin. Brezhnev's and Kosygin's behaviour during these events was reminiscent of Khrushchev's during the Cuban crisis, though even more muddle-headed. The pattern was the same. In the first phase there was needless provocation of the other side and a reckless move toward the "brink"; in the next, sudden panic and a hasty retreat; and then, frantic attempts to save face and cover up the traces. Having excited Arab fears, encouraged them to risky moves, promised to stand by them, and having brought out their own naval units into the Mediterranean to counter the moves of the American Sixth Fleet, the Russians then tied Nasser hand and foot.

Why did they do it? As the tension was mounting, the "hot line" between the Kremlin and the White House went into action. The two super powers agreed to avoid direct intervention and to curb the parties to the conflict. If the Americans went through the motions of curbing the Israelis, they must have done it so perfunctorily or with so many winks that the Israelis felt, in fact, encouraged to go ahead with their plan for the pre-emptive blow. (We have, at any rate, not heard of the American ambassador waking up the Israeli prime Minister to warn him that the Israelis must not be the first to open fire). The Soviet curb on Nasser was heavy, rude, and effective. Even so, Nasser's failure to take elementary military precautions remains something of a puzzle. Did the Soviet ambassador in the course of his nocturnal visit tell Nasser that Moscow was sure that the Israelis would not strike first? Had Washington given Moscow such an assurance? Was Moscow so gullible as to take it at face value and act on it? It seems almost incredible that this should have been so; but only some such version of the events can account for Nasser's inactivity and for Moscow's stunned surprise at the outbreak of hostilities.

Behind all this bungling loomed the central contradiction in Soviet policy. On the one hand the Soviet leaders see in the preservation of the international *status quo,* including the social *status quo,* the essential condition of their national security and of "peaceful coexistence." They are therefore anxious to keep at a "safe distance" from storm centers of class conflict in the world and to avoid dangerous foreign entanglements. On the other hand they cannot, for ideological and power-political reasons, altogether avoid dangerous entanglements. They cannot quite keep at a safe distance when American neocolonialism clashes directly or indirectly with its Afro-Asian and Latin American enemies, who look to Moscow as their friend and protector. In normal times this contradiction is only latent; Moscow works for *detente* and rapprochement with the U.S., and it cautiously aids and arms its Afro-Asian and Cuban friends. But sooner or later the moment of crisis comes, and the contradiction explodes in Moscow's face. Soviet policy must then choose between its allies and *proteges* working against the *status quo,* and its own commitment to the *status quo.* When the choice is pressing and ineluctable, it opts for the *status quo.*

The dilemma is real and, in the nuclear age, dangerous enough; but it confronts the United States as well, for the U.S. is just as much interested in avoiding world war and nuclear conflict as is the U.S.S.R. This, however, limits U.S. freedom of action and of political-ideological offensive far less than it restricts Soviet freedom. Washington is far less afraid of the possibility that some move by one of its *proteges* or its own military intervention might lead to a direct confrontation of the super powers. After the Cuban crisis and the war in Vietnam, the Arab-Israeli war has once again sharply illuminated the difference.

**One critical problem is obviously whether the Israelis have
ever had any chance of establishing normal or merely tolerable
relations with the Arabs. Did they ever have any option at all?
To what extent was the last war the outcome of a long chain
of irreversible events?**

To some extent the present situation has been determined by the whole
course of Arab-Israeli relations since the Second World War and even since
the First. Yet I believe that some options were open to the Israelis. Allow me
to quote a parable with the help of which I once tried to present this
problem to an Israeli audience.

A man once jumped from the top floor of a burning house in which many
members of his family had already perished. He managed to save his life; but,
as he was falling to the ground, he hit a person standing down below and
broke that person's legs and arms. The jumping man had no choice; yet to
the man with the broken limbs he was the cause of his misfortune. If both
behaved rationally, they would not become enemies. The man who escaped
from the blazing house, having recovered, would have tried to help and
console the other sufferer; and the latter might have realized that he was the
victim of circumstances over which neither of them had control. But look
what happens when these people behave irrationally. The injured man blames
the other for his misery and swears to make him pay for it. The other one,
afraid of the crippled man's revenge, insults him, kicks him, and beats him up
whenever they meet. The kicked man again swears revenge and is again
punched and punished. The bitter enmity, so whimsical at first, hardens and
comes to overshadow the whole existence of both men and to poison their
minds.

You will, I am sure, recognize yourselves (I said to my Israeli audience),
the Israeli remnants of European Jewry, in the man who jumped from the
blazing house. The other character represents, of course, the Palestinian
Arabs, more than a million of them, who have lost their lands and their
homes. They are resentful; they gaze from across the frontiers on their old
native places; they raid you stealthily and swear revenge. You punch and
kick them mercilessly; you have shown that you know how to do it. But
what is the sense of it? And what is the prospect?

The responsibility for the tragedy of European Jews, for Auschwitz,
Majdanek, and the slaughters in the ghetto, rests entirely on our Western
bourgeois "civilization," of which nazism was the legitimate, even though
degenerate, offspring. Yet it was the Arabs who were made to pay the price
for the crimes the West committed toward the Jews. They are still made to
pay it; for the "guilty conscience" of the West is, of course, pro-Israeli and
anti-Arab. How easily Israel has allowed itself to be bribed and fooled by the
false "conscience money."

A rational relationship between Israelis and Arabs might have been possible if Israel had at least attempted to establish it, if the man who jumped

from the burning house had tried to make friends with the innocent victim of his descent and compensate him. This did not happen. Israel never even recognized the Arab grievance. From the outset Zionism worked toward the creation of a purely Jewish state and was glad to rid the country of its Arab inhabitants. No Israeli government has ever seriously looked for any opportunity to remove or assuage the grievance. They refused even to consider the fate of the huge mass of refugees unless the Arab states first recognized Israel, unless, that is, the Arabs surrendered politically before starting negotiations. Perhaps this might still be excused as bargaining tactics. The disastrous aggravation of Arab-Israeli relations was brought about by the Suez War, when Israel unashamedly acted as the spearhead of the old bankrupt European imperialisms in their last common stand in the Middle East, in their last attempt to maintain their grip on Egypt. The Israelis did not have to align themselves with the shareholders of the Suez Canal Company. The pros and cons were clear; there was no question of any mixture of rights and wrongs on either side. The Israelis put themselves totally in the wrong, morally and politically.

On the face of it, the Arab-Israeli conflict is only a clash of two rival nationalisms, each moving within the vicious circle of its self-righteous and inflated ambitions. From the viewpoint of an abstract internationalism nothing would be easier than to dismiss both as equally worthless and reactionary. However, such a view would ignore the social and political realities of the situation. The nationalism of the people in semicolonial or colonial countries fighting for their independence must not be put on the same moral-political level as the nationalism of conquerors and oppressors. The former has a historic justification and progressive aspect which the latter has not. Clearly, Arab nationalism, unlike Israeli, still belongs to the former category.

Yet even the nationalism of the exploited and oppressed should not be viewed uncritically, for there are various phases in its development. In one phase the progressive aspirations prevail; in another reactionary tendencies come to the surface. From the moment independence is won or nearly won, nationalism tends to shed its revolutionary aspect altogether and turns into a retrograde ideology. We have seen this happening in India, Indonesia, Israel, and to some extent even in China. Even in the revolutionary phase each nationalism has a streak of irrationality, an inclination to exclusiveness, national egoism, and racism. Arab nationalism, despite all its historic merits and progressive functions, also contains such ingredients.

The June crisis has revealed some of the basic weaknesses of Arab political thought and action: the lack of political strategy, a proneness to emotional self-intoxication, and an excessive reliance on nationalist demagogy. These weaknesses were among the decisive causes of the Arab defeat. By indulging in threats to destroy Israel and even threats of "extermination"—and how empty these threats were has been amply demonstrated by the Arabs' utter military unpreparedness—some of Egypt's and Jordan's propagandists provided plenty of grist to Israeli chauvinism and enabled Israel's government to work up the mass of its people into the paroxysm of fear and ferocious aggressiveness which then burst upon Arab heads.

It is a truism that war is a continuation of policy. The Six-Day War has shown up the relative immaturity of the present Arab regimes. The Israelis owe their triumph not merely to the pre-emptive blow but also to a more modern economic, political, and military organization. To some extent the war drew a balance on the decade of Arab development since the Suez War and revealed its grave inadequacies. The modernization of the socio-economic structures of Egypt and the other Arab states and of Arab political thinking has proceeded far more slowly than people inclined to idealize the present Arab regimes have assumed.

The persisting backwardness is, of course, rooted in socio-economic conditions. But ideology and methods of organization are in themselves factors of weakness. I have in mind the single-party system, the cult of Nasserism, and the absence of free discussion. All of this has greatly hampered the political education of the masses and the work of socialist enlightenment. The negative results have made themselves felt on various levels. When major decisions of policy depend on a more or less autocratic leader, there is in normal times no genuine popular participation in the political processes, no vigilant and active consciousness, no initiative from below. This has had many consequences, even military ones. The Israeli pre-emptive blow, delivered with conventional weapons, would not have had such a devastating impact if Egypt's armed forces had been accustomed to rely on the initiative of individual officers and soldiers. Local commanders would then have taken the elementary defensive precautions without waiting for orders from above. Military inefficiency reflected here a wider and deeper, social-political weakness. The military-bureaucratic methods of Nasserism also hamper the political integration of the Arab movement of liberation. Nationalist demagogy flourishes only all too easily; but it is no substitute for a real impulse to national unity and for a real mobilization of popular forces against the divisive, feudal, and reactionary elements. We have seen how, during the emergency, excessive reliance on a single leader made the fate of the Arab states dependent in fact on the intervention of the great powers and accidents of diplomatic manoeuvre.

**To return to Israel, what use is it going to make of victory? How do the Israelis visualize their further role in that part of the world?**

Paradoxically and grotesquely, the Israelis appear now in the role of the Prussians of the Middle East. They have now won three wars against their Arab neighbours, just as the Prussians a century ago defeated all their neighbours within a few years—the Danes, the Austrians, and the French. The succession of victories bred in them an absolute confidence in their own efficiency, a blind reliance on the force of their arms, chauvinistic arrogance, and contempt for other peoples. I fear that a similar degeneration—for degeneration it is—may be taking place in the political character of Israel. Yet, as the Prussia of the Middle East, Israel can be only a feeble parody of the original. The Prussians were at least able to use their victories for uniting in their *Reich* all German-speaking peoples living outside the Austro-Hungarian Empire. Germany's neighbours were divided among themselves by interest, history, religion, and language. Bismarck, Wilhelm II, and Hitler could play them off against one another. The Israelis are surrounded by Arabs only. Attempts to play the Arab states against one another are bound to fail in the end. The Arabs were at loggerheads with one another in 1948, when Israel waged its first war; they were far less divided in 1956, during Israel's second war; and they formed a common front in 1967. They may prove far more firmly united in any future confrontation with Israel.

The Germans have summed up their own experience in the bitter phrase: "Man kann sich totsiegen!" "You can rush yourself victoriously into your grave." This is what the Israelis have been doing. They have bitten off much more than they can swallow. In the conquered territories and in Israel there are now nearly one and a half million Arabs, well over 40 per cent of the total population. Will the Israelis expel this mass of Arabs in order to hold "securely" the conquered lands? This would create a new refugee problem, more dangerous and larger than the old one. Will they give up the conquered territories? No, say most of their leaders. Ben Gurion, the evil spirit of Israeli chauvinism, urges the creation of an "Arab Palestinian state" on the Jordan, which would be an Israeli protectorate. Can Israel expect that the Arabs will accept such a protectorate, that they will not fight it tooth and nail? None of the Israeli parties is prepared even to contemplate a binational Arab-Israeli state. Meanwhile great numbers of Arabs have been "induced" to leave their homes on the Jordan, and the treatment of those who have stayed behind is far worse than that of the Arab minority in Israel, who were kept under martial law for nineteen years. Yes, this victory is worse for Israel than a defeat. Far from giving Israel a higher degree of security, it has rendered it much more insecure. If Arab revenge and extermination are what the Israelis feared, they have behaved as if they were bent on turning a bogey into an actual menace.

## Did Israel's victory bring any real gain to the United States? Has it furthered the American ideological offensive in Afro-Asia?

There was a moment, at the cease-fire, when it looked as if Egypt's defeat had led to Nasser's downfall and to the undoing of the policy associated with his name. If that had happened, the Middle East would have almost certainly been brought back into the Western sphere of influence. Egypt might have become another Ghana or Indonesia. This did not happen however. The Arab masses, who came out in the streets and squares of Cairo, Damascus, and Beirut to demand that Nasser should stay in office, prevented it. This was one of those rare historic popular impulses that redress or upset a political balance within a few moments. This time, in the hour of defeat, the initiative from below worked with immediate impact. There are only very few cases in history when a people stood by a defeated leader in this way. The situation is, of course, still fluid. Reactionary influences will go on working within the Arab states to achieve something like a Ghanaian or Indonesian coup. But for the time being neocolonialism has been denied the fruit of Israel's "victory."

**Moscow's influence and prestige have, as a result of these events, suffered a great reverse. Is this a permanent loss or a temporary one, and is it likely to have an effect on political alignments in Moscow?**

"The Russians have let us down!" was the bitter cry that came from Cairo, Damascus, and Beirut in June. When the Arabs saw the Soviet delegate at the United Nations voting in unison with the Americans for a cease-fire to which no condition for a withdrawal of Israeli troops was attached, they felt utterly betrayed. "The Soviet Union will now sink to the rank of a second or fourth-rate power," Nasser was reported to have told the Soviet ambassador. The events appeared to justify the Chinese accusation of Soviet collusion with the United States. The debacle aroused an alarm in Eastern Europe as well. "If the Soviet Union could let down Egypt like this, may it not also let us down when we are once again confronted by German aggression?" the Poles and the Czechs wondered. The Yugoslavs, too, were outraged. Tito, Gomulka, and other leaders rushed to Moscow to demand an explanation and a rescue operation for the Arabs. This was all the more remarkable as the demand came from the "moderates" and the "revisionists," who normally stand for "peaceful coexistence" and rapprochement with the U.S. Yet they were the ones who were speaking of Soviet "collusion with American imperialism."

The Soviet leaders had to do something. The fact that the intervention of the Arab masses had saved the Nasser regime unexpectedly provided Moscow with fresh scope for manoeuvre. After the great letdown, the Soviet leaders again came to the fore as the friends and protectors of the Arab states. A few spectacular gestures, breaking off diplomatic relations with Israel, and speeches at the United Nations cost them little. Even the White House showed "understanding" for their "predicament," for the "tactical necessity" which presently brought Kosygin to the United Nations Assembly.

However, something more than gestures was required to restore the Soviet position. The Arabs demanded that the Soviet Union should at once help them to rebuild their military strength, the strength they had lost through compliance with Soviet advice. They asked for new planes, new tanks, new guns, new stocks of munitions. But apart from the cost—the value of the military equipment lost by Egypt alone is put at a billion pounds—the reconstitution of the Arab armed forces carries, from Moscow's viewpoint, major political risks. The Arabs refuse to negotiate with Israel; they may well afford to leave Israel to choke on its victory. Rearmament is Cairo's top priority. Israel has taught the Egyptians a lesson; next time the Egyptian air force may strike the pre-emptive blow. And Moscow has had to decide whether it will supply the weapons for the blow.

Moscow cannot favour the idea of such an Arab retaliation, but neither can it refuse to rearm Egypt. Yet Arab rearmament will almost certainly tempt Israel to interrupt the process and strike another pre-emptive blow, in which case the Soviet Union would once again be faced with the same dilemma. If Egypt were to strike first, the United States would almost certainly intervene. The Sixth Fleet would not look on from the Mediterranean if the Israeli air force were knocked out and the Arabs were about to march into Jerusalem or Tel Aviv. If the U.S.S.R. again kept out of the conflict, it would irretrievably destroy its international power position.

A week after the cease-fire the Soviet chief of staff was in Cairo; and Soviet advisers and experts crowded the hotels there, beginning to work on the reconstitution of Egypt's armed forces. Yet Moscow cannot face with equanimity the prospect of an Arab-Israeli competition in pre-emptive blows and its wider implications. The Soviet experts in Cairo probably were making haste slowly, while Soviet diplomacy tried to "win the peace" for the Arabs after it had lost them the war. But even the most clever playing for time cannot solve the central issue of Soviet policy. How much longer can the Soviet Union adapt itself to the American forward push? How far can it retreat before the American economic, political, and military offensives across the Afro-Asian area? Not for nothing did *Krasnaya Zuezda* already in June suggest that the current Soviet conception of peaceful coexistence might be in need of some revision. The military, and not they alone, fear that Soviet retreats are increasing the dynamic of the American forward push and that, if this goes on, a direct Soviet-American clash may become inevitable. If Brezhnev and Kosygin do not manage to cope with this issue, changes in leadership are quite possible. The Cuban and Vietnamese crises contributed to Khrushchev's downfall. The full consequences of the Middle Eastern crisis have yet to unfold.

## What solutions do you see to this situation? Can the conflict still be resolved in any rational manner?

I do not believe that it can be so resolved by military means. To be sure, no one can deny the Arab states the right to reconstitute their armed forces to some extent. But what they need far more urgently is a social and political strategy and new methods in their struggle for emancipation. This cannot be a purely negative strategy dominated by the anti-Israeli obsession. They may refuse to parley with Israel as long as Israel has not given up its conquests. They will necessarily resist the occupation regime on the Jordan and in the Gaza Strip. But this need not mean a renewal of war.

The strategy that can yield the Arabs far greater gains than those that can be obtained in any Holy War or through a pre-emptive blow, a strategy that would bring them real victory, a civilized victory, must be centered on the imperative and urgent need for an intensive modernization of the structure of the Arab economy and of Arab politics and on the need for a genuine integration of Arab national life, which is still broken up by the old, inherited, and imperialist-sponsored frontiers and divisions. These aims can be promoted only if the revolutionary and socialist tendencies in Arab politics are strengthened and developed.

Finally, Arab nationalism will be incomparably more effective as a liberating force if it is disciplined and rationalized by an element of internationalism that will enable the Arabs to approach the problem of Israel more realistically than hitherto. They cannot go on denying Israel's right to exist and indulging in bloodthirsty rhetoric. Economic growth, industrialization, education, more efficient organization, and more sober policies are bound to give the Arabs what sheer numbers and anti-Israeli fury have not been able to give them, namely, an actual preponderance which should almost automatically reduce Israel to its modest proportions and its proper role in the Middle East.

This is, of course, not a short-term programme. Yet its realization need not take too much time; and there is no shorter way to emancipation. The short cuts of demagogy, revenge, and war have proved disastrous enough. Meanwhile, Arab policy should be based on a direct appeal to the Israeli people over the heads of the Israeli government, on an appeal to the workers and the kibbutzim. The Israeli people should be freed from their fears by clear assurances and pledges that Israel's legitimate interests are respected and that Israel may even be welcome as a member of a future Middle Eastern federation. This would cause the orgy of Israeli chauvinism to subside and would stimulate opposition to Eshkol's and Dayan's policy of conquest and domination. The capacity of Israeli workers to respond to such an appeal should not be underrated.

More independence from the great-power game is also necessary. That game has distorted the social-political development of the Middle East. I have shown how much American influence has done to give Israel's policy its present repulsive and reactionary character. But Russian influence has also done something to warp Arab minds by feeding them with arid slogans and encouraging demagogy, while Moscow's egoism and opportunism have fostered disillusionment and cynicism. If Middle East policy continues to be merely a plaything of the great powers, the prospect will be bleak indeed. Neither Jews nor Arabs will be able to break out of their vicious spirals. This is what we, of the Left, should be telling both the Arabs and the Jews as clearly and bluntly as we can.

**The crisis clearly caught the Left by surprise and found it disoriented and divided, both in Great Britain and in France, and, it seems, in the United States as well. In the U.S. fears have been expressed that the division over Israel might even split the movement against the war in Vietnam.**

Yes, the confusion has been undeniable and widespread. I shall not speak here of such "friends of Israel" as messrs. Mollet and his company, who, like Lord Avon and Selwyn Lloyd, saw in this war a continuation of the Suez campaign and revenge for their discomfiture in 1956. Nor shall I waste words on the right-wing Zionist lobby in the Labour party. But even on the "extreme Left" of that party men like Sidney Silverman behaved as if to illustrate someone's saying: "Scratch a Jewish left-winger, and you find only a Zionist."

The confusion showed itself even further on the Left and affected people with an otherwise unimpeachable record of struggle against imperialism. A French writer known for his courageous stands against the wars in Algeria and Vietnam called for solidarity with Israel, declaring that, if Israel's survival demanded American intervention, he would favour it and even raise the cry "Vive le President Johnson." Didn't it occur to him how incongruous it was to cry "A bas Johnson!" in Vietnam and "Vive!" in Israel? Jean-Paul Sartre also called for solidarity with Israel, though with reservations, but then spoke frankly of the confusion in his own mind and the reasons for it. During the Second World War, he said, as a member of the Resistance he learned to look upon the Jew as a brother to be defended in all circumstances. During the Algerian war the Arabs were his brothers, and he stood by them. The present conflict was therefore for him a fratricidal struggle in which he was unable to exercise cool judgment and was overwhelmed by conflicting emotions.

We must exercise our judgment, however and must not allow it to be clouded by emotions and memories, however deep or haunting. We should not allow even invocations of Auschwitz to blackmail us into supporting the wrong cause. I am speaking as a Marxist of Jewish origin whose next-of-kin perished in Auschwitz and whose relatives live in Israel. To justify or condone Israel's wars against the Arabs is to render Israel a very bad service and, indeed, to harm its own long-term interests. Israel's security, let me repeat, was not enhanced by the wars of 1956 and 1967; it was undermined and compromised. The "friends of Israel" have in fact abetted Israel on a ruinous course.

They have also, willy-nilly, abetted the reactionary mood that took hold of Israel during the crisis. It was only with disgust that I could watch on television the scenes from Israel in those days: the displays of the conquerors' pride and brutality, the outbursts of chauvinism, and the wild celebrations of the inglorious triumph—all contrasting sharply with the pictures of Arab suffering and desolation, the treks of Jordanian refugees, and the bodies of Egyptian soldiers dying of thirst in the desert. I looked at the medieval figures of the rabbis and khassidim jumping with joy at the Wailing Wall; and I felt how the ghosts of talmudic obscurantism—and I know these only too well—crowded in on the country, and how the reactionary atmosphere had grown dense and stifling. Then came the many interviews with General Dayan, the hero and saviour, with the political mind of a regimental sergeant-major, ranting about annexations and venting a raucous callousness about the fate of the Arabs in the conquered areas. ("What do they matter to me?" "As far as I am concerned, they may stay or they may go.") Already wrapped in a phony military legend—the legend is phony for Dayan neither planned nor conducted the six-day campaign—he cut a rather sinister figure, suggesting the candidate for the dictator's post. The hint was conveyed that if the civilian parties get too "soft" on the Arabs this new Joshua, this mini-de Gaulle, will teach them a lesson, himself take power, and raise Israel's "glory" even higher. Behind Dayan there was Beigin, minister and leader of the extreme right-wing Zionists, who had long claimed even Trans-Jordania as part of "historic" Israel. A reactionary war inevitably breeds the heroes, the moods, and the consequences in which its character and aims are faithfully mirrored. On a deeper historical level the Jewish tragedy finds in Israel a dismal sequel. Israel's leaders exploit in self-justification, and overexploit, Auschwitz and Treblinka; but their actions mock the real meaning of the Jewish tragedy.

European Jews paid a horrible price for the role they had played in past ages, and a role not of their own choosing, as representatives of a market economy, of "money," among peoples living in a natural, moneyless, agricultural economy. They were the conspicuous carriers of early capitalism, traders and moneylenders, in precapitalist society. As modern capitalism developed, their role in it, though still conspicuous, became less than secondary. In Eastern Europe the bulk of the Jewish people consisted of poverty-stricken artisans, small traders, proletarians, semiproletarians, and outright paupers. But the image of the rich Jewish merchant and usurer (the descendant, also, of Christ's crucifiers) lived on in gentile folklore and remained engraved on the popular mind, stirring distrust and fear. The Nazis seized this image, magnified it to colossal dimensions, and constantly held it before the eyes of the masses.

August Bebel once said that anti-Semitism is the "socialism of the fools." There was plenty of that kind of "socialism" about, and all too little of the genuine socialism, in the era of the Great Slump, the era of mass unemployment and mass despair, of the 1930s. The European working classes were unable to overthrow the bourgeois order; but the hatred of capitalism was intense and widespread enough to force an outlet for itself and focus on a scapegoat. Among the lower middle classes, the lumpenbourgeoisie, and the lumpenproletariat, a frustrated anticapitalism merged with fear of communism and neurotic xenophobia. These moods fed on crumbs of a mouldering historic reality which nazism used to the utmost. The impact of Nazi

Jew-baiting was so powerful in part because the image of the Jew as the alien and vicious "bloodsucker" was to all too many people still an actuality. This also accounted for the relative indifference and the passivity with which so many non-Germans viewed the slaughter of the Jews. The socialism of the fools gleefully watched Shylock led to the gas chamber.

Israel promised not merely to give the survivors of the European Jewish communities a "national home" but also to free them from the fatal stigma. This was the message of the kibbutzim, the Histardrut, and even Zionism at large. The Jews were to cease to be unproductive elements, shopkeepers, economic and cultural interlopers, carriers of capitalism. They were to settle in "their own land" as "productive workers."

They now appear in the Middle East once again in the invidious role of agents, not so much of their own, relatively feeble, capitalism as of powerful Western vested interests, and as *proteges* of neocolonialism. This is how the Arab world sees them, not without reason. Once again they arouse bitter emotions and hatreds in their neighbours, in all those who have ever been or still are victims of imperialism. What a fate it is for the Jewish people to be made to appear in this role! As agents of early capitalism, they were still pioneers of progress in feudal society; as agents of the late, overripe, imperialist capitalism of our days, their role is altogether lamentable; and they are placed once again in the position of potential scapegoats. Is Jewish history to come full circle in such a way? This may well be the outcome of Israel's "victories"; and Israel's real friends must warn it of this.

The Arabs, on the other hand, need to be put on guard against the socialism or the anti-imperialism of the fools. We trust that they will not succumb to it, that they will learn from their defeat and recover to lay the foundations of a truly progressive, socialist Middle East.

# Part Three

# An Israeli View

# The Arab-Israeli War of 1967:*
# An Answer to Isaac Deutscher

## Simcha Flapan

In Isaac Deutscher's article about the 1967 Israel-Arab conflict we recognize the trait that made him one of the leading Marxist historians of our times: a sharp observing eye, a clear exposition, and a passionate dedication to the cause of socialism. Nevertheless, it also contains elements that are rather clearly incompatible with his Marxist rejection of Marxist clichès, his care for exact detail, and his subtle analysis of complicated situations. What he has to say about the international context, the dilemmas of Soviet policy, and the weakness of the Arab national liberation movements shows an acute understanding. But when he deals with the Jewish-Arab conflict, he gets involved in oversimplifications which obscure certain rather important aspects of the problem and are not free of partisanship, and even tends to distort the facts.

Particularly when speaking of Israel, Deutscher abandons all pretensions to objectivity and displays a vehement bitterness and a disgust which are hard to understand. "A frenzy for war," "arrogance and fanaticism," "religious obscurantism," "ferocious aggressivity," "the pride and brutality of conquerors," and similar invectives flow from his pen whenever he mentions Israel. One is tempted to feel that his outbreaks conceal deep anger against the arrogance of the Israelis who have dared win the war. This is not

*Published by the International Department of the United Workers' Party—
MAPAM—, Tel Aviv, 1968. By permission of the publisher.

the reaction of a socialist to chauvinism and reaction, for in that case why was he disgusted only by the "medieval silhouettes" of rabbis at the Wailing Wall and not by the imams who preach the jihad in the mosques? Why did he not see the fanaticism of the crowds in Cairo, Damascus, and Baghdad, roaring "We want war?" Why was he not shocked by the warlike frenzy and hysterics of the Arab world, its leaders and masses alike?

Here his partisanship is simply revolting. He regards General Dayan as a Middle Eastern Marshal Ky, even less scrupulous than the original. Deutscher thus equates a traitor to his own people, who has appealed to a foreign power in order to oppress and assassinate his fellow countrymen and to annihilate their aspirations to independence, to a man who, notwithstanding his blunt and sometimes even brutal speeches, his wrong ideas and political tendencies, nevertheless was and still is an Israeli patriot defending his own people against the threat of aggression by its neighbors. Why highlight the "sinister figure" of Dayan and leave the real builders of Israel's victory in the shade: General Rabin, a son of the people and the working class, who has raised his voice against the intoxication of victory and hatred of the enemy; the people's army of Israel, without any military caste or soldier's mentality, always inspired by the tradition of voluntary service, brotherhood, and democracy of the War of Independence and the Socialist hopes of 1948; the Israeli people with its youth and its Kibbutzim, who by their discipline, calmness and solidarity maintained the country's economy and services while all men capable of bearing arms were at the borders?

The image of Israel, which the world observed throughout the crisis and which contrasted so sharply with the hysterical propaganda and war fever of the neighboring countries, is something Deutscher completely and deliberately ignores. He is shocked by the rush to the Wailing Wall; to him it appears to show that the phantom of "talmudic obscurantism" descends all over the country. How could Deutscher, who knows his Jewish history after all, be unaware of the fact that for the *majority* of the Jews the Wailing Wall is not a religious symbol, but stands for the stubborn fight for independence which a small people waged and fought two thousand years ago against a colonial empire and which ended by the expulsion of this people from its native land? Since the dispersion, "next year in Jerusalem" has not merely been a prayer text but the expression of an unceasing hope for a national revival.

I do not intend to underestimate the danger that legitimate national aspirations may be abused, may be transformed into religious mysticism and used to strengthen chauvinistic political trends. All I wish to show is that there is an a priori note of hostility in the way Deutscher interprets the Israeli "attitude" during and after the war. The case of the Egyptian soldiers dying of thirst in the desert, which Deutscher quotes as proof of Israeli cruelty, is a striking example of his partisanship. That the war was cruel and involved unspeakable suffering for soldiers and civilians alike goes without saying. But, after all, none other than the Israeli authorities informed world opinion of the disaster, alerted the International Red Cross, and offered it every possible aid in saving human lives.

## Myth of Imperialist Agent

Deutscher concludes his article by solemnly warning Israel of the tragic consequences of playing the part of an agent of colonialism amid the Arab world. He reminds us of the terrible price Jews paid for their involuntary role of representatives of a capitalist economy in a less developed society. The image of Shylock continued to pursue them even when they became a mass of proletarians and little shopkeepers. Nowadays the myth and image which pursue Israel like a curse are that of the "imperialist agent." "Not without reason," Deutscher says; and yet, there is no more truth in this legend than there was in the portrait of Shylock which the Nazis used in arousing anti-Semitism, that "socialism of idiots," and inflating it to the monstrous dimensions that made the gas chambers possible. Anti-Zionism has become the "anti-imperialism of idiots."

Deutscher, in fact, helps to propagate that poisonous myth by providing us with an image that is not only contrary to fact but contrary even to plain logic. If the word *colonialism* has any meaning, it indicates a form of domination or exploitation. Now Israel does not exercise any control over the Arab states, neither materially nor politically; it does not handle their raw materials or natural resources; it does not invest capital in them, does not exploit their labor, does not even trade with them, and is not present in those countries in any form. What kind of colonialism is that?

Again, why should the West or the United States use Israel as its agent, when they themselves are present and very effectively involved in the Arab world, maintain military bases there, exploit its oil, monopolize its trade, supply the larger part of the economic, military, and technical aid it receives? Is Israel responsible for the difficulties of the republican regime in Yemen? Does it prevent the nationalization of oil in Kuwait, Iraq, and Saudi Arabia? Does it prevent the Middle East from using its enormous revenues for economic and social development? Is it an obstacle to the new agrarian reform in Syria and in Egypt, or to those countries' progress in industrialization and social evolution? Does Israel keep the social revolution in Algeria, Morocco, and Tunisia in check? And yet, that slander of "Israeli imperialism" has poisoned the minds of the Arab world in Africa and Asia and has become "official currency" in many groups of the European and North American left.

The rather Western-oriented foreign policy of Israel, which was due as much to Arab belligerency as to its own statesmen, can by no means explain the way in which the socialist and progressive camp regards Israel. Dozens of

Afro-Asian states are less independent, more reactionary, linked with imperialist blocs, accepting their military presence and serving their economic interests, without their existence being questioned and without being vilified and denounced as tools of imperialism and bases of aggression. Only Israel, always one of the most oppressed peoples, that eternal scapegoat of every reaction, that first victim of fascism, that country born from an anti-imperialist struggle with the blessing of the socialist world, that nation of workers engaged in advanced socialist experiments, has been branded in the whole world as an agent of colonialism and as the new Shylock of the nonaligned world.

Small wonder that Jewish progressives, and not Jewish progressives alone, with an impeccable record of fighting for socialism and for freedom of oppressed peoples, have risen in disgust and bitterness and have even threatened to cry, "Long live Johnson," when they saw how the socialist world approved the "Holy War" of the Arabs against Israel in the disguise of a struggle against imperialism. The paradox was not theirs but that of the socialist world, which, having agreed to the devaluation of its own ideals, was ready to enter into an alliance with reactionary and chauvinist appeals to genocide. It is sad to see a man like Deutscher incapable of understanding these warnings.

The weakness of his analysis consists in its proceeding from the *effects of the war* on the relations between imperialist and socialist international forces. He judges the origins of the war by its effects. But the origins and causes of the war, unlike its results, are to be found not only in the international context but also in the dynamics of the local conflict itself, in the political aims, the theories, and the strategies which determined the actions of the parties involved. It is this aspect of the problem which is important for discovering the errors, faults, and mishaps which have produced the result. The fact that the allied forces occupied Berlin does not mean that they started the Second World War and in no way reduces Hitler's responsibility for it.

If I undertake to present an analysis of the war which is different from, and in some respects contrary to, Deutscher's, it is not with the intention of objecting to all of Deutscher's conclusions, but rather because oversimplification and partisanship inhibit the self-criticism which is so necessary for socialists if they are to free themselves of the fallacious theories and wrong tactics which have helped to transform the conflict into an actual war. Deutscher rightly demands that Arab nationalism should abandon the "bloodthirsty rhetoric" and its "anti-Israeli furor," recognize Israel's right to exist, and assure the people of Israel that its legitimate interest "shall be respected" and that "Israel will even be able to occupy a place in the future Federation of the Middle East." Nevertheless, he presents such an image of Israel that, far from making a change of attitude on the part of the Arabs easier, he rather reinforces the thesis that the fight against Israel is part of the fight against imperialism. If, as Deutscher claims, Israel is really a docile instrument of American imperialism, dependent completely upon its subsidies, is "firmly dedicated to anti-Communism," is guided in its attitude by implacable hostility to Arab emancipation and by the theory that "Israel's security is a function of periodically recurrent wars" designed to reduce the Arab states to a state of impotence—if that is the case, then why should Israel be spared in the fight against imperialism, and why should it not be doomed to disappear with imperialism?

This thesis has determined the political thought and action of the Arabs; it has supplied the principles of the strategy which led to the war and their defeat. If the thesis is valid, if dependence on American imperialsim is an inherent factor of Israel's structure and if inevitable hostility to Arab ambitions is an integral part of Zionism, then a change of strategy is impossible. If the recent war was nothing but an Israeli aggression allied with the policy of the United States, then the Arabs must not, as Deutscher advises them, agree to Israel's existence, but regard the defeat as merely a lost battle and resume the struggle.

In this article I shall try to show that the image presented by Deutscher and his analysis of Israel's relations with the United States, as well as his study of the war, are wrong and that they do not correspond to reality but, on the other hand, that he is right in insisting on the need for a basic revision of Arab policy.

## Game with Many Players

Deutscher presents the Jewish-Arab confrontation as a game between two chess players, each with a great power looking over his shoulder and telling him how to play. Actually, the Middle East should rather be compared to a chessboard on which not two, but a large number of players try to play simultaneously, each using the few pawns he holds in accordance with his personal interests and so creating a confused and extremely tense situation. All the elements of the crisis existed long before it broke out. The brittle *status quo* that was established after the Suez campaign of 1956 led to the accumulation of a continuously increasing amount of explosive. At the beginning of 1967, I defined the situation in the Middle East as follows:

> Paradoxically, the most serious danger of the Israel-Arab conflict is that the two sides pursue a policy designed to maintain the status quo . . . Under the circumstances, the status quo means a disastrous armaments race which accelerates from day to day and will soon reach the stage of atomic weapons. The big powers flood the Middle Eastern countries with arms, trying to involve them in political and military alliances, and influence the direction of their development. . . . The arms race has assumed dimensions out of all proportion to economic

resources and real security needs. A vicious cricle has been created: The big powers profit by the conflict between the nations of the Middle East by involving them in an arms race which in turn sharpens and poisons the conflict. . . . Notwithstanding their hate propaganda against Israel, the majority of Arab leaders do not actually want war. In the case of some of them, one can even discern attempts to draw back and disengage from the Palestinian problem. But that is precisely the reason why the Palestinians and Ba'athists of Syria insist on halting this process and creating a situation in which the Arab States will be forced to intervene with all their military strength. For the Palestinians, this is the last chance to save their doctrine of the liberation of Palestine by armed struggle. The members of El Fatah want war at any price. . . . For them it matters little that the Arab countries have no chance of winning it and that they risk a defeat that would involve the destruction of all their economic achievements. For the Palestinian extremists, even a lost war is a victory.

The Arab governments do not really want war, but by trying to use the Fatah groups for other purposes they play their game. The Syrians encourage them in order to re-establish the pan-Arab policy and overthrow King Hussein's regime with their assistance; King Hussein tolerates them to a certain extent in the hope that Israel will react against Syria, which is the main source of the encouragement of terrorism; the Egyptians keep them under control at home, but are sympathetic to their fight against Hussein and believe that guerrilla war against Israel would be favourable to the establishment of a pan-Arab joint command under Egyptian control. . . . The big powers, in turn, do not want war, but encourage it by their diplomacy. The United States is increasingly concerned over the "ultra-socialist" policy of Syria and the Sixth Fleet is cruising near the Lebanese coast in a state of alert; the USSR, for the same reason, has made haste to take the new Syrian regime under its wing. One wrong evaluation, one wrong step, and the Middle East is in flames.[1]

As we shall see, wrong evaluations and wrong steps have not been lacking in the drama which has developed, and it is important to highlight them. The question of knowing who lit the fire and what made the war inevitable is of more than academic importance, and we shall try to answer it by analysing the play of forces which led to the outbreak of war.

Deutscher regards the crisis as a chain of facts which started with the Israeli threat against Syria and led to the preventive attack against Egypt, both actions being designed to obtain American protection and support. The pattern is simple: the United States needed a kind of "Marshal Ky" in the Middle East in order to defeat the enemies of American neocolonialism, and General Dayan came on the stage to play that role. Israel might have had its

---

[1] Simcha Flapan, "The Israel-Arab Conflict," *Les Temps Modernes*, no. 253 (1967).

fears and its own motives, but it did not act on its own behalf. It is a plausible pattern and very tempting for many leftist groups, but actually it is only a convenient means of evading reality, truth, and self-criticism.

Actually, there is no direct link between the Israeli "threats" against Syria and the outbreak of war three weeks later. During that interval, the crisis changed completely in nature, content, and implications. As a matter of fact, we can distinguish two stages or two different crises in this conflict: the first, from May 14 to May 23, originated directly from the alleged plan to attack Syria; the other, from May 23 to June 5, resulted from the blockade of the Tiran Straits. *While the first crisis did not inevitably produce war and could have been solved peacefully, the second made war inevitable.* Naturally, the two crises were related, and the increasing seriousness of the first was what produced the second, but in the course of this process there occurred a basic and qualitative change: a fatal and disastrous decision was made, not by Israel but by Egypt.

What was the difference between the two crises? The first was, according to the Egyptian-Syrian propaganda, a confrontation not between Israel and the Arabs but between "the reactionary and pro-imperialist forces in the Middle East and the forces of revolutionary nationalism and socialism." In these terms, Israel was not the only agent of reaction: it was presented as conspiring with the leaders of Arab reaction—King Hussein of Jordan, King Faisal of Saudi Arabia, King Hassan II of Morocco, Bourguiba of Tunisia, and the feudal rulers of Southern Arabia, all servants of American imperialism. Still in the same terms, the socialist forces consist of the revolutionary states—the United Arab Republic, Syria, Algeria, and the Arab masses were called upon to rise and overthrow their reactionary governments.

This presentation sees American imperialism as playing the main role, with its policy of fighting for the overthrow of the revolutionary regimes and the annihilation of the anticolonialist liberation movements. Israel is accused of preparing, *together with Jordan*, for a military action against the revolutionary regime of Damascus. Nasser explains the mobilization of his troops and their movement in the direction of the Israel border by the need to discourage Israel from attacking Syria and, if necessary, to defend that country. The Arab workers are called upon to blow up military installations, pumping stations, and outlets of pipelines in case of British or American military intervention. There is an appeal to the peoples of Southern Arabia to intensify their struggle against British imperialism and to the workers of Saudi Arabia to rise against Faisal. At the same time, a violent campaign is mounted against Hussein of Jordan. *Nasser refuses the offer of convening an Arab summit conference or the Arab Defence Council,* claiming that he cannot reveal his plans to governments whose policies are linked with those of London and Washington. This propaganda results in aggravating tension not only between Israel, Syria, and Egypt, but also between Egypt and other Arab states, particularly Jordan and Saudi Arabia. On May 21, a serious incident breaks out on the Syrian-Jordanian border, followed by a concentration of troops, the expulsion of ambassadors, and a campaign of mutual recrimination. During this time, the Palestinian question is practically not mentioned except by the Palestinians themselves. The stress is on the defence of the Ba'athist regime in Syria, which is seen as threatened by an American-Israeli-Jordanian plot (according to the Syrian radio, the Jordanian mercenaries and Syrian officers who had tried a coup in September, 1966, were supposed to invade Syria following an Israeli military operation).

Notwithstanding the aggressive tone of Syrian and particularly Palestinian propaganda, all military (mobilization and concentration of troops along the Israeli border) and political (withdrawal of United Nations forces in Gaza and Sinai) steps taken by Nasser during this time are represented as shows of force merely designed to discourage and intimidate. There were no appeals to wage total war against Israel, no calls for a holy war in the mosques. One could even notice a certain hesitation in respect of political decisions which might have complicated the situation, and a certain lack of coordination between the political and military authorities.

The first letter demanding the withdrawal of the United Nations Emergency Force was addressed by General Fawzi to the officer commanding those forces, General Rikhye on May 16. The letter—or rather, telegram,—was drawn up in terms which U Thant described as "unclear." It did not demand the evacuation of the Gaza Strip and Sinai by the U.N. forces, but the withdrawal of observer posts on the border. It is now evident that the demand referred only to the Israeli-Egyptian borders: Sharm-el-Sheikh was not mentioned. One version goes so far as to claim that Fawzi demanded that the U.N. troops should be concentrated in the Gaza Strip and Sharm-el-Sheikh. On May 26, Egyptian journalist Hassanein Haykal revealed that the Egyptian troops had not waited for a reply before occupying all the border positions.[2]

U Thant's reaction to this demand is perhaps the strangest episode of the whole affair. He not only rejected it, answering that this retreat would lead to the total evacuation of UN forces, but hurried to publish his reply (on May 17), forcing Nasser either to withdraw the demand or accept the consequences of U Thant's ultimatum. The next day Mahmud Riyadh, Egypt's foreign minister, demanded the total evacuation of U.N. forces from Gaza and the United Arab Republic. The Egyptian troops occupied Sharm-el-Sheikh on May 20, but it took Nasser until May 23, at four o'clock to announce his intention of closing the Gulf of Aqaba to Israeli shipping. The hesitations, doubts, and second thoughts which preceded this fateful

---

[2] *Al Ahram*, May **26, 1967.**

decision are apparent from the very form in which it was announced. There were, in fact, two versions of the "historic" declaration of Nasser's. In the one he merely announced a blockade against any ship flying the Israeli flag; but the formula was soon amended, and the blockade was extended to the passage of oil and strategic materials in non-Israeli ships.

There is nothing surprising about these hesitations. Nasser was obviously aware of the consequences his decision entailed. To quote his own words:

> Occupying Sharm-el-Sheikh meant a conflict with Israel. The move also indicated that we were ready to start a general war against Israel. It was no question of an isolated operation, and we had to take this fact into consideration when we went to Sharm-el-Sheikh. The actual operation was organized on this basis.[3]

The blockade meant the end of the first stage and the start of a new crisis of a totally different nature. The first crisis had a decidedly "anti-imperialist" aspect and amounted to an essentially defensive move against a real or imaginary threat. Sharm-el-Sheikh marks a peak, because it symbolizes the elimination of the last trace of the Suez War. But Sharm-el-Sheikh also has a totally different aspect: it symbolizes the whole Jewish-Arab conflict and is an expression of the refusal to recognize the existence of Israel, the insistence on maintaining a state of war, and the Arab determination to wipe out all traces of "Zionist aggression." The occupation of Sharm-el-Sheikh and the re-establishment of the blockade against Israeli shipping are a turning point in the conflict. From this moment, the question is no longer one of defending revolutionary Syria against an imperialist plot, but of the Palestinian problem and the eternal rights of the Arab people of Palestine. It was not until the announcement of the blockade of May 23, that Nasser shifted the Palestine problem to the forefront as the most important and most decisive issue.

To quote his own words:

> The Arabs insist on their rights and are determined to re-establish the rights of the people of Palestine. For several years, many people have cast doubts on our intentions on the subject of Palestine. But talking is easy and acting is hard, very hard. The battle of 1956 left us wounded. Britain, Israel, and France had attacked us then. In 1956 we suffered serious losses. Later, the union [with Syria] was established; then there occurred the secession of 1961. . . . Then, the revolution of Yemen broke out. We considered that it was our duty to assist our brethren. . . . We waited for the day when we would be *completely ready* and sure to be capable of taking decisive measures if we intended to take up the struggle against Israel. . . . Recently, we have felt strong enough to win, God willing, if we should take up the struggle against

[3] Text of speech made on May 26, 1967, at the Central Committee of the International Confederation of Arab Trade Unions.

Israel. We therefore decided to act. ... If Israel engages in aggression ... the battle will be general and our main objective will be the destruction of Israel.[4]

This turn involved a basic change of tactics, new alliances, new ideology, and even a new terminology. Earlier, on May 14, the day when the Egyptian Army was ordered to move to the Israeli border, Nasser wrote to the Union of Arab Students in London on the occasion of "Palestine Day": "Imperialism, Zionism, and reaction cannot be separated. The three components of the enemy alliance form a single whole. None of them can exist without its two other allies." That was the burden of Arab propaganda in the first period. The fight against Israel was part of the anti-imperialist fight. Now, the question became one of allying oneself with reaction and neutralizing imperialism in order to conduct the war against Zionism by turning the whole power of the Arab world against an isolated enemy.

Anti-imperialist terminology was therefore abandoned and replaced by another language: Arab honour, Arab dignity, the great Arab nation, Arab heroism, Islam, became the sacred values which were to support the "Holy War" against Israel. The reactionary Arab governments, which were reviled and condemned the day before, suddenly became impatiently awaited brothers who were to help in bringing about the "day of reckoning."

One after the other, they were entreated, threatened, blackmailed to join the anti-Israeli alliance. The results did not disappoint. Within a few days, a wave of enthusiasm and war hysteria unfolded on the Arab continent, from the Atlantic to the Persian Gulf. All rushed to take part in the "Holy Alliance." King Hassan II placed a military unit at the disposal of the U.A.R., Bourguiba made haste to declare that his differences with Nasser "never had applied to the actual basis of the Palestinian problem." Algeria sent volunteers and aircraft, Lebanon and Kuwait promised active support and expressed their solidarity, Saudi Arabia decided to send troops to Aqaba, and King Hussein, the "Zionist agent," the "imperialist spy and plotter," rushed to Cairo to sign a military treaty that handed the command of the Jordanian Army over to the Egyptian chief of staff. Israel was completely surrounded. In the mosques, the imams called upon the people to join the Holy War. Shukairy, chief of the Palestine Liberation Organization, made a triumphant entry into Jerusalem and declared: "There will be no survivors." The atmosphere is reflected very clearly in a speech by President Aref of Iraq:

This is the opportunity for wiping out our shame. ... The armies of the liberated Arab countries are awaiting this day impatiently; they are inspired by the sincere desire and will to wipe out this shame, to wipe out Israel, and to bring a million homeless people back to their own country."

[4] *Ibid.*

## Suing for American Support

Once the Arab alliance was a fact, efforts were made to neutralize the United States, or even gain its support. The image of America as the imperialist power that made counterrevolutions in order to fight the progressive regimes in Africa, Asia, and Latin America and brutally suppressed any attempt to throw off the yoke of colonial exploitation, that conducted a genocidal war against the people of Vietnam, was amended. Ghana, Indonesia, Vietnam, Greece, Cuba—all the theatres of the plots and wars directed by the United States—suddenly disappeared from Arab propaganda in which only a few days before they had been in the forefront. All the United States is accused of now is supporting Israel, being partisan and unfair, and lacking understanding for the Arabs. Here is what Nasser had to say about the Americans in his famous press conference of May 28:

> In the first days of the revolution of 1952, we took the United States for the champion of the liberty and independence of other nations. . . . The Vice-President of the United States has said that Israel is a kind of lighthouse illuminating the world. . . . We regard the United States as partisan and as taking Israel's side a hundered per cent. Of course that will affect our relations with her. We have consistently offered our friendship to the people of the United States. There is no problem between them and us. The problem is between Israel and us. The United States is the greatest power in the world, and everyone expects to see her act in accordance with that position. Unfortunately . . . she has taken the side of Israel, and completely abandoned the Arabs. What have we done to the U.S.A.? We have always wanted her friendship; we have held out our hands to her and have cooperated with her in the economic field. The basic problem between the United States and us is Israel.

Different aims require different methods. In the earlier stage, Arab propaganda had appealed to the masses and the workers to blow up the oil installations and pipelines in case of war. Now Nasser says:

> I do not approve of the destruction of Arab property and of installations in Arab countries. We need them; they are our fortune and not that of the United States. To destroy them would be folly. It has been a great pleasure for me to accept the offer of the Foreign Minister of Kuwait . . . to halt oil production completely if we should be attacked or if the West or the United States should intervene.

The threat of blowing up the oil installations and pipelines, which was a method of fighting imperialism, was converted into a means of blackmail designed to bring the Arab oil interests, willingly or unwillingly, into the alliance and to neutralize the United States in the Arab-Israeli conflict. The move was fully successful in both respects. Having made an agreement with Nasser to safeguard their oil revenues at the cost of a war with Israel, a price which they were only too ready to pay, the reactionary Arab heads of state started a campaign designed to induce the United States to remain neutral. They succeeded. If one follows American reactions to the different stages of the struggle, one notes a development from open support of Israel and hostility to the Egyptian and Syrian governments to complete neutrality and the desire to reach an agreement with Nasser, from the inclination to intervene by force to the rejection of force and nonintervention. Naturally, this change of attitude was not brought about only by the Arabs. A major role was played by Soviet policy, which had as its main aim the prevention of an escalation which might have led to the oubreak of a new world war. But if the Soviets were the basic cause of the absence of American military intervention, Arab-American oil interests resulted in diverting the political line of the United States in the direction of accepting the blockade and the new political situation inaugurated by Nasser in exchange for a few insignificant concessions to Israel (such as permission to carry oil on non-Israeli ships).

The Americans did not fail to understand Nasser's barely disguised appeal. While in the first stage they had reacted with strong support for Israel, they changed their tune as of May 23. That day, Eugene Rostow asked Israel to wait 48 hours before acting. There were those in Israel who thought that this meant that the United States realized how hard it would be to wait *more* than 48 hours. But two days later Johnson asked Eshkol to wait another fortnight before taking action and promised to intervene effectively to break the blockade in cooperation with other naval powers. On June 1, Hubert Humphrey, Robert McNamara, and Dean Rusk informed the Foreign Relations Committee of the American Congress that the United States had no immediate plan for breaking the blockade by force or for acting alone, and preferred to find a solution within the framework of the United Nations. The importance of this change in the American attitude is fully apparent if one compares the "ultimatum" presented by the new United States ambassador, Richard Nolte, and rejected by the foreign minister of the U.A.R., Mahmud Riyadh, on May 23 (United Nations forces were to remain; no Egyptian force was to occupy Sharm-el-Sheikh unless the U.A.R. government ensured free shipping for all; Egyptian troops were to withdraw from Gaza and the Israeli borders—see *Al Ahram,* May 26, 1967), with the agreement which the special envoy of the United States, Charles Yost, reached a fortnight later (on June 3) with the same minister (diplomatic efforts with a view to be submitted to a peaceful solution, the navigation problem to be submitted to the International Court at The Hague, and Zakhariya Mahi-ed-Din to go to Washington with a view to further arrangements).

This amounted to accepting the blockade by Nasser, who had concentrated 80,000 troops and 1,200 tanks on the Israeli border, while the Iraqi

Army entered Jordan and Saudi Arabian forces approached Aqaba. The whole Arab world prepared for total war, encouraged by Soviet support and by the isolation of Israel, which had been left to its fate by its Western allies. For Israel, this was a kind of Munich, but without the illusions that prevailed in certain circles in 1938. No one, either in Israel or in the Arab states, doubted that Nasser was serious when he stated on May 28, at the high point of the crisis:

> The question now is not that of the Gulf of Aqaba, the Tiran Straits or the withdrawal of the UN troops but the question of the Palestinian people. It is the aggression of 1948, with the co-operation of Great Britain and the United States. . . . We demand for the Palestinian people the absolute right to start the war of liberation in order to re-establish its rights to its country. . . . The existence of Israel as such is an act of aggression.

Or on May 26:

> I could never have said anything of the kind [our basic objective will be the destruction of Israel] five or even three years ago. If I had said so and had been incapable of accomplishing it, my words would have been hollow and without value. . . . Today . . . I say these things because I am confident. I know what we have here and what Syria has. I also know that other States—Iraq, for instance—have sent their troops to Syria. Algeria will send troops, so will Kuwait. . . . That is Arab power.

All through the first stage, it still was possible to reach a peaceful solution. First of all, the danger of an Israeli invasion of Syria with the purpose of overthrowing the regime was imaginary. True, high officers and ministers sometimes offered very provocative threats without concern for their possible consequences. The right-wing parties, Herut and Rafi, demanded strong measures in order to contain the terrorist wave that came from Syria. But did Israel really plan to attack Syria? " We know nothing about it," Deutscher replies, and he adds that even if there had been nothing to it, "its [Israel's] attitude made the threat as plausible as the Arab threats were to the Israelis." But the Israelis knew the difference between threatening words and threats accompanied by concentrations of troops. There was no concentration of Israeli troops on the Syrian frontier. Nasser himself, who justified his troop movements by the legend of the concentration of Israeli forces, often forgets to mention it. A political analysis would show that the plan to attack Syria was incompatible with the character and the total actions of the Eshkol government. This was the first government without Ben-Gurion, Peres, Dayan, without the "activists" who were most pessimistic about the prospects of peace and for whom the only solution was to buy more and more powerful arms and to use them from time to time in order to *prevent* Arab aggression.

## Israel's Role in the Crisis

The Eshkol government had no general peace policy; it merely made efforts to reduce tension. It asked the Soviet Union more than once to calm down the Syrian Ba'athist regime; it even agreed to revive the Israeli-Syrian Armistice Commission and put forward proposals designed to settle the differences which might have led to clashes. All these efforts came to naught when the Ba'ath decided to encourage a "popular war" for the liberation of Palestine. After criticism from Herut and Rafi, Eshkol allowed reprisals against Fatah to reach a disproportionate extent (attack on Samoah in Jordan, use of aircraft against Syria on April 7).

Whatever one may think of the efficacy of military reprisals in the fight against terrorism, these were, after all, nothing but reprisals without any political purpose as far as the Arab governments were concerned. There was not a single action against "socialist" Egypt for the simple reason that Nasser kept the Fatah units under tight control. If there was a major raid against Jordan, the favorite of the West, the reason was simply that it did not follow Egypt's example. Moreover, it was not the first time that Israel was accused of planning an attack against Syria; as a matter of fact, this had long been one of the favourite subjects of the Arab and Soviet press. Why, then, were the Arabs panic-stricken, and why did they have recourse to such measures, if there was no troop concentration at all? The reason was no doubt the difficult situation of the governments of Egypt and Syria in their own countries and in the whole Arab world.

The Ba'athist government that had come into power in February, 1966, was threatened by an increasing opposition which objected to its reforms as well as to its dictatorial habits. Strikes, demonstrations by the merchants and by religious circles, and attempts at take-over produced a profound anxiety. In September, 1966, Colonel Hatoun attempted to take over the government and failed. On April 25, 1967, an atheist article published in the journal of the Syrian Army produced such violent reactions that the government was forced to resort to severe repressive measures. Arab reaction and American imperialism were accused of fostering the trouble and of having plotted a counterrevolution. Egypt was encumbered by a grave economic crisis due to crushing military expenses and to the delay of food supplies and credits from the United States. Nasser had to deal with opposition on the part of the Moslem Brotherhood and part of the Army. In the Arab world he was the target of a malevolent campaign against "his passive attitude and calm in the face of the Israeli menace and actions." Fear of plots of subversion fomented by the United States and the reactionary Arab leaders was very much alive. In this situation, it was decided—probably in coordination with the Soviets—to organize a show of force. Warnings of "the Israeli danger" were the most suitable diversionary move to silence Arab reaction.

That the danger was not real is, in the first place, shown by the fact that the Israeli attack never took place, though nothing ever happened which could have prevented it. The mobilization and concentration of Egyptian troops on the Israeli border were regarded by the Israeli press, government, and army as simply a demonstration, spectacular, but not a serious gesture. The troops that entered Sinai and Gaza were at first too few and too lightly armed to present a problem. Israel was not disturbed and could have attacked Syria if it had wanted. It did not do so because it had no intention of doing so. Even the withdrawal of the United Nations forces was not considered in Israel as proof that Nasser was ready to involve himself in a major war. Part of the Israeli press even thought that the withdrawal of those forces did not necessarily render the situation more serious. Israel did not approach U Thant and did not ask for an emergency session of the Security Council.

Concern in Israel only emerged when the numbers of men and tanks assumed dangerous proportions. Herut and Rafi then accused Eshkol of having misled public opinion about Nasser's intentions. Eshkol was concerned, but not dismayed; he assumed a cautious attitude, was prepared for any eventuality, but avoided any step likely to push Nasser into irreversible action. The decisive days came with the occupation of Sharm-el-Sheikh by the Egyptian Army on May 20. Would Nasser close the straits to Israeli shipping? Day after day, the Egyptians stepped up their manpower and armaments. The Israeli General Staff realized that they had not foreseen this development and were now convinced that Nasser wanted war and asked for action.

The government decided not to miss any chance for a peaceful solution. Eshkol presented the text of the speech he was to deliver the next day in the Knesset to the cabinet for approval. At the suggestion of Minister Shapiro, *all references to passage through the Straits of Tiran and any expression which might be considered as offensive were struck out.* Political and military personalities were requested to refrain from provocative attitudes. The purpose of all this was not to push Nasser into making any irrevocable statements. On May 22, Eshkol stated in the Knesset: "We have no intention of attacking any Arab country or of endangering its security, territory or rights. Nor shall we intervene in any form whatsoever in their internal affairs." He proposed to return to the previous situation on both sides of the border. *He made no reference whatsoever to the shipping problem and no warning was given that a blockade would be regarded as an act of aggression and a* casus belli. If Nasser's purpose really was what he had stated in the beginning—to prevent Israel from attacking Syria—the moment had now come to end the crisis. He could have declared that he had achieved his end, that Israel had been forced to give up its aggressive plans, and that the troops could go home. That same evening, Nasser, his vice-presidents, and his military chiefs met until late at night to discuss their future line of action, and the decision which was to lead to war and disaster was taken. We are not acquainted with any particulars of this discussion.

What is clear is that Nasser misinterpreted Eshkol's caution and moderation: he took them for signs of fear and weakness. In later speeches he was to reveal some of his reactions, based on the experience of 1956. In 1955, Ben-Gurion had not reacted immediately to the blockade of the straits, but had waited for a whole year for a military pact to be concluded with England and France, providing the vulnerable Tel Aviv region with an air umbrella. This time, Israel had no allies. France was neutral and even showed itself sympathetic to the Arabs. England was not ready to act. The United States could be neutralized by pressure on the oil lobby. Eshkol was not Ben-Gurion. The Egyptian Army was more powerful and better equipped (see Nasser's speeches of May 26 and 29, and his press conference of May 28).

Nasser had achieved his purpose in the course of the first stage. He could have remained the victor and at the same time saved the peace, if he had resisted the temptation of going on to the next stage, the stage of a total offensive against Israel. The development of the second stage made war inevitable, though Israel still tried to find a political solution after the announcement of the blockade. The army asked for immediate action before it was too late. Three times the government decided to postpone military action in the hope of inducing Israel's friends to take political steps capable of breaking the blockade. The foreign minister travelled from one capital to another, and was given promises that evaporated at the same time as Nasser accumulated new alliances. Federal Germany declared that the blockade didn't concern it because it was not a member of the United Nations. France announced that the problem of Israeli shipping involved the thorny questions of law. Britain was not ready to act otherwise than together with the United States. The United States, in turn, soon abandoned all plans of helping Israel when its Arab allies responded to Nasser's appeal to form a joint front against Israel. The failure of the political efforts made a profound impression on public opinion in Israel. Israel felt abandoned, betrayed, in mortal danger. For the first time, a *real fear* was felt in the streets of Israel. One cannot understand Israel's attitude before, after, and during the crisis if one disregards this psychological factor.

There was no need for propagandists, as Deutscher says, to play on the fear. On the contrary, the propagandists, the government, the army, did all they could to reassure, to re-establish confidence and to prevent panic. The fear was real, not because of the traumatic influences left behind by the Nazi concentration camps, or because of the terrifying threats of the Arabs, or even because of the bloody fighting against the Arabs in 1929, 1936, and 1948. The fear was real because the danger was real, and Jews have a sixth sense for feeling such danger. Now, after the lightning victory and the complete collapse of the Arab armies, one is inclined to deny that danger and to present the Arab threat as an enormous bluff. But the fact is that 1,200 tanks, hundreds of bombers and missiles, if they could have been operated by a large army encouraged by a first succcess, would have been an extremely serious danger for Israel. Victory was possible because the people fought with a determination and a courage which can only be inspired by a deep and real fear. That fear also explains the popular pressure for the establishment of a National Unity Government and the return of Dayan to the Ministry of Defence. Eshkol resisted this pressure to the last. Only after the formation of a military alliance between the socialist Nasser and the feudal King Hussein, and after the disappearance of the last hopes of international intervention, a unity government was formed in Israel, two days before the war.

War had become inevitable, not only because Israel could not consent to a blockade imposed by force which was the first step in a merciless struggle for the elimination of all traces of "the agression of 1948," but also because Nasser proved incapable of controlling the situation and ending the crisis by any political compromise whatsoever. In the face of the enormous army which impatiently awaited the order to march, of the Palestinians with their itching trigger-finger who roared for revenge, of the whole Arab world that had fallen prey to a hysterical war frenzy, Nasser could not possibly draw back, even if he had wanted to. He was caught in his own net. If he had tried to stop midway, he would have been swept away by his army, by the chauvinist and reactionary Arabs who for years had tried to make him depart from his "antifeudal and anti-imperialist" road in order to push him into a Palestinian war, some in the hope that it would cost him his position, others because they regarded him as the best-qualified leader for playing that part. But Nasser believed sincerely in his mission in the Arab world. His decision to close the straits was not solely induced by a propaganda war in which the Syrian Ba'ath and King Hussein vied with each other in defying him to take the decisive step. At the beginning of June, the crisis could no longer be kept under control, there was no way back.

Deutscher's version, according to which, after the joint American-Soviet decision not to intervene in the conflict and to make Egypt and Israel desist from taking warlike action, Nasser gave up the idea of military action and so became the victim of Soviet credulity, of American duplicity, and of "Israel's treacherous attack," is not based on any fact. From the beginning, Nasser's strategy was based not on preventive action but on a counteroffensive after an Israeli attack (sse his statement on the blockade of May 23), which, he was sure, was bound to come. In his speech of July 9 he revealed that two days before the war he had warned the head of his air force to be ready for an enemy air attack within 48 or 72 hours. Nasser's spokesman, Hassanein Haykal, had already written on May 24:

> From now on we must expect to see the enemy strike the first blow against us in battle. . . . We must make an effort to reduce its effects as much as possible. The second blow will then follow. But that blow will

be struck by us against the enemy in order to reply to him and discourage him. And it will be the most powerful blow we are able to strike.

Nasser had worked out a perfectly reasonable strategy, but he was unaware of two things: he did not know how corrupt, incompetent, disorderly, demoralized, and full of political opposition his own army was; and he did not imagine that the first attack of the Israelis would with one blow destroy his main strength, the air force.

## Role of the U.S.S.R.

In Cuba there was a real threat of invasion against a small country by the most powerful nation in the world. At the price of clumsy efforts and gropings, the Soviets succeeded in eliminating that danger. In the Middle East, it was the question of the *imaginary* threat of a little country against far larger neighbors. In the first stage of the crisis, this so-called threat was held in check; the blockade of Aqaba had nothing to do with anti-imperialist designs. It was directed against Israeli, not against British or United States ships. A small state, to the establishment of which the Soviet Union had contributed to a considerable extent, was challenged, not British or American military bases, not the Sixth Fleet or the oil companies.

It is quite certain that the first stage of the crisis was carefully organized and coordinated with the Soviets. On the other hand, it is now clear that the aims and tactics of the second phase were neither prepared nor discussed with the Soviets. They were not informed of the decision to block the straits until very shortly before it was made public. The Soviets did not entirely approve of Nasser in matters of the Palestinian problem. During the Security Council debate the week before the war, they supported the Arabs enthusiastically but did not say a word in favour of the blockade or other suggestions as the retreat from Al Awja and Eilat, which were proposed by the Arabs. The Soviet Union continued to speak in terms of the first stage: threats against Syria, imperialist intrigues, etc. While assuring the Arabs of its support, it was feverishly engaged in preventing the start of hostilities (note from Kosygin to Eshkol and Nasser) and making sure of the nonintervention of the great powers in the event of war breaking out.

The behaviour of the Soviet Union during the crisis may be explained in terms of its Middle East policy since 1956. It entered the scene in this region by a wide flanking movement encircling the signatories of the Baghdad Pact (1955) by means of the supply of arms to the new military regime in Egypt. The strategy consisted of supporting the neutralist elements of the Arab world while exploiting the Israeli-Arab coflict. Large supplies of arms enabled the Soviets to penetrate in depth, and produced anti-imperialist movements and attempts at social change. But the price was the aggravation of the Israeli-Arab conflict, which in turn led to an ever more dangerous arms race. Arms purchases became a more and more serious obstacle to economic and social progress and strengthened militarist groups and trends.

To be fair to the Soviets, they were aware of the dangers resulting from the use of the Israeli-Arab conflict and cooperation with the Pan-Arab and basically middle-class officers' caste. They tried, not without some success, to stress the reformist character of the regime, to broaden its social base, to direct its efforts toward development and progressive economic reform, and, with less success, to adopt a more realistic and tolerant attitude toward Israel. The influence of the Soviets had become a decisive factor in the political and military affairs of the Middle East. But its strength was also its weakness. By relying on the middle-class military regimes and not on socialist forces and popular organizations, the Soviet Union rendered itself unable to take roots and form sound cadres among the masses. The military regimes depended on the political, economic, and military aid of the U.S.S.R., but they themselves decided on policy, on the extent of social development and social change. These matters were not left to the Soviets. The more the Soviets invested, the more was their future linked to that of those regimes.

Finally, the Soviets became prisoners of the aid they had given: the larger that aid was, the less decisive their influence. The regimes themselves were torn between contrasting tendencies. They were a mixture of socialism, Pan-Arabism, militarism, and chauvinism. As far as Israel was concerned, they alternately proved themselves inclined toward realism and revenge. Like the Arab reactionaries, they never hesitated to have recourse to the "Zionist enemy" for a diversion in case of difficulties. Moscow asked the communists and socialists to cooperate with these regimes and to swim with the nationalist current. In those conditions, the socialists could not prevent the sudden transition from an anti-imperialist to an anti-Israeli policy, the more so as in theory, at least, Israel and Zionism were defined as imperialistic phenomena.

When President Nasser provoked the Israeli-Arab confrontation, the Soviets had to pay the price for their confusion in matters of doctrine and their political opportunism. They could not afford to lose the horse on which they had bet for ten years. They also did not want to see themselves dragged along on too dangerous a course. They were doomed to support the political activity of the Arabs with all their power, while using all means to restrain their military action. This effort was completely useless. War could not be avoided because of that very political support.

There is not the slightest doubt that if at the decisive moment, before or immediately after the announcement of the blockade, the Soviets had adopted a resolute and clear attitude of "anti-imperialism—yes; war against Israel—no," the war would not have taken place. Nevertheless, $3 billion worth of military equipment (the equivalent of three Aswan Dams) which had been acquired in the course of ten years at the expense of education, public health, living standards, and industrialization, were transformed into a heap of scrap or enriched the arsenals of the Israeli Army. The failure of the Egyptian Army was the failure of a social system and of an ideology: the system of a military bourgeoisie that had been nationalized under the guise of "Arab socialism," and the ideology of Pan-Arab chauvinism under the guise of "anti-imperialism." If that system and that ideology are not thrown on the scrap heap, there is not a single chance for peace and socialism in the Middle East. But such a possibility still seems remote. There are few encouraging signs. The United Arab Republic has undergone a terrible shock; if the regime of the "military bourgeoisie" collapses, will it be replaced by a more democratic, more socialist regime, or by an alliance of the Muslim Brotherhood with pro-American generals? The future will tell.

The U.S.S.R. is making efforts to save Nasser, to push him toward an alliance with the Left and a settlement with Israel. But at the same time, it still pursues its poisonous campaign against Israel and Zionism, in which Nazi and anti-Semitic arguments are used with no more shame than in Arab propaganda. Such a campaign will certainly not help to achieve the desired aim.

## Americans, Jews, and Arabs

This analysis differs from that of Deutscher, because he oversimplifies the relations among Americans, Jews, and Arabs. Nothing is more mistaken than the thesis that turns Israel into the sole or principal pawn of the United States in the Middle East. The United States has in the Middle East a much more important Arab engagement, to whatever extent it may be interested in Israel. Out of the fourteen Arab states in the Middle East and North Africa, only three (the U.A.R., Syria and Algeria) follow a neutralist policy and have the support of the Soviet Union. The others are to varying degrees oriented toward the West and the United States in political, economic, and military affairs. The two most important American bases are in Saudi Arabia (Dahran) and in Libya (Wheelus). The Arab states in the Middle East and in North Africa are for the United States one of the most important zones from the economic (oil) as well as from the strategic point of view. The American companies hold the lion's share in the production of crude oil and in refining in the Middle East; Arab oil accounts for 27 percent of world production and 60 percent of known reserves. Out of 100 million tons of refined products, the American companies account for 44 percent and they own 55 percent of the crude oil production. In the four main oil-producing countries—Kuwait, Saudi Arabia, Iran and Iraq—American interests amount to 50 percent, 100 percent, 30 percent, and 25 percent, respectively. The oil revenues of those countries are from 70 to 90 percent of their total income.

When they are compared with these giant interests, all American investments in Israel seem insignificant. The "oil lobby" in the United States is less mobile, but far more powerful, than the "Zionist lobby." For all the importance of the Jewish vote in the presidential elections, American policy has always been ambivalent when it came to Zionism. It was the United States that attempted to "freeze" the decisions of the United Nations in November, 1947, and to prevent the establishment of a Jewish state. The representative of the United States in the Security Council secured the adoption of a resolution which called for the tabling of the partition plan and its replacement by an international mandate. On the eve of the declaration of independence, the State Department exercised pressure in order to obtain the postponement of the declaration. The Provisional Israeli Government resisted this pressure and proclaimed the establishment of the state of Israel.

Afterward, during the years of the cold war (1950-55), the United States made every effort to involve the Arab states in all manner of political and military alliances (Middle East Defense Organization, Baghdad Pact, etc.). To that end, John Foster Dulles, who was then secretary of state, was ready to deprive Israel of the Negev and force the return of the Arab refugees (Dulles-Eden Plan; see Eden's speech at Guildhall in 1954). This American plan—which, incidentally, failed because of the increasing neutralist trends in the Arab states—played a part in assuring the victory of the military activism of Ben-Gurion over the diplomatic solutions preached by Sharett. The American efforts aiming at a conciliation with or gaining the support of the Arab neutralists pushed Ben-Gurion into an alliance with France, which reached its peak in the Suez campaign of 1956. The United States made haste to condemn that war, and American pressure rather than Soviet threats made Ben-Gurion withdraw his troops from Sinai and the Gaza Strip. It should be noted here that, contrary to all predictions, President Eisenhower did not hesitate to adopt this decidedly anti-Israeli policy shortly before the presidential elections, showing by his success that the Jewish vote in the United States was not so decisive as had been believed.

American policy maintained a careful equilibrium in its relations with Israel and the Arabs. Only in 1954 did the United States agree to lift the embargo on arms destined for Israel that had been in force since 1948—that is to say, since the outbreak of the war the Arab states had started in order to prevent the creation of Israel. Even then, the supply of arms to Israel was compensated for by the supply of arms to Jordan, Iraq, and Saudi Arabia and by training facilities for their military cadres. While the Soviet Union supplied large quantities of arms to the United Arab Republic, the United States hoped, by the supply of grain and a grant of economic aid, to prevent Nasser's neutralism from leading to socialist development and to an alliance with the Soviet bloc. When it became evident that these efforts were in vain the United States started an offensive against the dangerous new trends, less by trying to stimulate Israel than by stimulating Arab reaction.

The Arab leaders who were pro-Western and had the support of the Americans, and whose feudal and monarchist regimes were "threatened" by the opposition of the masses, started a slander campaign against Nasser: he was accused of "neglecting" and "betraying" Palestine and of displaying cowardice in the face of the increasing military strength of Israel, of doing nothing against Israel's economic development plans, of permitting the passage of Israeli ships through the Straits of Tiran, of hiding behind United Nations forces in Gaza, and of using his enormous military power in a fratricidal war in Yemen instead of employing it for the liberation of Palestine. The reactionary and chauvinist party of Shukeiry and the other Palestinian groups played a major role in this propaganda. This diversionary move of the Arab reactionaries also found enthusiastic support among the "revolutionary Ba'ath" of Syria and the Algerian F.L.N., who gave the slogan of the Palestinian war of liberation pride of place in the fight for socialism. American imperialism, in its struggle against socialist progress in the Arab world, found powerful allies among the Arabs themselves and did not have to rely on Israel.

If the United States sought to exploit the Israeli-Arab conflict to serve imperialist policies, its real ally remains Arab feudalism, reaction, and capitalism, with which the U.S. shares $6 billion of petroleum revenue each year. It was the realization of these relations which induced the Arab summit conference at Khartoum to define a new strategy of attempting to resume the dialogue with the United States. Notwithstanding appearances, which seem to confirm the popular thesis of Washington's support of Israel against the whole Arab world, the Arab leaders know full well that it would suffice for them to give the United States an assurance that social reform and anti-imperialist policies will be stopped, in order for America to make haste to take its place at the head of the campaign designed to eliminate all traces of "Israeli aggression," as it did in 1956. American-Arab relations are typically colonialist. On the one hand, the imperialist power faces the exploited and impoverished masses of peasants, workers, and minor intellectuals, whose opposition produces the anti-imperialist national liberation movements, but on the other hand there are organic links between the American companies (with their $2.5 billion in investments) and the class of landowners, oil kings, merchants, and state bureaucrats and the army. Nothing of that kind is to be found in the relations between the United States and Israel. They are not based on oil or on natural resources able to attract large-scale American investment. American exports to the Arab countries are three or four times as large as those to Israel and consist mainly of manufactured goods or of equipment offering wide possibilities of investment.

## Measuring Israeli Dependence

Admittedly, the cost of absorbing immigration, of economic development, and of–defence required the import of large amounts of capital to Israel, and these sums include the gifts of American Jews and loans by the American government. But in comparison with the money paid by Germany in the form of reparations, the part played by U.S. government loans is minor. Moreover, the American Jewish community has never tried to involve Israel in the world politics of the American government; on the contrary, several American Zionist leaders have insisted that Israel follow a neutralist policy (Newman, Silver, Nahum Goldmann). Finally, need we say that the majority of American Jewry—Zionist and non-Zionist—is fighting actively against the Vietnam War? The idea that American capital as such has created a sort of colonial-type dependence and deprived Israel of its sovereignty in the political and economic spheres is not only wrong but neither a Marxist nor a dialectic thesis. As a matter of fact, it is not the capital but the economic structure, the social system, and the political power which determine the type of relationship. Investing capital in a feudal, backward economy is one thing; injecting money into a developed economy and advanced social system is another. In the latter case what decides is the level of consciousness, organization and activity of the working masses, the relative power of the classes, and the character of the political system.

The influx of American capital in the French economy has not turned France into a colony unable to have an independent foreign policy or to plan its economy according to its own national interests. In the case of Israel, the evolution was decided not by capital but by immigration. Now, this was not an immigration of capitalists. The great majority of immigrants consisted of impoverished Jews, workers, artisans, member of the middle class in process of being proletarized. Nearly half of them came from Eastern Europe with a history of class struggle, socialist education, and political consciousness. The conditions of poverty and backwardness which prevailed in Israel and which made the country unattractive and unprofitable for capital investment still further underscored the need for proletarization and the importance of the role of the working class. Thus, there resulted a unique development: an economy with a capitalist structure, containing the maximum number of planning elements and of cooperative and socialist achievements that could be found in a capitalist country—91 percent of the land, all sources of energy, most of the natural resources (water, electricity, mines, oil) are nationalized; workers' enterprises occupy key positions in the economy (24 percent of industry, 80 percent of agriculture, most of public transport, the main building and public-works enterprises, etc.); a system of national insurance covers all risks; there is progressive labour legislation and the highest proportion of trade unionists (70 percent) with a highly advanced system of mutual and medical insurance; and, last but not least, there are more than 200 kibbutzim, which, though representing only 4 percent of the population, nevertheless control 35 percent of agriculture, 8 percent of industry, and play a predominant role in political life in Israel. The labour parties hold the majority of seats in the Knesset and in all government coalitions. The use of American farm machinery in the kibbutzim does not affect their socialist character, and the advantages of collective labour have shown themselves capable of compensating for the heavy interest charged by the capitalist banks.

The effect of this dependence on the capital and gifts of the United States Jews, which, incidentally, is a result of the Arab boycott, has not been able to hamper the growing development of Israeli economic independence. Though the deficit in the balance of payments grew, in absolute figures, from $220 million in 1949 to $525 million in 1965, the percentage of imports covered by Israeli exports has during the same period grown from 12 percent to 50 percent. At the same time, the American share in Israeli trade has not grown (36 percent of imports, 17 percent of exports), while trade with the Afro-Asian countries has grown considerably (in 1965, 18 percent exports and 7 percent of imports), notwithstanding the Arab boycott. Deutscher regards the insufficiency of food production and the absence of a heavy steel and metal industry as proof of American domination of the Israeli economy. A glance at Israeli statistics will show that the country already produces all it consumes in the field of dairy produce, fruit, vegetables, poultry, etc., and is rapidly proceeding towards self-sufficiency in meat, oils, and cereals. As for a steel industry, Deutscher seems to forget that Israel has no metal ores and that heavy industry in a small country has specific problems of its own.

Nevertheless, if the index of industrial production in 1965 stood at 241.7 (taking 1958 as the base year), the index of mining and quarry production was 314, the basic metallurgic industries index was 261, the index of production of machine tools, 447, that of electrical machinery, 312. The increasing economic independence of Israel also appears in the decrease of the share of foreign capital in the development budget (from 61.6 percent in 1962-63 to 47 percent in 1966-67), while self-financing rose from 39.4 percent to 53 percent. True, the influx of capital has led to waste, to a lack of planning, to insufficient savings and productivity, and has made possible a living standard for the Israelis that is beyond the means of the country. It is also correct that the new liberalism designed to attract investment has produced a shift toward the middle class in Israeli society, has given rise to a wave of parasites who have grown rich by speculation, has enabled the banks to make exaggerated profits, and has set up an economic and social dividing line between the different sectors of the Jewish community as well as between Jews and Arabs. All this is a serious threat to the socialist values of Israel. But these dangers, real as they are, have not yet destroyed its essentially progressive character and can be stopped. They do not automatically affect Israeli policy.

Not all Israeli governments have staked the future of the existence of the country on their "Western orientation," to use Deutscher's formula. Between 1948 and 1951, Israel's policy was officially one of neutrality, of non-involvement with either bloc, and of friendship with both. Hundreds of thousands of Jews have come from Eastern Europe while the capital came from the United States. During the succeeding years, policy wavered between the United States and Europe, but the present Eshkol government has made many efforts in the direction of independence and of improving relations with the East: resistance to American pressure in favour of the establishment of diplomatic relations with Saigon, recognition of the Oder-Neisse frontier, total backing for the Afro-Asian bloc in its fight against "apartheid" and colonialsim (South Africa, Rhodesia, etc.). The difference between the Eshkol and Ben-Gurion governments has been recognized and appreciated by the U.S.S.R. and the other socialist countries, as is shown by the resumption of Jewish immigration from the Soviet Union and the intensification of economic and cultural relations between Israel and Eastern Europe until June, 1967.

Nor is it correct, as Deutscher maintains, that Israel is implacably hostile to Arab aspirations. He disregards the binationalist trend of Zionists before 1948, which united the Left of the working class (Hashomer Hatzair and others) with liberal circles (Magnes, Buber, etc.). Between 1948 and 1952, Sharett undertook serious negotiations with the Arabs, to whom he proposed the return of part of the refugees. He opposed the Sinai campaign and the policy of large-scale military reprisals. After the departure of Ben-Gurion, one can discern a certain effort by Eshkol and Abba Eban to return to Sharett's view: a more flexible approach to the refugee problem, the abolition of military government in the Arab regions of Israel, more serious interest in moderate and realistic trends in the Arab world, etc. While the "activists" regarded the "Bourguiba trend" as a serious source of danger, Eban, on the contrary, saw it as a cause for hope. By choosing this particular moment for a major confrontation with Israel, the Arab leaders have struck a severe blow against those who strove for a policy of moderation and peace. They seem to have justified the activist thesis which claims that moderation would be regarded as "weakness" and would invite aggression.

## The Choices between Both Sides

For the Arab socialists and progressives, June, 1967, was a double disaster. As Arabs, they share the humiliation of their fellow countrymen, the bitterness and the tragic consequences of defeat; as socialists, they are horrified by the thought that all their achievements may be swept away and they themselves persecuted by a reactionary regime of pro-Western and pro-American generals or, worse, by a return of the Muslim Brotherhood, who would not hesitate to unleash a great bloodbath in the Indonesian style. Their political situation is complex, their doctrinal confusion total. They are confronted by two solutions, one as painful as the other. One is to continue regarding Israel as Enemy No. 1 by reason of its being the vanguard of imperialsim. This results either in a "Chinese" strategy of pursuing and "Vietnamizing" the war; or in a reconciliation with the United States, the only power which, according to Arab opinion, is capable of "making Israel return to its old borders." In the present circumstances, those who favour the "Chinese" solution have no chance of winning out. Reconciliation with the United States is more likely, with all that would result from it: change of government, a halt to all "social reform," perhaps even a process of denationalization and of abolition of agrarian reform. The other solution is to give up the anti-Israeli doctrine and to reach a settlement with Israel in order to save socialism in Egypt. In 1917 the Bolsheviks, at Brest Litovsk, "gave ground to win time." The Egyptian socialists need not go so far: Israel does not demand the annexation of Sinai; its only condition for a settlement is free passage for its ships through the Suez Canal, and it would pay cash for that passage. If one considers that the Suez Canal is open to the ships of all nations, including the most imperialistic, that concession to Israel cannot be regarded as a capitulation to imperialism; but psychologically, it must be an agonizing choice.

Israel's situation, on the other hand, is not the best. Right-wing nationalist, clerical, and military trends have tried to exploit the exultation of victory in order to justify a policy of annexation. The ideas and plans for a "Greater Israel," "historical frontiers," or a "new era in Jewish history" have grown like mushrooms after the rain. Intellectuals, workers, scientists, and journalists have supplied sentimental, religious, historical, political, and rational motivations. The Israeli left wing has received a severe blow precisely at the moment when the Eshkol-Ben-Gurion controversy came to a head in its confrontation between moderation and extremism. Nasser chose to let the gunpowder speak. More than anything else, this has contributed to persuading the Israeli people that a policy of peace is impossible, that the desire for peace is taken by the Arabs for weakness, and that, on the other hand, a policy of force and deterrence guarantees security and even offers advantages. The peace party cannot pride itself on any result, not even in a peace party in the Arab world. The "activists" can at least claim that they have settled the security problems and secured Israel's supremacy for some time to come.

The Soviet Union's unconditional support of Arab policy has also contributed to the isolation of the Left. The great fear of pre-war days is responsible for the unanimous resolution not to return to the nightmare of before June 5, and not to retreat from the occupied territories without peace. This attitude is so deeply engrained that no government can afford to disregard it, and even the risk of a tragic cycle of resistance and suppression cannot change it.

Jewish and Arab behaviour and psychology have never been so far apart. Nevertheless, even the tragic experience of the war has certain positive aspects. The Arabs have confronted the dynamic and irreversible reality of Israel. The Jews have been confronted with the reality of the refugee problem and the need to resolve the problem of the Arabs of Palestine, which no military victory can eliminate. Both may have understood how useless and dangerous it is to be a pawn in the game of the great powers.

Now it is up to world socialism to act. To do so there is need for an attitude of true objectivity, of patience, of friendship, and of mutual understanding. It is necessary to detach oneself from bitterness and from the prejudices born of disappointed sympathies and hopes. Above all, it is necessary to understand that, even after its great victory, Israel remains a minority within the Arab world—that is to say, the weaker side whose existence is definitely not assured; while the Arab world, notwithstanding its momentary setback, has its whole future ahead of it.

# Part Four

# Soviet Views

# Aggressor's Troops Must Be Withdrawn and Peace Restored in the Near East*

Aleksei N. Kosygin

Representatives of nearly all the nations of the world have gathered for the emergency special Session of the U.N. General Assembly to consider the grave and dangerous situation which took shape recently in the Near East, a situation which is causing profound anxiety everywhere.

True, hostilities are not in progress there now. The fact that a cease-fire was achieved is a definite success for the peaceloving forces. To a large measure the credit for this is due also to the Security Council though it failed to fulfill completely its duty in conformity with the U.N. Charter. The aggression is continuing. The armed forces of Israel are occupying territory belonging to the U.A.R., Syria and Jordan.

At any moment, as long as the Israeli troops continue their occupation of the territories they have seized, and until urgent measures have been taken to liquidate the aftermath of aggression, military conflict can erupt with new force at any minute.

Precisely because of this the Soviet Union initiated the convocation of an emergency Session of the General Assembly. We note with satisfaction that many states have supported our proposal. They have shown an understanding of the danger with which the situation is fraught, and a desire to strengthen peace.

*From U.N., *Official Records of the General Assembly, Fifth Emergency Special Session,* agenda item 5, document A/6717, June 19, 1967.

The General Assembly has a responsible task—to adopt decisions which will pave the way to the restoration of peace in the Near East. This task concerns all states, irrespective of the differences in their social and political systems, philosophical views, geographical position or to what groupings they belong. The problem facing us can be solved only if the diversity and complexity of the contemporary world do not eclipse the common issues that unite states and nations and, above all, the need to avert a catastrophic war.

What problem is arousing the greatest anxiety among all nations today? We think that all the participants in the General Assembly will agree that the nations are anxious most of all about how to avoid this catastrophe.

No nation wants war. Today no one doubts that should a new world war break out it would inevitably be a nuclear war. Its consequences would be disastrous for many countries and peoples of the world. The more farsighted statesmen of various lands, outstanding thinkers and scientists have from the first day of the existence of nuclear weapons warned of this.

The nuclear age has created a new reality in problems of war and peace; it has placed an immeasurably greater reponsibility on the states in everything that is relating to these problems. No political or military leader can argue against that if he has not lost the ability to think soberly, that more so since military men have a better concept than others as to the consequences of a nuclear war.

However, in real life, international relations are crammed with facts which prove that certain states have quite a different approach to this. Attempts at interferring in the internal affairs of independent countries and peoples, at imposing on them political concepts and alien views on social systems from the outside have not ended. Everything is done to breathe life into military blocs. The system of military bases—the strongholds of aggression spread all over the world—is being modernised and improved. Navies are cruising thousands of kilometres away from their own shores and threatening the security of states throughout the entire regions of the world.

Even in those cases, when the aggravation of tension or the appearance of hotbeds of war danger is caused by conflicts between relatively small states, big powers quite often stand behind them. This is true not only of the Near East, where aggression has been committed by Israel, backed by bigger imperialist powers, but of other regions of the globe as well.

For nearly three years now the United States of America, having cast off all disguise, has carried out direct aggression against the Vietnamese people.

The war is being waged to impose on the Vietnamese people an order which is to the liking of foreign imperialist circles. It is no exaggeration to say that the world has condemned those who are to blame for this war. There is a way to settle the Vietnamese problem and it is a simple way: the U.S.A. must get out of Vietnam, must withdraw its troops. Above all, it must immediately and unconditionally stop bombing the Democratic Republic of Vietnam. No declarations about readiness to seek a peaceful settlement of the Vietnamese problem will sound convincing until this is done. The declarations the U.S. leaders make must not be in contradiction to the real activities of the U.S.A. It is necessary to take into account that the continuation of the war in Vietnam increases the danger of military conflict spreading beyond the. limits of the region and is fraught with the ominous danger that this conflict could turn into a broad-scale military confrontation of powers. This precisely is the danger of the present course of the United States of America . . .

This is a far from complete list of events which keep international life at fever point and which sometimes lead to major aggravations and the emergence of hotbeds of war.

If we analyse the events in the Near East, we cannot but reach the conclusion that the war between Israel and Arab states is not the result of misunderstanding or lack of understanding of each other by the parties concerned. Nor is it just a local conflict. The events which took place recently in the Near East in connection with the armed conflict between Israel and the Arab states must of necessity be considered within the context of the general international situation.

I do not wish to dwell on particulars, but it is necessary to speak of the main facts, in order to make a correct appraisal of all that has happened.

What did the last year demonstrate in relation between Israel and the Arab states? Continuous aggravation of tensions and attacks that grew in scope by Israeli troops on one or another of Israel's neighbours.

On November 25, 1966, the Security Council censured the Government of Israel for its thoroughly planned "large-scale military action" against Jordan, committed in violation of the U.N. Charter, and issued a warning that should such actions be repeated, the Security Council would have to consider "the further and more effective steps as envisaged in the Charter." However, Israel refused to heed this lesson.

On April 7, (1967), Israeli troops attacked the Syrian Arab Republic. It was a major military operation involving aircraft, tanks and artillery. Following this Israel provoked new military clashes on the border with Jordan.

At the time, a number of states warned Israel once more that it would be held responsible for the consequences of the policy it was pursuing. But even then the Israeli Government did not reconsider its course. Its political leaders openly threatened "broader military actions against the Arab countries." The Prime Minister of Israel made it clear that the April armed attack on Syria was not to be the final measure and that Israel itself would choose the methods and the time for new similar actions. On May 9, 1967, the Israeli Parliament empowered the Government of Israel to carry out military operations against Syria. Israeli troops began to advance to the Syrian borders and mobilisation was effected.

At the time, information started to come to the Soviet Government and I think not only to us, that the Israeli Government planned to strike a swift blow against Syria at the end of May with the aim of smashing it and then to transfer hostilities to the territory of the United Arab Republic.

When the war preparations had entered the final stage, the Government of Israel suddenly began to pronounce, both confidentially and publicly, assurances of its peaceful intentions. It declared that it did not intend to begin hostilities, and did not want conflict with its neighbours. Literally several hours before the attack on the Arab states the Minister of Defence of Israel swore that his Government was seeking a peaceful settlement. "Let diplomacy work," this Minister said at a time when Israeli pilots had already received orders to bomb the cities of the United Arab Republic, Syria and Jordan. What unprecedented perfidy!

On June 5, Israel launched war against the United Arab Republic, Syria and Jordan. The Government of Israel violated the U.N. Charter, the norms of international law and demonstrated that all its peaceloving declarations were utterly false.

Everyone knows what followed.

I shall remind you here, at the headquarters of the United Nations Organisation, only of how brazenly the aggressor ignored the demands of the Security Council for an immediate cease-fire.

On June 6, the Security Council established a deadline for the termination of hostilities. Israeli troops continued their offensive and Israeli aircraft bombed peaceful Arab cities and villages.

On June 9, a new categorical demand was issued by the Security Council for a cease-fire. Israel ignored this, too. The Israeli army opened an offensive against the defence lines of Syria aimed at effecting a breakthrough to Damascus, the capital of this state.

The Security Council had to adopt yet another, and its fourth, decision, a number of states had to sever diplomatic relations with Israel and give a firm warning that sanction would be applied, before the Israeli troops stopped hostilities. The major part of the territory of the Arab states, which is now practically under Israeli occupation, was seized after the Security Council had adopted the decision on the immediate termination of hostilities.

There is irrefutable proof to show that Israel bears the responsibility for unleashing the war, for all who suffered from it and for its consequences.

But if anyone needs further evidence that the war in the Near East was unleashed by Israel and that Israel is the aggressor, Israel itself has provided the proof. It is impossible to explain in any other way the refusal of the Israeli Government to support the Soviet Union's proposal to convene an emergency Session of the U.N. General Assembly. If the Government of Israel felt no guilt before the nations of the world, it would not fear our discussion and the decisions which the General Assembly is bound to adopt.

Israel has no arguments to justify its aggression. Its attempts to justify itself—like those of its advocates to whitewash its policies and actions—based on declarations that the attack on the Arab states was a forced step, that, allegedly, the other side left Israel no other course of action, are all false.

If Israel had claims against its neighbours, it should have come here, to the United Nations Organisation, and sought a peaceful settlement here, as it is authorised by the U.N. Charter. After all, Israel claims the right to use all the rights and privileges which accrue from being a member of the United Nations Organisation. But rights cannot exist without responsibilities.

More and more information is pouring in on the atrocities and violence being commmitted by the Israeli aggressors on the territories they have seized. What is happening on the Sinai Peninsula, in the Gaza area, in the western part of Jordan, and Syrian territory occupied by Israeli troops, recalls the monstrous crimes committed by the fascists during World War II. The indigenous Arab population is being ousted from Gaza, Jerusalem and other areas. As, in its time, Nazi Germany appointed Gauleiters in the regions it had occupied, so the Israeli Government is setting up an occupational administration in the territories it has seized and appointing its military governors there.

The Israeli troops are razing villages and destroying hospitals and schools. Civilians are being left without food and water, or any means of subsistence. The shooting of POW's and even women and children has been reported and ambulances with wounded have been burned.

The United Nations Organisation cannot ignore these crimes. The Security Council has already approached the Government of Israel with the demand that the preservation, safety, and wellbeing of the inhabitants in the regions it has seized be guaranteed. This resolution in itself is an indictment of the aggressor. The United Nations Organisation must force Israel to respect international laws. Those organising and carrying out crimes on the occupied territories of the Arab countries must be severely punished.

True to its principle of assisting victims of aggression, of supporting peoples who are fighting for their independence and freedom, the Soviet Union has come out strongly in defence of Arab states. We warned the Government of Israel, both before the aggression began and during the war, that if it decided to take upon itself the responsibility of unleashing a military conflict, it would have to pay in full measure for the consequences. We still firmly adhere to this stand.

There must be no political zigzags when we speak of war and peace and of defending peoples' rights. Of course, in order to settle one or another problem, states sometimes outline several possible ways. But in problems like this, which the emergency Session of the General Assembly is now considering, there exists no alternative for a resolute condemnation of aggression, and of those forces behind it, no alternative for the elimination of the aftermath of aggression. Otherwise it is impossible to end aggression, to discourage those who would care to launch such ventures in the future.

One may ask, why does the Soviet Union take such a resolute stand against Israel? No, gentlemen, the Soviet Union is not against Israel, but against the aggressive policies which are being conducted by ruling circles of that state.

Throughout the 50 years of its existence, the Soviet Union has treated all nations—big and small—with respect. Every nation has the right to create its own independent national state. This is one of the main principles of the policy the Soviet Union pursues.

It was this that determined our attitude towards Israel as a state when in 1947 we voted for the decision of the U.N.O. to create on the territory of Palestine, a former British colony, two independent states—one Jewish and one Arab. Guided by this principle, the Soviet Union established diplomatic relations with Israel.

While supporting the right of nations to self-determination, the Soviet Union condemns, just as vigorously, attempts by any state to conduct an aggressive policy in relation to other countries—a policy of seizing foreign lands and enslaving the people there.

What policy does the state of Israel pursue? Unfortunately, throughout the major part of its history, the ruling Israeli circles have conducted a policy of seizure and expanding their territory at the expense of the territories of the neighbouring Arab states, and ousting or even destroying the indigenous population of those lands.

It was so in 1948-1949, when Israel forcibly seized a considerable part of the territory of the Arab state, which was to be set up according to the U.N. decision. About a million people were driven out of their native land and doomed to hunger, suffering and poverty. All these years these people have lived like exiles, deprived of their motherland and means of subsistence. The acute problem of the Palestine refugees, which resulted from the policies of Israel, remains unsettled to this day, and tends constantly to aggravate tension in that area.

The same occurred in 1956, when Israel took part in the aggression against Egypt. At that time its troops invaded Egyptian territory as they have done now. At that time, too, Israel tried to retain the areas it had seized, but had to retreat beyond the armistice line under the powerful pressure brought to bear on it by the United Nations Organisation, by the majority of its members.

The members of the United Nations Organisation are well aware that throughout the years that followed, Israel has been committing acts of aggression against the United Arab Republic, Syria and Jordan. There has been no other issue about which it has been necessary to convene the Security Council so often, as that of conflicts between Israel and the Arab states.

As we can see, the aggressive war unleashed today by Israel against the Arab countries is a direct continuation of policies which the ruling extremist circles have imposed on their country throughout the entire existence of the Israeli state. It is against this aggressive policy that the Soviet Union has acted firmly and consistently, along with the other socialist and all peaceloving states. It is the duty of the United Nations Organisation to force Israel to submit to the demands of the nations. If U.N.O. fails to do this, it will be failing to fulfil its highest duty, in the name of which it was created, and faith in the Organisation will be undermined.

Israel can establish its place among the nations of the world only by taking the path of peace, by abandoning its aggressive policies towards its neighbours.

We would not be consistent or fair in appraising Israel's policy, if we did not say with complete certainty, that, in its actions, Israel enjoys support from certain imperialist circles outside the country. More than that, these influential circles have made statements and indulged in practical activities which the extremists in Israel could interpret only in one way—as a direct encouragement to commit acts of aggression.

How else, for example, can we estimate the fact that on the eve of the Israeli aggression, a plan was being hurriedly worked out in the U.S.A. and Great Britain—and which was widely reported in the press—on establishing an international naval force to bring pressure to bear on the Arab states? How else can we estimate the military demonstrations of the 6th U.S. Fleet off the shores of the Arab states and the increase in British naval and air forces in the Mediterranean and in the Red Sea area, or the stepped-up deliveries of modern armaments and ammunition for the Israeli army? . . .

At present, the extremely bellicose circles in Tel Aviv are declaring that their seizure of Arab territories provides them with—as they brazenly state—the basis for making new demands on the Arab countries and nations. An unbridled anti-Arab propaganda campaign, supported by the press of certain Western countries, is being carried on in Israel. The force of arms is being lauded, new threats are being made against neighbouring countries, and it is being said that Israel will not heed any decisions, not even those adopted by the present Session of the U.N. General Assembly, if they do not conform to its demands.

The aggressor is in a state of intoxication. Plans devised long before to reshape the map of the Near East, are being brought to the fore. The Israeli leaders are declaring that Israel will not leave the Gaza area, or the western banks of the Jordan River. They are declaring that Israel intends to retain under its control the entire city of Jerusalem and say that, should the Arab countries not submit to Israeli demands, Israeli troops will simply remain where they are now.

What is the attitude of the governments of the U.S.A. and Great Britain to the Israeli claims? For all practical purposes, in this case, too, they are taking the stand of encouraging the aggressor. How else can the aggressor interpret their position in the Security Council which hampered the adoption of a proposal on the immediate withdrawal of the Israeli troops behind the armistice line? Declarations of support for the political independence and territorial integrity of the Near Eastern countries so lavishly made by the U.S. representatives can have meaning only if those who utter them reject in no uncertain way the territorial claims of the aggressor and favour the immediate withdrawal of his troops.

By putting forward a programme of annexation, Israel completely loses all sense of reality and embarks on a very dangerous path. Any attempt to consolidate the results of aggression is bound to fail. We are confident that the United Nations will reject attempts to impose a settlement on the Arab peoples that might jeopardise their legitimate interests or humiliate them. Territorial conquests, if they were recognised by various states, would only lead to new and perhaps bigger conflicts while peace and security in the Near East would remain an illusion. Such a situation cannot be permitted to arise, and one can rest assured that this will not happen. Attempts to consolidate the fruits of aggression will in the long run rebound against Israel and its people.

By occupying U.A.R., Jordanian and Syrian territories, Israel is continuing to throw out a challenge to the United Nations and all peaceloving states. Therefore the main task of this Assembly is to condemn the aggressor and take measures for the immediate withdrawal of Israeli troops beyond the armistice line. In other words, the task is to clear all the territories of Arab countries of the Israeli invaders.

The Israeli aggression has resulted in paralysing the work of the Suez Canal, an important international waterway which has been transformed by the invaders into a front line.

The Soviet Union voices a categorical demand that the Israeli troops be immediately removed from the shores of the Suez Canal and from all occupied Arab territories.

Only the withdrawal of Israeli forces from the areas they have seized can change the situation in favour of a detente and the creation of conditions for peace in the Near East.

Is it not clear that unless this is done and the Israeli invaders evicted from the territory of Arab states, there can be no hope of settling other unsolved problems in the Near East?

Those who unleashed the war against the Arab states should not cherish hopes that they will gain advantages from this.

The United Nations, called upon to serve the cause of preserving peace and international security, must use all its influence and all its prestige to end aggression.

In its demand to condemn aggression and withdraw troops from the seized territories of the U.A.R., Syria and Jordan, the Soviet Government proceeds from the necessity to maintain peace not only in the Near East. It should not be forgotten that there are many regions in the world where there are bound to be those eager to seize foreign territories, where principles of territorieal integrity and respect for the sovereignty of states are far from being honoured. If Israel's claims are not rebuffed today, tomorrow new aggressors, big or small, may attempt to overrun the lands of other peaceful countries . . . .

There is another important aspect of the aggression perpetrated by Israel. The point is that this aggression was aimed at toppling the existing regimes in the U.A.R., Syria and other Arab countries, which by their determined struggle to strengthen their national independence and make progress have evoked the hatred of the imperialists and the solidarity and support of the peoples which have embarked on the path of independent development. Therefore, to permit the actions of Israel against the Arab states to go unpunished would mean opposing the cause of national liberation of peoples and the interests of many states of Asia, Africa and Latin America.

The Soviet Union does not recognise Israel's seizure of territories. True to the ideals of peace, freedom and independence of people, the Soviet Union will undertake all measures within its power, both in the United Nations and outside it, to eliminate the consequences of aggression and promote the establishment of a lasting peace in this region. This is our firm and principled course. This is our joint course together with other socialist countries.

On June 9, the leaders of Communist and Workers' Parties and governments of seven socialist countries declared their full and complete solidarity with the just struggle of the states of the Arab East. Unless the Government of Israel ceases its aggression and withdraws its troops beyond the armistice line, the socialist states "will do everthing necessary to aid the peoples of the Arab countries to deal a firm rebuff to the aggressor, to safeguard their legitimate rights, to quench the hotbed of war in the Near East and restore peace in that region."

No state, however far removed from the area of the aggression, can remain aloof from the problem which is being discussed by the present emergency session. The problem concerns war and peace. In the present tense international situation hours or minutes can settle the fate of the world. If the dangerous developments in the Near East, South-East Asia or any other place where peace is being violated, are not halted, if conflicts are permitted to spread, the only possible outcome today or tomorrow will be a big war, and no single state will be able to remain on the sidelines.

No state or government, if it is genuinely concerned about peace and the prevention of a new war, can reason that if some event takes place far from its borders it can regard it with equanimity. Indeed it cannot. A seemingly small event or "local wars" may grow into big military conflicts. This means that every state and government should not only refrain from all actions that would bring about new complications, it must do all it can to prevent any aggravation of the situation, especially the emergence of hotbeds of war. Should they appear, however, it must try and quench them. This should be stressed especially in connection with the recent events in the Near East which have greatly complicated the already complex and dangerous international situation.

The Arab states, which fell victim to aggression, are entitled to expect that their sovereignty, territorial integrity, legitimate rights and interest, that were violated by the armed attack, will be restored in full and without delay. We repeat that this means, first of all, the withdrawal of Israeli forces from the occupied territories. This is the crucial question today, without which there can be no detente in the Near East.

Elimination of the consequences of aggression also means restitution of the material damage inflicted by the aggressor upon those attacked and whose lands were occupied. The Israeli troops and aircraft destroyed homes, industrial projects, roads and transport facilities in the U.A.R., Syria and Jordan. Israel is in duty bound to reimburse the full cost of all it destroyed and to return all captured property. It is in duty bound to do this within the shortest possible time.

Can the General Assembly measure up to the tasks that face it, can it cope with them? Yes, it can. The General Assembly should say its weighty word in favour of justice and peace.

The Soviet Union and its delegation are ready to work together with other countries, whose representatives have assembled in this hall. They are ready to work together with all other states and delegations in order to attain this aim.

Much depends on the efforts of the big powers. It would be good if their delegations also found a common language in order to reach decisions meeting the interests of peace in the Near East and throughout the world.

Guided by the lofty principles of the United Nations Charter and the desire to eliminate the consequences of aggression and restore justice as quickly as possible, the Soviet Government submits the following draft resolution to the General Assembly:

The General Assembly,

stating that Israel, by grossly violating the United Nations Charter and the universally accepted principles of international law, has committed a premeditated and planned aggression against the United Arab Republic, Syria and Jordan, has occupied a part of their territory and inflicted great material damage upon them,

noting that in contravention of the resolutions of the Security Council on the immediate cessation of all hostilities and a cease-fire of June 6, June 7 and June 9, Israel continued to conduct offensive military operations against the afore-said states and expanded the territory it had seized,

noting further that although at the present time hostilities have ceased, Israel is continuing to occupy the territory of the U.A.R., Syria and Jordan, thus failing to halt the aggression and throwing out a challenge to the United Nations and all peaceloving states,

regarding as inadmissible and illegitimate the presentation by Israel of territorial claims to the Arab states, which prevents the restoration of peace in the area,

1. Resolutely condemns Israel's aggressive actions and its continuing occupation of a part of the territory of the U.A.R., Syria and Jordan, which constitutes an act of recognised aggression;

2. Demand that Israel should immediately and unconditionally withdraw all its forces from the territory of the afore-said states to positions beyond the armistice lines, as stipulated in the general

armistice agreements, and should respect the status of the demilitar-
ised zones, as prescribed in those armistice agreements;

3. Also demand that Israel should restitute in full within the
shortest possible time all the damage inflicted by its aggression upon
the U.A.R., Syria and Jordan, and their nationals, and should return to
them all seized property and other material assets;

4. Appeals to the Security Council to undertake, on its part,
immediate and effective measures to eliminate all the consequences
of the Israeli aggression.

The Government of the Soviet Union expresses the hope that the General
Assembly will make a decision that will be effective in ensuring the
inviolability of the sovereignty and the territorial integrity of the Arab states,
the restoration and consolidation of peace and security in the Near East.

The convening of the General Assembly emergency Session is a fact of
great international significance. Should the General Assembly prove incapable of reaching a decision in the interests of peace, this will be a heavy
blow to the expectations of mankind regarding the possibility of settling
major international problems by peaceful means, by diplomatic contacts and
negotiations. No state, which is genuinely concerned about the future of its
people, can fail to take this into consideration.

All peoples must feel assured that the United Nations is capable of
achieving the aims proclaimed in its Charter, and of safeguarding peace on
earth.

# The Soviets: The puppet*

## Le Nouvel Observateur

Soviet intelligence was disturbed by the Israeli plan to make a raid into Syria to destroy the nests of the Palestinian commandos and eventually push onward to Damascus to overthrow the Syrian government. It was with Soviet approval that Nasser massed his troops on the Sinai frontier to demonstrate to the Israelis that, if they launched an offensive against Syria, that country would not fight alone. Nasser believed this would discourage Israel from initiating the attack.

On the other hand, Nasser made the grave decisions of demanding the withdrawal of the U.N. "blue helmets" from the Suez Canal zone and blockading the Gulf of Aqaba on his own and then informed the U.S.S.R. about them. The Soviets told him that by playing these two cards at this time he was running the risk of unpredictable reactions. But he seemed confident, and U Thant's decision to withdraw the U.N. forces, which came sooner than expected, appeared to justify this confidence. At that point the U.S.S.R. advised Nasser that it was only committed to neutralizing the United States—that is, it would respond with an escalation equal to any escalation Washington might undertake—and that its support would not go beyond that.

When it appeared that the Israelis considered the blockade of the Gulf of Aqaba as a *casus belli* and that the situation had become grave, the hot line

*From "The Soviets: The Puppet," *Atlas,* August, 1967, pp. 17-20, by permission of the publisher. This report is attributed to a high Soviet *fonctionnaire* and was obtained in Moscow by a reporter for *Le Nouvel Observateur* (Paris).

between Washington and Moscow began operating. Kosygin and Johnson agreed to work on their allies—the one on Egypt and Syria, the other on Israel—in order to prevent them from resorting to arms. They also decided to keep military forces out of the theater of operations, to take the measures necessary to avoid contact between these forces, and to immediately get in touch should an incident occur so that it would not degenerate into a serious conflict. (This is why Washington promptly notified Moscow when planes took off from the Sixth Fleet after an American vessel had been attacked through an error by the Israelis.)

Nasser, knowing Soviet reservations, promised he would not be the first to attack, but he committed the error of believing that the agreement between the two big powers allowed him all the time he needed for diplomatic maneuvers. In fact, he was partially a victim of his own propaganda, which claimed that the Tel Aviv government was merely Washington's pawn. He did not want to believe that this pawn might act on its own. Furthermore, he made a major mistake in neglecting the military side of the crisis. It did not even occur to him to put his airfields in a state of alert. This lack of foresight (or sabotage by some top officers hostile to Nasser) caused the destruction of the excellent military material the U.S.S.R. had given Egypt. The truth is the U.S.S.R. had overrated the ability of the commanding staff and logistics of the Egyptian military apparatus. Since 1956, the Egyptian army units up to battalion level had made great progress in terms of courage and maneuverability, but the shortcomings above this level turned out to be shocking.

The second exchange on the hot line between Johnson and Kosygin dealt with an American proposal for a general settlement of the Middle East problem. Wanting to protect their oil interests on the Arab peninsula and their political positions in Jordan, the Americans proposed to settle the question of freedom of navigation in the Gulf of Aqaba by a compromise between the Israeli and Arab viewpoints. The Israelis would be compensated by substantial economic and financial aid from the United States, and a large-scale plan of economic aid similar to that which had been projected for the "Alliance for Progress" in Latin America would be launched for the benefit of all Arab countries, including Egypt and Syria. The Soviet Union was invited to make a parallel effort. Kosygin replied that he needed more facts, but that *a priori* he was not opposed to the project. In order to test the reactions of the Egyptians to the plan, Johnson invited one of the men closest to Nasser, Zakaria Mohieddin, to come to Washington. On the advice of the Soviet Union, Mohieddin accepted the invitation, which only strengthened Nasser's convictions that hostilities would not erupt. In addition, the Israelis skillfully hoodwinked him. At the very moment when Dayan was making the final preparations for his lightning offensive, he stated at a press conference that his country would not attack first. But in fact the Israelis had decided to act and confront the world with the *fait accompli* of their military victory.

The drama unfolded at dawn on Monday, June 5. Almost all of the

Jordanian and Syrian air forces and two-thirds of the Egyptian air force were destroyed on the ground. Dramatic conversations took place in Cairo between Nasser and the Soviet ambassador and in Moscow between the Egyptian ambassador and the top members of the Soviet collective leadership, which had been called into an emergency meeting. The Egyptians demanded that the Soviets immediately replace their destroyed air force. But where were the new craft to be landed? All the Egyptian airfields were under fire by Israeli planes except Luxor and Aswan in Upper Egypt, and these fields were poorly equipped to handle such attacks. The Egyptians suggested sending the planes to the Sudan, to Iraq or to Libya; the Soviets refused because the two or three airfields in the Sudan and Iraq were small and inadequate. As for sending Soviet planes into Libya, a few miles from the American base, Wheelus Field, Washington would regard it as provocation— and the U.S.S.R. did not want war with the United States.

The dialogues between the Egyptians and the Soviets grew strained. They accused the U.S.S.R. of abandoning them in the hour of need. The U.S.S.R. replied that it had committed itself to supporting Egypt against American action but not against Israel, whose power they had underestimated. After the success of the Israeli offensive the Soviet Union decided, without consulting the Egyptians, that it could accept an immediate cease-fire in the Security Council because the Arab positions on the ground were still not catastrophic. De Gaulle, who was in communication with Kosygin, shared this view.

The Egyptians mistakenly believed they could take the first punch thrown by the Israelis in ground fighting. Once that danger had passed, they would begin a long war which they could win due to the large area and numerical superiority of the Arab world. The U.S.S.R. told them they were substituting their wishes for realities, since their tanks would be beaten without air cover. Nasser did not want to believe this and launched his counteroffensive, which failed. He closed the door on the only reasonable solution: to pay the price in ground fighting under the least disadvantageous conditions possible and gain precious time during which he would be able to quietly rebuild his air force.

As Nasser continued his desperate struggle, the U.S.S.R. became aware that the Arab world and a large part of the Third World, not to mention the Chinese, disapproved of the inadequacy of Soviet support to Egypt. Suddenly, some of Soviet leaders began to think of taking the risk of limited military action on behalf of Egypt within the framework of a "prudent challenge" to the United States. However, this solution was finally rejected. (As elsewhere, the pressure of Jewish opinion made its weight felt in the U.S.S.R. right up to the leading circles.)

Events following the war prove the imperialism of Israeli policy, and the Soviet attitude toward Tel Aviv will get even tougher. The Israelis are now the mad dogs of the Middle East. You don't kill a mad dog; he has a right to live, but you do have to punish him. We now firmly believe that this punishment is required to bring Israel to its senses and that undoubtedly it will take place some day. The Israelis have pointed out the road the Arabs must take: to launch a surprise air attack one day on the vulnerable territory of Israel.

The political and diplomatic struggle the U.S.S.R. is going to wage alongside the Arabs, especially the Syrians and the Egyptians, will be difficult. As for the Americans, the U.S.S.R. shall exploit to the utmost the blackmailing of their oil interests and navigation through the Suez Canal.

The Soviet Union shall fight at all the conference tables to force the Israelis to evacuate the territories they conquered. And the Soviets shall wage an incessant propaganda war, particularly among the young Arab generation, against all the cowards, opportunists, and elements linked to the Anglo-Americans who show any readiness to cooperate with Israel—as long as Israel does not agree to the concessions that the U.S.S.R. shall demand of it.

The Soviet Union knows that its prestige has suffered terribly among the Arabs. The most intelligent will come to understand that it was impossible for the U.S.S.R. to act otherwise. When reason finally prevails over emotions, the progressive Arab leaders will have to admit that, if the Americans are now the target of spontaneous, vigilant hatred in the Arab world, there is only one great power that can help the Arabs recover from the disaster—the Soviet Union. One may say that the big winner in this crisis has been Mao Tse-tung. But let us be serious. Who can pull Egypt and Syria out of the hornets' nest and, to start with, rebuild their air forces? The Chinese?

# Part Five

# The United Nations View

# The Withdrawal of the United Nations Emergency Force*

## United Nations Secretary-General

1. This report on the withdrawal of the United Nations Emergency Force (UNEF) is submitted because, as indicated in my statement on 20 June 1967 to the fifth emergency special session of the General Assembly (1527th plenary meeting), important questions have been raised concerning the actions taken on the withdrawal of UNEF. These questions merit careful consideration and comment. It is in the interest of the United Nations, I believe, that this report should be full and frank, in view of the questions involved and the numerous statements that have been made, both public and private, which continue to be very damaging to the United Nations and to its peace-keeping role in particular. Despite the explanations already given in the several reports on the subject which have been submitted to the General Assembly and to the Security Council, misunderstandings and what, I fear, are misrepresentations persist, in official as well as unofficial circles, publicly and behind the scenes.

2. A report of this kind is not the place to try to explain why there has been so much and such persistent and grossly mistaken judgement about the withdrawal of UNEF. It suffices to say here that the shattering crisis in the Near East inevitably caused intense shock in many capitals and countries of the world, together with deep frustration over the inability to cope with it. It is, of course, not unusual in such situations to seek easy explanations and

*From U.N. *Official Records of the General Assembly, Fifth Emergency Special Session, Annexes,* June 26, 1967.

excuses. When, however, this tactic involves imputing responsibility for the unleashing of major hostilities, it is, and must be, a cause for sober concern. The objective of this report is to establish an authentic, factual record of actions and their causes.

3. The emphasis here, therefore, will be upon facts. The report is intended to be neither a polemic nor an apologia. Its sole purpose is to present a factually accurate picture of what happened and why. It will serve well the interests of the United Nations, as well as of historical integrity, if this presentation of facts can help to dissipate some of the distortions of the record which, in some places, apparently have emanated from panic, emotion and political bias.

## CHRONOLOGY OF RELEVANT ACTIONS

4. Not only events but dates, and even the time of day, have an important bearing on this exposition. The significant events and actions and their dates and times are therefore set forth below.

### 16 May 1967

5. *2000 hours GMT (2200 hours Gaza local time).* A message from General Fawzi, Chief of Staff of the United Arab Republic Armed Forces, was received by the Commander of UNEF, Major-General Rikhye, requesting withdrawal of "all UN troops which install OPs along our borders" (A/6730, para. 6, sub-para. 3 [a]). Brigadier Mokhtar, who handed General Fawzi's letter to the Commander of UNEF, told General Rikhye at the the time that he must order the immediate withdrawal of United Nations troops from El Sabha and Sharm el-Sheikh on the night of 16 May since United Arab Republic armed forces must gain control of these two places that very night. The UNEF Commander correctly replied that he did not have authority to withdraw his troops from these positions on such an order and could do so only on instructions from the Secretary-General; therefore, he must continue with UNEF operations in Sinai as hitherto. Brigadier Mokhtar told the Commander of UNEF that this might lead to conflict on that night (16 May) between United Arab Republic and UNEF troops, and insisted that the Commander issue orders to UNEF troops to remain confined to their camps at El Sabha and Sharm el-Sheikh. General Rikhye replied that he could not comply with this request. He did, of course, inform the contingent commanders concerned of these developments. He also informed United Nations Headquarters that he proposed to continue with UNEF activities as established until he received fresh instructions from the Secretary-General.

6. *2130 hours GMT (1730 hours New York time).* The Secretary-General received at this time the UNEF Commander's cable informing him of the above-mentioned message from General Fawzi. The UNEF Commander was immediately instructed to await further instructions from the Secretary-

General and, pending this later word from him, to "be firm in maintaining UNEF position while being as understanding and as diplomatic as possible in your relations with local U.A.R. officials."

7. *2245 hours GMT (1845 hours New York time).* The Permanent Representative of the United Arab Republic visited the Secretary-General at this time at the latter's urgent request. The Secretary-General requested the Permanent Representative to communicate with his Government with the utmost urgency and to transmit to it his views (A/6730, para. 6, sub-para. 3 [c]). In particular, the Secretary-General requested the Permanent Representative to obtain his Government's clarification of the situation, pointing out that any request for the withdrawal of UNEF must come directly to the Secretary-General from the Government of the United Arab Republic.

8. *2344 hours GMT.* The UNEF Commander further reported at this time that considerable military activity had been observed in the El Arish area since the afternoon of 16 May 1967.

### *17 May 1967*

9. *0800 hours GMT (0400 hours New York time).* The Commander of UNEF reported then that on the morning of 17 May, thirty soldiers of the Army of the United Arab Republic had occupied El Sabha in Sinai and that United Arab Republic troops were deployed in the immediate vicinity of the UNEF observation post there. Three armoured cars of the United Arab Republic were located near the Yugoslav UNEF camp at El Sabha and detachments of fifteen soldiers each had taken up positions north and south of the Yugoslav contingent's camp at El Amr. All UNEF observation posts along the armistice demarcation line and the international frontier were manned as usual, but in some places United Arab Republic troops were also at the line.

10. *1030 hours GMT (0630 hours New York time).* The Commander of UNEF reported then that troops of the United Arab Republic had occupied the UNEF observation post at El Sabha and that the Yugoslav UNEF camps at El Quseima and El Sabha were now behind the positions of the army of the United Arab Republic. The Commander of UNEF informed the Chief of the United Arab Republic Liaison Staff of these developments, expressing his serious concern at them. The Chief of the United Arab Republic Liaison Staff agreed to request the immediate evacuation of the observation post at El Sabha by United Arab Republic troops and shortly thereafter reported that orders to this effect had been given by the United Arab Republic military authorities. He requested, however, that to avoid any future misunderstandings, the Yugoslav observation post at El Sabha should be withdrawn immediately to El Quseima camp. The Commander replied that any such withdrawal would require the authorization of the Secretary-General.

11. *1200 hours GMT (0800 hours New York time).* The Chief of the United Arab Republic Liaison Staff at this time conveyed to the Commander of UNEF a request from General Muhammed Fawzi, Chief of

Staff of the Armed Forces of the United Arab Republic, for the withdrawal of the Yugoslav detachments of UNEF in the Sinai within twenty-four hours. He added that the UNEF Commander might take "forty-eight hours or so" to withdraw the UNEF detachment from Sharm el-Sheikh. The Commander of UNEF replied that any such move required instructions from the Secretary-General.

12. *1300 hours GMT.* The Commander of UNEF then reported that a sizable detachment of troops of the United Arab Republic was moving into the UNEF area at El Kuntilla.

13. *2000 hours GMT (1600 hours New York time).* The Secretary-General at this date held an informal meeting in his office with the representatives of countries providing contingents to UNEF to inform them of the situation as then known. There was an exchange of views. The Secretary-General gave his opinion on how he should and how he intended to proceed, observing that if a formal request for the withdrawal of UNEF were to be made by the Government of the United Arab Republic, the Secretary-General, in his view, would have to comply with it, since the Force was on United Arab Republic territory only with the consent of the Government and could not remain there without it. Two representatives expressed serious doubts about the consequences of agreeing to a peremptory request for the withdrawal of UNEF and raised the questions of consideration of such a request by the General Assembly and an appeal to the United Arab Republic not to request the withdrawal of UNEF. Two other representatives stated the view that the United Arab Republic was entitled to request the removal of UNEF at any moment and that that request would have to be respected regardless of what the General Assembly might have to say in the matter, since the agreement for UNEF's presence had been concluded between the then Secretary-General and the Government of Egypt. A clarification of the situation from the United Arab Republic should therefore be awaited.

14. *2150 hours GMT (1750 hours New York time).* The Secretary-General at this time saw the Permanent Representative of the United Arab Republic and handed to him an *aide-mémoire*, the text of which is contained in paragraph 6 of document A/6730. The Secretary-General also gave to the Permanent Representative of the United Arab Republic an *aide-mémoire* calling to the attention of his Government the "good faith" accord, the test of which is contained in paragraph 7 of document A/6730.

*18 May 1967*

15. *1321 hours GMT (0921 hours New York time).* The Commander of UNEF reported at this time that his Liaison Officer in Cairo had been informed by an ambassador of one of the countries providing contingents to UNEF that the Foreign Minister of the United Arab Republic had summoned the representatives of nations with troops in UNEF to the Ministry for

Foreign Affairs and informed them that UNEF had terminated its tasks in the United Arab Republic and in the Gaza strip and must depart from the above territory forthwith. This information was confirmed by representatives of some of these countries at the United Nations.

16. Early on 18 May the UNEF sentries proceeding to man the normal observation post at El Sabha in Sinai were prevented from entering the post and from remaining in the area by United Arab Republic soldiers. The sentries were then forced to withdraw. They did not resist by use of force since they had no mandate to do so.

17. *1100 hours GMT.* United Arab Republic soldiers at this time forced Yugoslav UNEF sentries out of their observation post on the international frontier in front of El Kuntilla Camp. One hour later, United Arab Republic officers arrived at the water point and asked UNEF soldiers to withdraw the guard.

18. *1220 hours GMT.* At this hour, United Arab Republic soldiers entered the UNEF observation post on the international frontier in front of El Amr Camp and forced the Yugoslav soldiers to withdraw. Later, two United Arab Republic officers visited El Amr Camp and asked the UNEF platoon to withdraw within fifteen minutes.

19. *1210 hours GMT.* United Arab Republic officers then visited the Yugoslav camp at Sharm el-Sheikh and informed the Commanding Officer that they had come to take over the camp and the UNEF observation post at Ras Nasrani, demanding a reply within fifteen minutes. The contingent commander replied that he had no instructions to hand over the positions.

20. *1430 hours GMT.* The UNEF Yugoslav detachment at El Quseima camp reported that two artillery shells, apparently ranging rounds from the United Arab Republic artillery, had burst between the UNEF Yugoslav camps at El Quseima and El Sabha.

21. *1030 hours New York time.* The Secretary-General met at this time with the Permanent Representative of Israel who gave his Government's views on the situation, emphasizing that the UNEF withdrawal should not be achieved by a unilateral United Arab Republic request alone and asserting Israel's right to a voice in the matter. The question of stationing UNEF on the Israel side of the line was raised by the Secretary-General and this was declared by the Permanent Representative of Israel to be entirely unacceptable to his Government.

22. *1600 hours GMT (12 noon New York time).* At this hour the Secretary-General received through the Permanent Representative of the United Arab Republic the following message from Mr. Mahmoud Riad, Minister of Foreign Affairs of the United Arab Republic:

> The Government of the United Arab Republic has the honour to inform Your Excellency that it has decided to terminate the presence of the United Nations Emergency force from the territory of the United Arab Republic and Gaza strip.

Therefore, I request that the necessary steps be taken for the withdrawal of the Force as soon as possible.

I avail myself of this opportunity to express to Your Excellency my gratitude and warm regards.

At the same meeting the Permanent Representative of the United Arab Republic informed the Secretary-General of the strong feeling of resentment in Cairo at what was there considered to be attempts to exert pressure and to make UNEF an "occupation force." The Secretary-General expressed deep misgivings about the likely disastrous consequences of the withdrawal of UNEF and indicated his intention to appeal urgently to President Nasser to reconsider the decision. Later in the day, the representative of the United Arab Republic informed the Secretary-General that the Foreign Minister had asked the Permanent Representative by telephone from Cairo to convey to the Secretary-General his urgent advice that the Secretary-General should not make an appeal to President Nasser to reconsider the request for withdrawal of UNEF and that, if he did so, such a request would be sternly rebuffed.

The Secretary-General raised the question of a possible visit by him to Cairo and was shortly thereafter informed that such a visit as soon as possible would be welcomed by the government of the United Arab Republic.

23. *1700 hours New York time.* The Secretary-General met with the UNEF Advisory Committee, set up under the terms of paragraphs 6, 8 and 9 of resolution 1001 (ES-I) of 7 November 1956, and the representatives of three countries not members of the Advisory Committee but providing contingents to UNEF, to inform them of developments and particularly the United Arab Republic's request for UNEF's withdrawal, and to consult them for their views on the situation. At this meeting, one of the views expressed was that the United Arab Republic's demand for the immediate withdrawal of UNEF from United Arab Republic territory was not acceptable and that the ultimate responsibility for the decision to withdraw rested with the United Nations acting through the Security Council or the General Assembly. The holders of this view therefore urged further discussion with the Government of the United Arab Republic as well as with other Governments involved. Another position was that the Secretary-General had no choice but to comply with the request of the Government of the United Arab Republic, one representative stating that the moment the request for the withdrawal of UNEF was known his Government would comply with it and withdraw its contingent. A similar position had been taken in Cairo by another Government providing a contingent. No proposal was made that the Advisory Committee should exercise the right vested in it by General Assembly resolution 1001 (ES-I) to request the convening of the General Assembly to take up the situation arising from the United Arab Republic communication. At the conclusion of the meeting, it was understood that the Secretary-General had no alternative other than to comply with the United Arab Republic's demand, although some representatives felt the

Secretary-General should previously clarify with that Government the meaning in its request that withdrawal should take place "as soon as possible." The Secretary-General informed the Advisory Committee that he intended to reply promptly to the United Arab Republic, and to report to the General Assembly and to the Security Council on the action he had taken. It was for the Member States to decide whether the competent organs should or could take up the matter and to pursue it accordingly.

24. After the meeting of the Advisory Committee, at approximately 1900 hours New York time on 18 May, the Secretary-General replied to the message from the Minister for Foreign Affairs of the United Arab Republic through that Government's Permanent Representative as follows:

I have the honour to acknowledge your letter to me of 18 May conveying the message from the Minister of Foreign Affairs of the United Arab Republic concerning the United Nations Emergency Force. Please be so kind as to transmit to the Foreign Minister the following message in reply:

Dear Mr. Minister,

Your message informing me that your Government no longer consents to the presence of the United Nations Emergency Force on the territory of the United Arab Republic, that is to say in Sinai, and in the Gaza Strip, and requesting that the necessary steps be taken for its withdrawal as soon as possible, was delivered to me by the Permanent Representative of the United Arab Republic at noon on 18 May.

As I have indicated to your Permanent Representative on 16 May, the United Nations Emergency Force entered Egyptian territory with the consent of your Government and in fact can remain there only so long as that consent continues. In view of the message now received from you, therefore, your Government's request will be complied with and I am proceeding to issue instructions for the necessary arrangements to be put in train without delay for the orderly withdrawal of the Force, its vehicles and equipment and for the disposal of all properties pertaining to it. I am, of course, also bringing this development and my actions and intentions to the attention of the UNEF Advisory Committee and to all Governments providing contingents for the Force. A full report covering this development will be submitted promptly by me to the General Assembly, and I consider it necessary to report also to the Security Council about some aspects of the current situation in the area.

Irrespective of the reasons for the action you have taken, in all frankness, may I advise you that I have serious misgivings about it for, as I have said each year in my annual reports to the General Assembly on UNEF, I believe that this Force has been an important factor in maintaining relative quiet in the area of its deployment during the past ten years and that its withdrawal may have grave implications for peace.

With warm personal regards,

*U THANT*

Please accept, Sir, the assurances of my highest consideration.

It is to be noted that the decision notified to the Government of the United Arab Republic in this letter as in compliance with the request to withdraw the Force. It did not, however, signify the actual withdrawal of the Force which, in fact, was to remain in the area for several more weeks.

25. Formal instructions relating to the withdrawal of UNEF were sent to the UNEF Commander by the Secretary-General on the night of 18 May (see annex).

26. Also on the Evening of 18 May the Secretary-General submitted his special report to the General Assembly (A/6730).

27. On 19 May the Secretray-General issued his report to the Security Council on recent developments in the Near East (S/7896).

*19 May 1967*

28. *1130 hours New York time.* The Secretary-General again received the Permanent Representative of Israel who gave him a statement from his Government concerning the withdrawal of UNEF, strongly urging the Secretary-General to avoid condoning any changes in the *status quo* pending the fullest and broadest international consultation.

29. On the afternoon of 22 May, the Secretary-General departed from New York, arriving in Cairo on the afternoon of 23 May. He left Cairo on the afternoon of 25 May, arriving back in New York on 26 May (see S/7906). While en route to Cairo during a stop in Paris, the Secretary-General learned that on this day President Nasser had announced his intention to reinstitute the blockade against Israel in the Straits of Tiran.

*17 June 1967*

30. The withdrawal of UNEF was completed. Details of the actual withdrawal and evacuation of UNEF are given in document 1/6730/Add.2.

## MAIN POINTS AT ISSUE

31. Comment is called for on some of the main points at issue even prior to the consideration of the background and basis for the stationing of UNEF on United Arab Republic territory.

### *The Causes of the Present Crisis*

32. It has been said rather often in one way or another that the withdrawal of UNEF is a primary cause of the present crisis in the Near East. This is, of course, a superficial and oversimplified approach. As the Secretary-General pointed out in his report of 26 May 1967 to the Security

Council (S/7906), this view "ignores the fact that the underlying basis for this and other crisis situations in the Near East is the continuing Arab-Israel conflict which has been present all along and of which the crisis situation created by the unexpected withdrawal of UNEF is the latest expression." The Secretary-General's report to the Security Council of 19 May 1967 (S/7896) described the various elements of the increasingly dangerous situation in the Near East prior to the decision of the Government of the United Arab Republic to terminate its consent for the presence of UNEF on its territory.

33. The United Nations Emergency Force served for more than ten years as a highly valuable instrument in helping to maintain quiet along the line between Israel and the United Arab Republic. Its withdrawal revealed in all its depth and danger the undiminishing conflict between Israel and her Arab neighbours. The withdrawal also made immediately acute the problem of access for Israel to the Gulf of Aqaba through the Straits of Tiran—a problem which had been dormant for over ten years only because of the presence of UNEF. But the presence of UNEF did not touch the basic problem of the Arab-Israel conflict—it merely isolated, immobilized and covered up certain aspects of that conflict. At any time in the last ten years either of the parties could have reactivated the conflict and if they had been determined to do so UNEF's effectiveness would automatically have disappeared. When, in the context of the whole relationship of Israel with her Arab neighbours, the direct confrontation between Israel and the United Arab Republic was revived after a decade by the decision of the United Arab Republic to move its forces up to the line, UNEF at once lost all usefulness. In fact, its effectiveness as a buffer and as a presence had already vanished, as can be seen from the chronology given above, even before the request for its withdrawal had been received by the Secretary-General from the Government of the United Arab Republic. In recognizing the extreme seriousness of the situation thus created, its true cause, the continuing Arab-Israeli conflict, must also be recognized. It is entirely unrealistic to maintain that that conflict could have been solved, or its consequences prevented, if a greater effort had been made to maintain UNEF's presence in the area against the will of the Government of the United Arab Republic.

### The Decision on UNEF's Withdrawal

34. The decision to withdraw UNEF has been frequently characterized in various quarters as "hasty," "precipitous," and the like, even, indeed, to the extent of suggesting that it took President Nasser by surprise. The question of withdrawal of UNEF is by no means a new one. In fact, it was the negotiations on this very question with the Government of Egypt which, after the establishment of UNEF by the General Assembly, delayed its arrival while it waited in a staging area at Capodichino airbase, Naples, Italy, for several days in November 1956. The Government of Egypt, understandably,

did not wish to give permission for the arrival on its soil of an international force, unless it was assured that its sovereignty would be respected and a request for withdrawal of the Force would be honoured. Over the years, in discussions with representatives of the United Arab Republic, the subject of the continued presence of UNEF has occasionally come up, and it was invariably taken for granted by United Arab Republic representatives that if their Government officially requested the withdrawal of UNEF the request would be honoured by the Secretary-General. There is no record to indicate that this assumption was ever questioned. Thus, although the request for the withdrawal of UNEF came as a surprise, there was nothing new about the question of principle nor about the procedure to be followed by the Secretary-General. It follows that the decision taken by him on 18 May 1967 to comply with the request for the withdrawal of the Force was seen by him as the only reasonable and sound action that could be taken. The actual withdrawal itself, it should be recalled, was to be carried out in an orderly, dignified, deliberate and not precipitate manner over a period of several weeks. The first troops in fact left the area only on 29 May.

### The Possibility of Delay

35. Opinions have also been frequently expressed that the decision to withdraw UNEF should have been delayed pending consultations of various kinds, or that efforts should have been made to resist the United Arab Republic's request for UNEF's withdrawal, or to bring pressure to bear on the Government of the United Arab Republic to reconsider its decision in this matter. In fact, as the chronology given above makes clear, the effectiveness of UNEF, in the light of the movement of United Arab Republic troops up to the line and into Sharm el-Sheikh, had already vanished before the request for withdrawal was received. Furthermore, the Government of the United Arab Republic had made it entirely clear to the Secretary-General that an appeal for reconsideration of the withdrawal decision would encounter a firm rebuff and would be considered as an attempt to impose UNEF as an "army of occupation." Such a reaction, combined with the fact that UNEF positions on the line had already been effectively taken over by United Arab Republic troops in pursuit of their full right to move up to the line in their own territory, and a deep anxiety for the security of UNEF personnel should an effort be made to keep UNEF in position after its withdrawal had been requested, were powerful arguments in favour of complying with the United Arab Republic request, even supposing there had not been other overriding reasons for accepting it.

36. It has been said that the decision to withdraw UNEF precipitated other consequences such as the reinstitution of the blockade against Israel in the Straits of Tiran. As can be seen from the chronology, the UNEF positions at Sharm el-Sheikh on the Straits of Tiran (manned by thirty-two men in all) were in fact rendered ineffective by United Arab Republic troops before the

request for withdrawal was received. It is also pertinent to note that in response to a query from the Secretary-General as to why the United Arab Republic had announced its reinstitution of the blockade in the Straits of Tiran while the Secretary-General was actually en route to Cairo on 22 May, President Nasser explained that his Government's decision to resume the blockade had been taken some time before U Thant's departure and it was considered preferable to make the announcement before rather than after the Secretary-General's visit to Cairo.

### The Question of Consultations

37. It has been said also that there was not adequate consultation with the organs of the United Nations concerned or with the Members before the decision was taken to withdraw the Force. The Secretary-General was, and is, firmly of the opinion that the decision for withdrawal of the Force, on the request of the host Government, rested with the Secretary-General after consultation with the Advisory Committee on UNEF, which is the organ established by the General Assembly for consultation regarding such matters. This was made clear by Secretary-General Hammarskjöld, who took the following position on 26 February 1957 in reply to a question about the withdrawal of the Force from Sharm el-Sheikh:

> An indicated procedure would be for the Secretary-General to inform the Advisory Committee on the United Nations Emergency Force, which would determine whether the matter should be brought to the attention of the Assembly.[1]

The Secretary-General consulted the Advisory Committee before replying to the letter of 18 May 1967 from the United Arab Republic requesting withdrawal. This consultation took place within a few hours after receipt of the United Arab Republic request, and the Advisory Committee was thus quickly informed of the decision which the Secretary-General had in mind to convey in his reply to the Foreign Minister of the United Arab Republic. As indicated in the report to the Security Council of 26 May 1967:

> The Committee did not move, as it was its right to do under the terms of paragraph 9 of General Assembly resolution 1001 (ES-I) to request the convening of the General Assembly on the situation which had arisen. (S/7906, para. 4)

38. Before consulting the Advisory Committee on UNEF, the Secretary-General had also consulted the Permanent Representatives of the seven

---

[1] *Official Records of the General Assembly, Eleventh Session, Annexes,* agenda item 66, document A/3563, annex I, B, 2.

countries providing the contingents of UNEF and informed them of his intentions. This, in fact, was more than was formally required of the Secretary-General in the way of consultation.

39. Obviously, many Governments were concerned about the presence and functioning of UNEF and about the general situation in the area, but it would have been physically impossible to consult all of the interested representatives within any reasonable time. This was an emergency situation requiring urgent action. Moreover, it was perfectly clear that such consultations were sure to produce sharply divided counsel, even if they were limited to the permanent members of the Security Council. Such sharply divided advice would have complicated and exacerbated the situation, and, far from relieving the Secretary-General of the responsibility for the decision to be taken, would have made the decision much more difficult to take.

40. It has been said that the final decision on the withdrawal of UNEF should have been taken only after consideration by the General Assembly. This position is not only incorrect but also unrealistic. In resolution 1000 (ES-I) the General Assembly established a United Nations command for an emergency international force. On the basis of that resolution the Force was quickly recruited and its forward elements flown to the staging area at Naples. Thus, though established, it had to await the permission of the Government of Egypt to enter Egyptian territory. That permission was subsequently given by the Government of Egypt as a result of direct discussions between Secretary-General Hammarskjöld and President Nasser of Egypt. There is no official United Nations document on the basis of which any case could be made that there was any limitation on the authority of the Government of Egypt to rescind that consent at its pleasure, or which would indicate that the United Arab Republic had in any way surrendered its right to ask for and obtain at any time the removal of UNEF from its territory. This point is elaborated later in this report (see paras. 71-80 below).

41. As a practical matter, there would be little point in any case in taking such an issue to the General Assembly unless there would be reasonable certainty that that body could be expected expeditiously to reach a substantive decision. In the prevailing circumstances, the question could have been validly raised as to what decision other than the withdrawal of UNEF could have been reached by the Assembly once United Arab Republic consent for the continued presence of UNEF was withdrawn.

42. As regards the practical possibility of the Assembly considering the request for UNEF's withdrawal, it is relevant to observe that the next regular session of the General Assembly was some four months off at the time the withdrawal request was made. The special session of the General Assembly which was meeting at the time could have considered the question, according to rule 19 of the Assembly's rules of procedure, only if two thirds or eighty-two members voted for the inclusion of the item in the agenda. It is questionable, to say the least, whether the necessary support could have been mustered for such a controversial item. There could have been no emergency

special session since the issue was not then before the Security Council, and therefore the condition of lack of unanimity did not exist.

43. As far as consultation with or action by the Security Council was concerned, the Secretary-General reported to the Council on the situation leading up to and created by the withdrawal of UNEF on 19 May 1967 (S/7896). In that report he characterized the situation in the Near East as "extremely menacing." The Council met for the first time after this report on 24 May 1967, but took no action.

44. As has already been stated, the Advisory Committee did not make any move to bring the matter before the General Assembly, and no representative of any Member Government requested a meeting of either the Security Council or the General Assembly immediately following the Secretary-General's reports (A/6730 and S/7896). In this situation, the Secretary-General himself did not believe that any useful purpose would be served by his seeking a meeting of either organ, nor did he consider that there was basis for him to do so at that time. Furthermore, the information available to the Secretary-General did not lead him to believe that either the General Assembly or the Security Council would not have decided that UNEF should remain on United Arab Republic territory, by force if necessary, despite the request of the Government of the United Arab Republic that it should leave.

### Practical Factors Influencing the Decision

45. Since it is still contended in some quarters that the UNEF operation should somehow have continued after the consent of the Government of the United Arab Republic to its presence was withdrawn, it is necessary to consider the factors, quite apart from constitutional and legal considerations, which would have made such a course of action entirely impracticable.

46. The consent and active co-operation of the host country is essential to the effective operation and, indeed, to the very existence, of any United Nations peace-keeping operation of the nature of UNEF. The fact is that UNEF had been deployed on Egyptian and Egyptian-controlled territory for over ten and a half years with the consent and co-operation of the Government of the United Arab Republic. Although it was envisaged in pursuance of General Assembly resolution 1125 (XI) of 2 February 1957 that the Force would be stationed on both sides of the line, Israel exercised its sovereign right to refuse the stationing of UNEF on its side, and the Force throughout its existence was stationed on the United Arab Republic side of the line only.

47. In these circumstances, the true basis for UNEF's effectiveness as a buffer and deterrent to infiltration was, throughout its existence, a voluntary undertaking by local United Arab Republic authorities with UNEF, that United Arab Republic troops would respect a defined buffer zone along the entire length of the line in which only UNEF would operate and from which United Arab Republic troops would be excluded. This undertaking was

honoured for more than a decade, and this Egyptian co-operation extended also to Sharm el-Sheikh, Ras Nasrani and the Straits of Tiran. This undertaking was honoured although UNEF had no authority to challenge the right of United Arab Republic troops to be present anywhere on their own territory.

48. It may be pointed out in passing that over the years UNEF dealt with numerous infiltrators coming from the Israel as well as from the United Arab Republic side of the line. It would hardly be logical to take the position that because UNEF has successfully maintained quiet along the line for more than ten years, owing in large measure to the co-operation of the United Arab Republic authorities, that Government should then be told that it could not unilaterally seek the removal of the Force and thus in effect be penalized for the long co-operation with the international community it had extended in the interest of peace.

49. There are other practical factors relating to the above-mentioned arrangement which are highly relevant to the withdrawal. of UNEF. First, once the United Arab Republic troops moved up to the line to place themselves in direct confrontation with the military forces of Israel, UNEF had, in fact, no further useful function. Secondly, if the Force was no longer welcome, it could not as a practical matter remain in the United Arab Republic, since the friction which would almost inevitably have arisen with that Government, its armed forces and with the local population would have made the situation of the Force both humiliating and untenable. It would even have been impossible to supply it. UNEF clearly had no mandate to try to stop United Arab Republic troops from moving freely about on their own territory. This was a peace-keeping force not an enforcement action. Its effectiveness was based entirely on voluntary co-operation.

50. Quite apart from its position in the United Arab Republic, the request of that Government for UNEF's withdrawal automatically set off a disintegration of the Force, since two of the Governments providing contingents quickly let the Secretary-General know that their contingents would be withdrawn, and there can be little doubt that other such notifications would not have been slow in coming if friction had been generated through an unwillingness to comply with the request for withdrawal.

51. For all the foregoing reasons, the operation, and even the continued existence of UNEF on United Arab Republic territory, after the withdrawal of United Arab Republic consent, would have been impossible, and any attempt to maintain the Force there would without question have had disastrous consequences.

## LEGAL AND CONSTITUTIONAL CONSIDERATIONS AND THE QUESTION OF CONSENT FOR THE STATIONING OF UNEF ON UNITED ARAB REPUBLIC TERRITORY

52. Legal and constitutional considerations were, of course, of great importance in determining the Secretary-General's actions in relation to the request of the Government of the United Arab Republic for the withdrawal of UNEF. Here again, a chronology of the relevant actions in 1956 and 1957 may be helpful.

53. *4 November 1956.* The General Assembly, at its first emergency special session in resolution 998 (ES-I), requested "the Secretary-General to submit to it within forty-eight hours a plan for the setting up, with the consent of the nations concerned, of an emergency international United Nations Force to secure and supervise the cessation of hostilities. . . ."

54. *5 November 1956.* The General Assembly, in its resolution 1000 (ES-I), established a United Nations Command for an emergency international Force, and, *inter alia*, invited the Secretary-General "to take such administrative measures as may be necessary for the prompt execution of the actions envisaged in the present resolution."

55. *7 November 1956.* The General Assembly, by its resolution 1001 (ES-I), *inter alia*, approved the guiding principles for the organization and functioning of the emergency international United Nations Force and authorized the Secretary-General "to take all other necessary administrative and executive action."

56. *10 November 1956.* Arrival of advance elements of UNEF at staging area in Naples.

57. *8-12 November 1956.* Negotiations between Secretary-General Hammarskjöld and the Government of Egypt on entry of UNEF into Egypt.

58. *12 November 1956.* Agreement on UNEF entry into Egypt announced and then postponed, pending clarification, until 14 November.

59. *15 November 1956.* Arrival of advance elements of UNEF in Abu Suweir, Egypt.

60. *16 November to 18 November 1956.* Negotiations between Secretary-General Hammarskjöld and President Nasser in Cairo on the presence and functioning of UNEF in Egypt and co-operation with Egyptian authorities, and conclusion of an *"aide-mémoire* on the basis for the presence and functioning of UNEF in Egypt" (the so-called "good faith accord").[2]

61. *24 January 1957.* The Secretary-General in a report to the General Assembly[3] suggested that the Force should have units stationed on both sides of the armistice demarcation line and that certain measures should be taken in relation to Sharm el-Sheikh. On *2 February 1957,* the General

---

[2] *Ibid.,* document A/3375, annex.
[3] *Ibid.,* document A/3512.

Assembly, by its resolution 1125 (XI), noted with appreciation the Secretary-General's report and considered that "after full withdrawal of Israel from the Sharm el-Sheikh and Gaza areas, the scrupulous maintenance of the Armistice Agreement required the placing of the United Nations Emergency Force on the Egyptian-Israel armistice demarcation line and the implementation of other measures as proposed in the Secretary-General's report, with due regard to the considerations set out therein with a view to assist in achieving situations conducive to the maintenance of peaceful conditions in the area."

   62. *7 March 1957.* Arrival of UNEF in Gaza.

   63. *8 March 1957.* Arrival of UNEF at Sharm el-Sheikh.

   64. In general terms the consent of the host country to the presence and operation of the United Nations peace-keeping machinery is a basic prerequisite of all United Nations peace-keeping operations. The question has been raised whether the United Arab Republic had the right to request unilaterally the withdrawal "as soon as possible" of UNEF from its territory or whether there were limitations on its rights in this respect. An examination of the records of the first emergency special session and the eleventh session of the General Assembly is relevant to this question.

   65. It is clear that the General Assembly and the Secretary-General from the very beginning recognized, and in fact emphasized, the need for Egyptian consent in order that UNEF be stationed or operate on Egyptian territory. Thus, the initial resolution 998 (ES-I) of 4 November 1956 requested the Secretary-General to submit a plan for the setting up of an emergency force, "with the consent of the nations concerned." The "nations concerned" obviously included Egypt (now the United Arab Republic), the three countries (France, Israel and the United Kingdom) whose armies were on Egyptian soil and the States contributing contingents to the Force.

   66. The Secretary-General, in his report to the General Assembly of 6 November 1956, stated, *inter alia:*

9. Functioning, as it would, on the basis of a decision reached under the terms of the resolution 337 (V) "Uniting for peace," the Force, if established, would be limited in its operations to the extent that consent of the parties concerned is required under generally recognized international law. While the General Assembly is enabled to *establish* the Force with the consent of those parties which contribute units to the Force, it could not request the Force to be *stationed* or *operate* on the territory of a given country without the consent of the Government of that country.[4]

   67. He noted that the foregoing did not exclude the possibility that the

---

[4] *Ibid., First Emergency Special Session, Annexes,* agenda item 5, document A/3302, para. 9.

Security Council could use such a Force within the wider margins provided under Chapter VII of the United Nations Charter. He pointed out, however, that it would not be necessary to elaborate this point further, since no use of the Force under Chapter VII, with the rights in relation to Member States that this would entail, had been envisaged.

68. The General Assembly in its resolution 1001 (ES-I) of 7 November 1956 expressed its approval of the guiding principles for the organization and functioning of the emergency international United Nations Force as expounded in paragraphs 6 to 9 of the Secretary-General's report. This included the principle of consent embodied in paragraph 9.

69. The need for Egypt's consent was also stated as a condition or "understanding" by some of the States offering to contribute contingents to the Force.

70. It was thus a basic legal principle arising from the nature of the Force, and clearly understood by all concerned, that the consent of Egypt was a prerequisite to the stationing of UNEF on Egyptian territory, and it was a practical necessity as well in acquiring contingents for the Force.

### The "Good Faith" Aide-Mémoire of 20 November 1956

71. There remains to be examined whether any commitments were made by Egypt which would limit its pre-existing right to withdraw its consent at any time it chose to do so. The only basis for asserting such limitation could be the so-called "good faith" *aide-mémoire* which was set out as an annex to a report of the Secretary-General submitted to the General Assembly on 20 November 1956.

72. The Secretary-General himself did not offer any interpretation of the "good faith" *aide-mémoire* to the General Assembly or make any statement questioning the remarks made by the Foreign Minister of Egypt in the General Assembly the following week (see paragraph 74 below). It would appear, however, that in an exchange of cables he had sought to obtain the express acknowledgement from Egypt that its consent to the presence of the Force would not be withdrawn before the Force had completed its task. Egypt did not accept this interpretation but held to the view that if its consent was no longer maintained the Force would be withdrawn. Subsequent discussions between Mr. Hammarskjöld and President Nasser resulted in the "good faith" *aide-mémoire*.

73. An interpretative account of these negotiations made by Mr. Hammarskjöld in a personal and private paper entitled *"aide-mémoire,"* dated 5 August 1957, some eight and a half months after the discussions, has recently been made public by a private person who has a copy. It is understood that Mr. Hammarskjöld often prepared private notes concerning significant events under the heading *"aide-mémoire,"* This memorandum is not in any of the official files. The General Assembly, the Advisory Committee on UNEF and the Government of Egypt were not informed of its

contents or existence. It is not an official paper and has no standing beyond being a purely private memorandum of unknown purpose or value, in which Secretary-General Hammarskjöld seems to record his own impressions and interpretations of his discussions with President Nasser. This paper, therefore, cannot affect in any way the basis for the presence of UNEF on the soil of the United Arab Republic as set out in the official documents, much less supersede those documents.

### Position of Egypt

74. It seems clear that Egypt did not understand the "good faith" *aide-mémoire* to involve any limitation on its right to withdraw its consent to the continued stationing and operation of UNEF on its territory. The Foregin Minister of Egypt, speaking in the General Assembly on 27 November 1956, one week after the publication of the "good faith" *aide-mémoire* and three days following its approval by the General Assembly, said:

> We still believe that the General Assembly resolution of 7 November 1956 still stands, together with its endorsement of the principle that the General Assembly could not request the United Nations Emergency Force to be stationed or to operate on the territory of a given country without the consent of the Government of the country. This is the proper basis on which we believe, together with the overwhelming majority of this Assembly, that the United Nations Emergency Force could be stationed or could operate in Egypt. It is the only basis on which Egypt has given its consent in this respect.[5]

He then added:

> . . . as must be abundantly clear, this Force has gone to Egypt to help Egypt, with Egypt's consent; and no one here or elsewhere can reasonably or fairly say that a fire brigade, after putting out a fire, would be entitled or expected to claim the right of deciding not to leave the house.[6]

### Analysis of the "Task" of the Force

75. In the "good faith" *aide-mémoire* the Government of Egypt declared that, "when exercising its sovereign rights on any matters concerning the presence and functioning of UNEF, it will be guided, in good faith, by its acceptance of General Assembly resolution 1000 (ES-I) of 5 November 1956."

---

[5] *Official Records of the General Assembly, Eleventh Session, Plenary Meetings,* 597th meeting, para. 48.
[6] *Ibid.,* para. 50.

76. The United Nations in turn declared "that the activities of UNEF will be guided, in good faith, by the task established for the Force in the aforementioned resolutions [1000 (ES-I) and 997 (ES-I)]; in particular, the United Nations, understanding this to correspond to the wishes of the Government of Egypt, reaffirms its willingness to maintain UNEF until its task is completed."

77. It must be noted that, while Egypt undertook to be guided in *good faith* by its acceptance of General Assembly resolution 1000 (ES-I), the United Nations also undertook to be guided in *good faith* by the task established for the Force in resolutions 1000 (ES-I) and 997 (ES-I). Resolution 1000 (ES-I), to which the declaration of Egypt referred, established a United Nations Command for the Force "to secure and supervise the cessation of hostilities in accordance with all the terms" of resolution 997 (ES-I). It must be recalled that at this time Israel forces had penetrated deeply into Egyptian territory and that forces of France and the United Kingdom were conducting military operations on Egyptian territory. Resolution 997 (ES-I) urged as a matter of priority that all parties agree to an immediate cease-fire, and halt the movement of military forces and arms into the area. It also urged the parties to the armistice agreements promptly to withdraw all forces behind the armistice lines, to desist from raids across the armistice lines, and to observe scrupulously the provisions of the armistice agreements. It further urged that, upon the cease-fire being effective, steps be taken to reopen the Suez Canal and restore secure freedom of navigation.

78. While the terms of resolution 997 (ES-I) cover a considerable area, the emphasis in resolution 1000 (ES-I) is on *securing and supervising the cessation of hostilities.* Moreover, on 6 November 1956 the Secretary-General, in his second and final report on the plan for an emergency international United Nations Force, noted that "the Assembly intends that the Force should be of a temporary nature, the length of its assignment being determined by the needs arising out of the present conflict."[7] Noting further the terms of resolution 997 (ES-I), he added that "the functions of the United Nations Force would be, when a cease-fire is being established, to enter Egyptian territory with the consent of the Egyptian Government, in order to help maintain quiet during and after the withdrawal of non-Egyptian troops, and to secure compliance with the other terms established in the resolution of 2 November 1956" (997 (ES-I)).[8]

79. In a cable delivered to Foreign Minister Fawzi on 9 or 10 November 1956, in reply to a request for clarification as to how long it was contemplated that the Force should stay in the demarcation line area, the Secretary-General stated: "A definite reply is at present impossible but the

[7] *Ibid., First Emergency Sepcial Session, Annexes,* agenda item 5, document A/3302, para. 8.

[8] *Ibid.,* para. 12.

emergency character of the Force links it to the immediate crises envisaged in resolution 2 November [997 (ES-I)] and its liquidation." This point was confirmed in a further exchange of cables between the Secretary-General and Dr. Fawzi on 14 November 1956.

80. The Foreign Minister of Egypt (Dr. Fawzi) gave his understanding of the task of the Force in a statement to the General Assembly on 27 November 1956:

> Our clear understanding—and I am sure it is the clear understanding of the Assembly—is that this Force is in Egypt only in relation to the present attack against Egypt by the United Kingdom, France and Israel, and for the purposes directly connected with the incursion of the invading forces into Egyptian territory. The United Nations Emergency Force is in Egypt, not as an occupation force, not as a replacement for the invaders, not to clear the Canal of obstructions, not to resolve any question or settle any problem, be it in relation to the Suez Canal, to Palestine or to any other matter; it is not there to infringe upon Egyptian sovereignty in any fashion or to any extent, but, on the contrary, to give expression to the determination of the United Nations to put an end to the aggression committed against Egypt and to the presence of the invading forces in Egyptian territory.[9]

81. In letters dated 3 November 1956 addressed to the Secretary-General, the representatives of both France and the United Kingdom had proposed very broad functions for UNEF, stating on behalf of their Governments that military action could be stopped if the following conditions were met:

(a) Both the Egyptians and Israel Governments agree to accept a United Nations Force to keep the peace.

(b) The United Nations decides to constitute and maintain such a Force until an Arab-Israel peace settlement is reached and until satisfactory arrangements have been agreed in regard to the Suez Canal, both agreements to be guaranteed by the United Nations.

(c) In the meantime, until the United Nations Force is constituted, both combatants agree to accept forthwith limited detachments of Anglo-French troops to be stationed between the combatants.[10]

These broad functions for the Force were not acceptable to the General Assembly, however, as was pointed out in telegrams dated 4 November 1956 from Secretary-General Dag Hammarskjöld to the Minister for Foreign Affairs of France and the Secretary of State for Foreign Affairs of the United Kingdom.[11]

---

[9] Ibid., Eleventh Session, Plenary Meetings, 597th meeting, para. 49.
[10] Ibid., First Emergency Special Session, Annexes, documents A/3268 and A/3269.
[11] Ibid., document A/3284, annexes 2 and 4.

82. Finally, it is obvious that the task referred to in the "good faith" *aide-mémoire* could only be the task of the Force as it had been defined in November 1956 when the understanding was concluded. The "good faith" undertaking by the United Nations would preclude it from claiming that the Egyptian agreement was relevant or applicable to functions which the Force was given at a much later date. The stationing of the Force on the armistice demarcation line and at Sharm el-Sheikh was only determined in pursuance of General Assembly resolution 1125 (XI) of 2 February 1957. The Secretary-General, in his reports relating to this decision, made it clear that the further consent of Egypt was essential with respect to these new functions. [12] Consequently, the understanding recorded in the "good faith" *aide-mémoire* of 20 November 1956 could not have been, itself, a commitment with respect to functions only determined in February and March 1957. It is only these later tasks that the Force had been performing during the last ten years—tasks of serving as a buffer and deterring infiltrators which went considerably beyond those of securing and supervising the cessation of hostilites provided in the General Assembly resolutions and referred to in the "good faith" *aide-mémoire*.

### The Stationing of UNEF on the Armistice Demarcation Line and at Sharm el-Sheikh

83. There remains to examine whether Egypt made further commitments with respect to the stationing of the Force on the armistice demarcation line and at Sharm el-Sheikh. Israel, of course, sought to obtain such commitments, particularly with respect to the area around Sharm el-Sheikh.

84. For example, in an *aide-mémoire* of 4 February 1957,[13] the Government of Israel sought clarification as to whether units of the United Nations Emergency Force would be stationed along the western shore of the Gulf of Aqaba in order to act as a restraint against hostile acts, and would remain so deployed until another effective means was agreed upon between the parties concerned for ensuring permanent freedom of navigation and the absence of belligerent acts in the Strait of Tiran and the Gulf of Aqaba. The Secretary-General pointed out that such "clarification" would require "Egyptian consent." He stated:

> The second of the points in the Israel *aide-mémoire* requests a "clarification" which, in view of the position of the General Assembly, could go beyond what was stated in the last report only after negotiation with Egypt. This follows from the statements in the debate in the General Assembly, and the report on which it was based, which

---

[12] *Ibid., Eleventh Session, Annexes,* agenda item 66, documents A/3512, para. 20, and A/3527, para. 5.
[13] *Ibid.,* document A/3527, annex I.

make it clear that the stationing of the Force at Sharm el-Sheikh, under such terms as those mentioned in the question posed by Israel, would require Egyptian consent.[14]

85. It is clear from the record that Egypt did not give its consent to Israel's proposition. The Secretary-General's report of 8 March 1957[15] recorded "arrangements for the complete and unconditional withdrawal of Israel in accordance with the decision of the General Assembly." There is no agreement on the part of Egypt to forgo its rights with respect to the granting or withdrawing of its consent to the continued stationing of the Force on its territory. On the contrary, at the 667th plenary meeting of the General Assembly on 4 March 1957, the Foreign Minister of Egypt stated:

At our previous meeting I stated that the Assembly was unanimous in expecting full and honest implementation of its resolutions calling for immediate and unconditional withdrawal by Israel. I continue to submit to the Assembly that this position—which is the only position the Assembly can possibly take—remains intact and entire. Nothing said by anyone here or elsewhere could shake this fact or detract from its reality and its validity, nor could it affect the fullness and the lawfulness of Egypt's rights and those of the Arab people of the Gaza Strip.[16]

86. The Foreign Minister of Israel, in her statement at the 666th meeting of the General Assembly, on 1 March 1957, asserted that an assurance had been given that any proposal for the withdrawal of UNEF from the Gulf of Aqaba area would come first to the Advisory Committee on UNEF (see paragraphs 95-98 below).

### Question of the Stationing of UNEF on Both Sides of the Armistice Demarcation Line

87. Another point having significance with respect to the undertakings of Egypt is the question of the stationing of UNEF on both sides of the armistice demarcation line. The Secretary-General, in his report of 24 January 1957 to the General Assembly,[17] suggested that the Force should have units stationed also on the Israel side of the armistice demarcation line. In particular, he suggested that units of the Force should at least be stationed

---

[14] *Ibid.*, document A/3527, para. 5.
[15] *Ibid.*, document A/3568.
[16] *Ibid., Eleventh Session, Plenary Meetings,* 667th meeting, para. 240.
[17] *Ibid., Eleventh Session, Annexes,* agenda item 66, document A/3512.

in the El Auja demilitarized zone[18] which had been occupied by the armed forces of Israel. He indicated that if El Auja were demilitarized in accordance with the Armistice Agreement and units of UNEF were stationed there, a condition of reciprocity would be the Egyptian assurance that Egyptian forces would not take up positions in the area in contravention of the Armistice Agreement.[19] However, Israel forces were never withdrawn from El Auja and UNEF was not accepted at any point on the Israel side of the line.

88. Following the Secretary-General's report, the General Assembly on 2 February 1957 adopted resolution 1125 (XI), in which it noted the report with appreciation and considered:

> ... that, after full withdrawal of Israel from the Sharm el-Sheikh and Gaza areas, the scrupulous maintenance of the Armistice Agreement requires the placing of the United Nations Emergency Force on the Egyptian-Israel armistice demarcation line and the implementation of other measures as proposed in the Secretary-General's report, with due regard to the considerations set out therein with a view to assist in achieving situations conducive to the maintenance of peaceful conditions in the area.

89. On 11 February 1957, the Secretary-General stated in a report to the General Assembly that, in the light of the implication of Israel's question concerning the stationing of UNEF at Sharm el-Sheikh (see paragraph 84 above), he "considered it important . . . to learn whether Israel itself, in principle, consents to a stationing of UNEF units on its territory in implementation of the functions established for the Force in the basic decisions and noted in resolution 1125 (XI) where it was indicated that the Force should be placed 'on the Egyptian-Israel armistice demarcation line.'"[20] No affirmative response was ever received from Israel. In fact, already on 7 November 1956 the Prime Minister of Israel, Mr. Ben Gurion, in a speech to the Knesset, stated, *inter alia,* "On no account will Israel agree to the stationing of a foreign force, no matter how called, in her territory or in any of the territories occupied by her. In a note to correspondents of 12 April 1957 a "United Nations spokesman" stated:

Final arrangements for the UNEF will have to wait for the response of

---

[18] *Article VIII of the Egyptian-Israel General Armistice Agreement provides, inter alia,* that an area comprising the village of El Auja and vicinity, as defined in the article, shall be demilitarized and that both Egyptian and Israel armed forces shall be totally excluded therefrom. The article further provides that on the Egyptian side of the frontier, facing the El Auja area, no Egyptian defensive positions shall be closer to El Auja than El Qouseima and Abou Aoueigila.

[19] *Official Records of the General Assembly, Eleventh Session, Annexes,* agenda item 66, document A/3512, paras. 15-22.

[20] *Ibid.,* document A/3527, para. 5.

the Government of Israel to the request by the General Assembly that the Force be deployed also on the Israeli side of the Armistice Demarcation Line.

90. In a report dated 9 October 1957 to the twelfth session of the General Assembly,[21] the Secretary-General stated:

> Resolution 1125 (XI) calls for placing the Force "on the Egyptian-Israel armistice demarcation line, " but no stationing of UNEF on the Israel side has occurred to date through lack of consent by Israel.

91. In the light of Israel's persistent refusal to consent to the stationing and operation of UNEF on its side of the line in spite of General Assembly resolution 1125 (XI) of 2 February 1957 and the efforts of the Secretary-General, it is even less possible to consider that Egypt's "good faith" declaration made in November 1956 could constitute a limitation of its rights with respect to the continued stationing and operation of UNEF on Egyptian territory in accordance with the resolution of 2 February 1957.

92. The representative of Israel stated at the 592d meeting of the General Assembly, on 23 November 1956:

> If we were to accept one of the proposals made here—namely, that the Force should separate Egyptian and Israel troops for as long as Egypt thought it convenient and should then be withdrawn on Egypt's unilateral request—we would reach a reduction to absurdity. Egypt would then be in a position to build up, behind the screen of this Force, its full military preparations and, when it felt that those military preparations had reached their desired climax, to dismiss the United Nations Emergency Force and to stand again in close contact and proximity with the territory of Israel. This reduction to absurdity proves how impossible it is to accept in any matter affecting the composition or the functions of the Force the policies of the Egyptian Government as the sole or even the decisive criterion.[22]

93. The answer to this problem which is to be found in resolution 1125 (XI) of 2 February 1957 is not in the form of a binding commitment by Egypt which the record shows was never given, but in the proposal that the Force should be stationed on both sides of the line. Israel in the exercise of its sovereign right did not give its consent to the stationing of UNEF on its territory and Egypt did not forgo its sovereign right to withdraw its consent at any time.

---

[21] *Ibid., Twelfth Session, Annexes*, agenda item 65, document A/3694, para. 15.

[22] *Ibid., Eleventh Session, Plenary Meetings*, 592d meeting, para. 131.

*Role of the UNEF Advisory Committee*

94. General Assembly resolution 1001 (ES-I) of 7 November 1956, by which the Assembly approved the guiding principles for the organization and functioning of UNEF, established an Advisory Committee on UNEF under the chairmanship of the Secretary-General. The Assembly decided that the Advisory Committee, in the performance of its duties, should be empowered to request, through the usual procedures, the convening of the General Assembly and to report to the Assembly whenever matters arose which, in its opinion, were of such urgency and importance as to require consideration by the General Assembly itself.

95. The memorandum of important points in the discussion between the representative of Israel and the Secretary-General on 25 February 1957 recorded the following question raised by the representative of Israel:

In connexion with the duration of UNEF, deployment in the Sharm el-Sheikh area, would the Secretary-General give notice to the General Assembly of the United Nations before UNEF would be withdrawn from the area, with or without Egyptian insistence, or before the Secretary-General would agree to its withdrawal?[23]

96. The response of the Secretary-General was recorded as follows:

On the question of notification to the General Assembly, the Secretary-General wanted to state his view at a later meeting. An indicated procedure would be for the Secretary-General to inform the Advisory Committee on the United Nations Emergency Force, which would determine whether the matter should be brought ·to the attention of the Assembly.[24]

97. On 1 March 1957 the Foreign Minister of Israel stated at the 666th plenary meeting of the General Assembly:

My Government has noted the assurance embodied in the Secretary-General's note of 26 February 1957 [A/3363, annex] that any proposal for the withdrawal of the United Nations Emergency Force from the Gulf of Aqaba area would first come to the Advisory Committee on the United Nations Emergency Force, which represents the General Assembly in the implementation of its resolution 997 (ES-I) of 2 November 1956. This procedure will give the General Assembly an opportunity to ensure that no precipitate changes are

---

[23] *Ibid., Eleventh Session, Annexes*, agenda item 66, document A/3563, annex I, A, 2.
[24] *Ibid.*, annex I, B, 2.

made which would have the effect of increasing the possibility of belligerent acts.[25]

98. In fact, the 25 February 1957 memorandum does not go as far as the interpretation given by the Foreign Minister of Israel. In any event, however, it gives no indication of any commitment by Egypt, and so far as the Secretary-General is concerned it only indicates that a procedure would be for the Secretary-General to inform the Advisory Committee which would determine whether the matter should be brought to the attention of the General Assemlby. This was also the procedure provided in General Assembly resolution 1001 (ES-I). It was, furthermore, the procedure followed by the Secretary-General on the withdrawal of UNEF.

## OBSERVATIONS

99. A partial explanation of the misunderstanding about the withdrawal of UNEF is an evident failure to appreciate the essentially fragile nature of the basis for UNEF's operation throughout its existence. UNEF in functioning depended completely on the voluntary co-operation of the host Government. Its basis of existence was the willingness of Governments to provide contingents to serve under an international command and at a minimum of cost to the United Nations. It was a symbolic force, small in size, with only 3400 men, of whom 1800 were available to police a line of 295 miles at the time of its withdrawal. It was equipped with light weapons only. It had no mandate of any kind to open fire except in the last resort in self-defense. It had no formal mandate to exercise any authority in the area in which it was stationed. In recent years it experienced an increasingly uncertain basis of financial support, which in turn gave rise to strong annual pressures for reduction in its strength. Its remarkable success for more than a decade, despite these practical weaknesses, may have led to wrong conclusions about its nature, but it has also pointed the way to a unique means of contributing significantly to international peace-keeping.

## ANNEX

*Cable Containing Instructions for the Withdrawal of UNEF*
*Sent by the Secretary-General to the Commander of UNEF*
*on 18 May 1967, at 2230 hours New York Time*

The following instructions are to be put in effect by you as of date and time

---

[25] *Ibid., Eleventh Session, Plenary Meetings,* **666th meeting, para. 8.**

of their receipt and shall remain operative until and unless new instructions are sent by me.

1. UNEF is being withdrawn because the consent of the Government of the United Arab Republic for its continued deployment on United Arab Republic territory and United Arab Republic-controlled territory has been rescinded.

2. Date of the commencement of the withdrawal of UNEF will be 19 May when the Secretary-General's response to the request for withdrawal will be received in Cairo by the Government of the United Arab Republic, when also the General Assembly will be informed of the action taken and the action will become public knowledge.

3. The withdrawal of UNEF is to be orderly and must be carried out with dignity befitting a Force which has contributed greatly to the maintenance of quiet and peace in the area of its deployment and has earned widespread admiration.

4. The Force does not cease to exist or to lose its status or any of its entitlements, privileges and immunities until all of its elements have departed from the area of its operation.

5. It will be a practical fact that must be reckoned with by the Commander that as of the date of the announcement of its withdrawal the Force will no longer be able to carry out its established functions as a buffer and as a deterrent to infiltration. Its duties, therefore, after 19 May and until all elements have been withdrawn, will be entirely nominal and concerned primarily with devising arrangements and implementation of arrangements for withdrawal and the morale of the personnel.

6. The Force, of course, will remain under the exclusive command of its United Nations Commander and is to take no orders from any other source, whether United Arab Republic or national.

7. The Commander, his headquarters staff and the contingent commanders shall take every reasonable precaution to ensure the continuance of good relations with local authorities and the local population.

8. In this regard, it should be made entirely clear by the Commander to the officers and other ranks in the Force that there is no discredit of the Force in this withdrawal and no humiliation involved for the reason that the Force has operated very successfully and with, on the whole, co-operation from the Government on the territory of an independent sovereign State for over ten years, which is a very long time; and, moreover, the reasons for the termination of the operation are of an overriding political nature, having no relation whatsoever to the performance of the Force in the discharge of its duties.

9. The Commander and subordinate officers must do their utmost to avoid any resort to use of arms and any clash with the forces of the United Arab Republic or with the local civilian population.

10. A small working team will be sent from Headquarters by the

Secretary-General to assist in the arrangements for, and effectuation of, the withdrawal.

11. The Commander shall take all necessary steps to protect United Nations installations, properties and stores during the period of withdrawal.

12. If necessary, a small detail of personnel of the Force or preferably of United Nations security officers will be maintained as long as necessary for the protection of United Nations properties pending their ultimate disposition.

13. UNEF aircraft will continue flights as necessary in connexion with the withdrawal arrangements but observation flights will be discontinued immediately.

14. Elements of the Force now deployed along the line will be first removed from the line, the IF and ADL, including Sharm el-Sheikh to their camps and progressively to central staging.

15. The pace of the withdrawal will of course depend upon the availability of transport by air, sea and ground to Port Said. The priority in withdrawal should of course be personnel and their personal arms and equipment first, followed by contingent stores and equipment.

16. We must proceed on the assumption that UNEF will have full co-operation of United Arab Republic authorities on all aspects of evacuation, and to this end a request will be made by me to the United Arab Republic Government through their Mission here.

17. As early as possible the Commander of UNEF should prepare and transmit to the Secretary-General a plan and schedule for the evacuation of troops and their equipment.

18. Preparation of the draft of the sections of the annual report by the Secretary-General to the General Assembly should be undertaken and, to the extent possible, completed during the period of withdrawal.

19. In the interests of the Force itself and the United Nations, every possible measure should be taken to ensure against public comments or comments likely to become public on the withdrawal, the reasons for it and reactions to it.

# Part Six

# Interpretations

# The June 1967 War:

# Miscalculation or Conspiracy?*

## Elias Sam'o

Every political event is a game, and every game has a number of players, rules, strategies, moves, and pay-offs. There are two kinds of games: zero-sum and non-zero-sum games. The essential difference between them is that in the first the net pay-off is always zero—that is, the gains of the winners are always equal to the losses of the losers—while in the second the net pay-off is not zero. In other words, in the second type it is possible to have all the players winning or losing depending on the players' motives, interests, strategies, and the amount of information available to each player about these factors.

The Middle East crisis of May-June, 1967, which resulted in a war, was no exception. However, although the crisis was a continuous process which culminated in a war, it actually consisted of two games, each of which was of a different kind played by different players.

## A Zero-Sum Game

The first game was a zero-sum game with essentially two players—Egypt and Israel. Its beginning is harder to determine than its abrupt end, which

*This is an exercise in conceptual thinking. Future findings might render this exercise futile. The only purpose is to encourage unconventional thinking with regard to the developments which led to the June 1967 War.

occurred on May 22, 1967. We could go back in history as far as 1948, when the state of Israel was created, to determine the beginning of the first game; but it seems that the most realistic date for the beginning would be the Suez War of 1956. The reason for selecting this date is rather obvious. The 1967 war was precipitated by two elements resulting from the Suez War: the creation of the United Nations Emergency Force (UNEF) in the Sinai and the opening of the Gulf of Aqaba for Israeli shipping. It was the changes in these two elements—the removal of UNEF and the closing of the gulf to the Israelis—which raised the level of tension to a breaking point.

Egypt and Israel played this first game for an extended period of over ten years. Even though there were other parties involved, their roles were short of full-fledged players. They were supporting players, informants, rumor-mongers, or simply subordinates to the main players; but they never sat at the table, nor did they have a hand of cards.

Israel made the first move by attacking Egypt on October 29, 1956, and the pay-off was very handsome. Two predetermined objectives were fulfilled: the destruction of Egyptian commando bases in the Sinai and the opening of the Gulf of Aqaba to Israeli shipping. Another by-product of the war was the stationing of the United Nations Emergency Force on the Egyptian-Israeli border inside Egypt. At this time, President Nasser did not have his chips on the table; he had to wait until May 16, 1967, to make his countermove. This is not to say that in 1967 Nasser was prepared for direct action. In fact, the record indicates that the *circumstances* in which Nasser found himself in early May, 1967, rather than his actual state of preparedness, dictated his moves. He had suspended the game for more than ten years, and there was no reason why he could not have waited for five years, or even more, had he been free to do so.

The circumstances which determined Nasser's behavior during May, 1967, consisted chiefly of two elements: the presence of UNEF and Israel's behavior toward other Arab states, particularly Syria and Jordan. The presence of UNEF since its deployment in 1956 had been a constant source of embarrassment to Nasser, especially vis-à-vis other Arab leaders. Some of Nasser's Arab antagonists did not hesitate to accuse him of hiding behind the UNEF cover. This problem became more acute in late 1966 and early 1967 as the result of Israeli actions against Syria and Jordan.

Although there had been numerous border incidents between Israel on the one hand and Jordan and Syria on the other, two in particular assumed major significance. On November 13, 1966, Israeli forces attacked the Jordanian village of Es Samu, killing eighteen and wounding fifty-four Jordanian soldiers and civilians. Five months later, on April 7, 1967, a limited exchange of fire between the Israelis and the Syrians escalated into an air battle over the Syrian capital of Damascus and ended with the destruction of six Syrian aircraft.

During the course of these events, Nasser remained ostensibly aloof and uninvolved, but the pressure on him from Syria, an ally, and Jordan, a rival, was increasing as the border incidents multiplied and intensified. However, it is likely that Nasser could have continued to withstand this pressure had the nature of the events not changed radically in the early days of May. Nasser could have, as he had done until then, remained calm and uninvolved as long as Israeli actions vis-á-vis Jordan and Syria could be written off as "teaching its neighbors a lesson." However, in early May it seemed to Nasser that Israeli policy was taking a new and very ominous turn. The new direction of the Israeli policy, as he perceived it at that time, was not "to teach a lesson," but to overthrow the Ba'athist regime in Syria. The president explained on June 9, 1967:

> There was an enemy plan to invade Syria, and the statements by his [Israeli] politicians and his military commanders declared that frankly. The Evidence was ample.
> The sources of our Syrian brothers and our own reliable information were categorical on this.
> Even our friends in the Soviet Union told the parliamentary delegation which was visiting Moscow early last month that there was a calculated intention. It was our duty not to accept this in silence. In addition to its being a question of Arab brotherhood, it was also a matter of national security. Who starts with Syria will finish with Egypt.[1]

Whether it was a question of "Arab brotherhood" or Egypt's security, Nasser could not and did not accept the impending Israeli attack against Syria in silence.

Nasser made his first move on May 16, when he ordered his forces to advance to the Israeli border. Simultaneously—and this was his second major move—Egyptian military authorities requested General Rikhye, the commander of UNEF, to withdraw all UNEF troops immediately. Two days later, on May 18, U.N. Secretary General U Thant received the following message from Mahmoud Riad, minister of foreign affairs of the U.A.R.:

> The Government of the United Arab Republic has the honour to inform Your Excellency that it has decided to terminate the presence of the United Nations Emergency Force from the territory of the United Arab Republic and Gaza strip.
> Therefore, I request that the necessary steps be taken for the withdrawal of the Force as soon as possible.[2]

---

[1] *New York Times*, June 10, 1967.
[2] *Official Records of the General Assembly, Fifth Emergency Special Session*, June 26, 1967, para. 22.

On that day the Secretary General complied with Egyptian demands and ordered the withdrawal of the UNEF.[3] Israel objected to U Thant's compliance with the Egyptian request to withdraw the force, even though it refused to have the Force stationed on its own side of the border.

Although Nasser's two moves—the mobilization and deployment of his forces in Sinai and the withdrawal of UNEF—raised the level of tension, the crisis was still manageable; although the stakes in the game were getting very high, the game was still in progress. It took four more days and one additional major bid by Nasser for the entire nature of the game to change in terms of the identity of the players, the rules of the game, and the nature of the pay-off. Nasser made his third move, which turned out to be his last bid. On May 22, in a speech delivered at air force headquarters in Sinai, he declared:

> The armed forces yesterday occupied Sharm el-Sheikh. What is the meaning of the armed forces' occupation of Shram el-Sheikh? It is an affirmation of our right and our sovereignty over the Aqaba Gulf. The Aqaba Gulf constitutes our Egyptian territorial waters. Under no circumstances will we allow the Israeli flag to pass through the Aqaba Gulf.

This was Nasser's last move before he was eliminated as a player. The second and more complex non-zero-sum game had begun.[4] Nasser made two further moves in an effort to recover his role as a player, but by then the game had progressed so far that the new players were viewing him not as a player but merely as a pay-off. Both of his attempts were made on May 28 in a press conference attended by many international correspondents. Answering questions concerning the massing of Egyptian troops on the Israeli border, Nasser suggested the revival of the Armistice Commission to supervise the withdrawal of Egyptian and Israeli forces from the front lines. On the question of the Gulf of Aqaba, he offered to let the International Court of Justice settle the dispute.

---

[3] Egypt's request to withdraw UNEF and U Thant's compliance created a number of controversies. One of these was whether Egypt really wanted the troops stationed at Sharm el-Sheikh to be withdrawn. Exactly three years later, in an interview in U.S. News and World Report (May 18, 1970, p. 61), Nasser said, "In 1967 when we asked U.N. forces to withdraw, we cited specifically the area from Rafah to Elath. We did not ask U.N. troops to withdraw from Sharm el-Sheikh, nor from all other areas. Because they did withdraw, this created a problem." However on May 22, 1967, in his famous Sinai speech in which he declared the closure of the Gulf of Aqaba, Nasser had stated that, "On May 16 we requested the withdrawal of the United Nations Emergency Force in a letter from Lt. Gen. Muhammad Fawzi. We then requested the complete withdrawal of UNEF."
[4] Answering a question during his press conference of May 28, 1967, Nasser said, "We have regained the rights which were ours in 1956. As I have already said, we have left the next move to Israel." He might have added the United States and the Soviet Union.

Thus, the first game, which began on October 29, 1956, ended on May 22, 1967, with the closure of the Gulf of Aqaba. What the Israelis had done in 1956—opening the gulf to Israeli shipping and forcing Egypt to station UNEF on its side of the border—was undone by May 22, 1967. Although it might appear that Nasser was merely evening an old account with the Israelis, his actions in the spring of 1967 were the result of far more complex considerations. Although Nasser was still the dominant leader in the Arab world, his popularity had been waning since the early 1960s. The secession of Syria from the U.A.R. in 1961 was considered a personal blow to his prestige. This was followed by his failure in the Yemen campaign. His insistence on keeping UNEF stationed on his border was interpreted by some Arab leaders as a sign of weakness and an abdication of his responsibility to the Arab nation. Finally, his refusal to respond to Israeli attacks against Syria and Jordan in the months preceding the June war had seriously threatened his stature as the only Arab leader who could speak with unquestioned authority to the Arab masses.

This was the situation in early May, 1967. It would soon change abruptly. By May 16, when the UNEF was ordered to withdraw, Nasser had recovered a considerable degree of prestige among the Arab masses; on May 22, with the closure of the Gulf of Aqaba, his banners were again raised all over the Arab world. Neither his envious allies nor his jealous rivals could dare to challenge him. Nasser was again the undisputed leader of the Arab masses. Even many of the Arab leaders—allies and rivals alike—submitted to him grudgingly. It was no surprise when King Hussein, one of his rivals, flew humbly to Cairo on May 30 to conclude a defense pact with him.

Nasser's undisputed leadership of the Arab world, which was one of the major consequences of the first game, set in motion the forces for the second game, playing a central role in the strategies of the new players. From the point of view of the superpowers, it is bad enough to have to deal with a strong national leader; but it is worse yet to have to deal with a regional hero. Nasser had become in late May the hero of the whole Arab world. In the eyes of the Arab masses, he had not only defeated Zionism but had also challenged American imperialism. Hussein's "capitulation" to Nasser was not an isolated event but only a link in a chain of reactions in the Arab world. From the American, Russian, and Israeli points of view, although the UNEF withdrawal and the closure of the gulf had triggered the confrontation, the context of this confrontation had been expanded. In late May the whole future of the Middle East was in question, and the key figure was Nasser. As far as these powers were concerned, the issue was not UNEF or the gulf, but rather the power of Nasser. This brings to an end the first game played between Egypt and Israel and sets the stage for the beginning of the second game, which started immediately after Nasser's declaration on May 22 of the closing of the Gulf of Aqaba.[5]

## A Non-Zero-Sum Game

There were three players in the new game: the United States, Israel, and the Soviet Union. The pay-off was Nasser and, behind him, the Arab world. The main rule in this game was to avoid a superpower confrontation that might lead to a world war. The strategy for the players was for each to at least maintain his interests and perhaps achieve some gains— either at the expense of one or both of the other players or, through cooperation with the other players, at the expense of Nasser and the Arab world. To appreciate the setting in which this tripartite game was played, a brief review of the interests and expectations of the three players is essential.

In recent years, the United States had become a major power in the Middle East, with substantial economic, political, and strategic interests in the region. Although there is no precise method of calculating all aspects of U.S. economic interests in the Middle East, in 1966 American trade and investment in the region produced a net inflow into the U.S. of some $1.6 billion, half of which was from oil investment. Oil in the Middle East (and North Africa) represents the single most important component of U.S. economic interest in the region. In fact, the Middle East accounts for two-thirds of the oil produced by American corporations outside the U.S. However, the importance of the Middle Eastern oil to the U.S. goes beyond its economic impact, for Middle Eastern oil is a major factor in the American global defense network. The region, which contains 76 percent of the known "free-world" oil reserves, supplies Japan with 85 percent of its oil needs and Western Europe with 76 percent.

> Oil from the Middle East and North Africa has for two decades fueled the land, sea and air forces which support U.S. containment policy throughout the Eastern Hemisphere—NATO components and the Sixth Fleet in Europe, Korea, Okinawa, the Seventh Fleet, Vietnam, and SEATO in Asia. The United States relies on this oil to maintain its commitments to the containment policy.[6]

---

[5] It could be suggested that the second game did not start in earnest until May 29, when Nasser delivered a speech to members of the National Assembly. He said, "Preparations have already been made. We are now ready to confront Israel. Now we are ready for the confrontation. We are now ready to deal with the entire Palestine question." Another possible date could be May 30, when King Hussein flew to Cairo to sign a defense pact with Nasser. The importance of these two events will become clear in the following pages.

[6] George Lenczowski, ed., *United States Interests in the Middle East* (Washington, D.C.: American Enterprise Institute for Public Policy Research, 1968), p. 2. I wish to acknowledge my indebtedness to this work in preparing this section of the paper.

Furthermore, in terms of its general strategic importance, the area is rated by David G. Nes, former chargé d'affaires of the United States Embassy in Cairo, as "far more important in defense of Western interests than the area to which the United States has presently committed more than half a million fighting men."[7] This strategic importance of the Middle East to the "free world" makes it imperative for U.S. foreign policy-makers to prevent the Soviet Union from penetrating the region. Russian dominance in the Middle East would mean not only denying NATO forces in Western Europe the flow of oil from the region but also counter-balancing the presence of the Sixth Fleet in the Mediterranean and possibly outflanking NATO forces from the south. A former Defense Department official, in emphasizing the importance of the Middle East to the U.S., stated that:

> While the United States has a policy of friendship, aid and protec-tion toward Israel, we have national interests of the highest impor-tance in the Arab world ... to encourage and strengthen the moderate Arab states in order to weaken the radical (Arab) potential and to avoid a polarization of power relationships in which the United States would have no friends in the Middle East except Israel, while the Soviet Union would gain uncontested influence and possibly control throughout the vast and populous Arab world.[8]

When analyzing the relationship between the Arab world and the United States, the ideological orientation of the different Arab states is of paramount importance. In 1967, the Arab world was divided ideologically into three camps: the "leftist," or "revolutionary," camp consisted of Egypt, Syria, Iraq, Yemen, and Algeria; the "traditionalist," or "conserva-tive," camp included Saudi Arabia, Jordan, Libya, Kuwait, and Morocco; and the "moderate," or "neutral," camp consisted of Lebanon, Tunisia, and the Sudan.

The "revolutionary" camp, though very important to short- and long-range American interests, has, for the most part, been beyond the reach of direct American influence. This was Nasser's domain. His leadership of this camp, though challenged at times, was fully recognized, and by May, 1967, he had become its undisputed spokesman. Syria and Iraq had signed defense pacts with him; in Yemen, he had some 40,000 soldiers fighting in support of the Republican government against the royalists; and Algeria supported his moves vis-á-vis Israel.

It was in the "conservative" camp that the U.S. had its greatest economic interests and political influence; the bulk of American oil investments lie in Saudi Arabia, Kuwait, and Libya. Although Nasser had

[7] *Ibid.*
[8] Townsend Hoopes, former deputy assistant secretary of defense for international security affairs, quoted in *New York Times*, August 18, 1967.

consistently constituted a threat to these regimes and, by extension, to American interests and influence, the threat in late May, 1967, seems to have reached a level of unacceptability as far as the United States was concerned.

To understand U.S. perception of the situation in late May, 1967, several important points should be noted. First, Nasser's relationship with the conservative camp had always been such that the greater his influence and adoration among the Arab people, the greater was his threat to the conservative regimes. Second, under Nasser's pressure in late May, this quasi-unified camp seemed to crumble. King Hussein, one of its main spokesmen, flew to Cairo on May 30 to sign a defense pact with Nasser.

This leads to the third and perhaps the most significant point from the American perspective. To appreciate this point, two considerations should be kept in mind; one is the Defense White Paper issued by Britain on February 22, 1966, declaring that in 1968, as part of reducing its military presence east of Suez, it would withdraw its forces from South Arabia. The other consideration is that, in 1967, Nasser had some 40,000 soldiers stationed in Yemen. British evacuation would have created a "power vacuum" in the South Arabian peninsula. This, coupled with the presence of Egyptian troops in Yemen and the existence in the peninsula of various pro-Nasser national liberation fronts, were regarded as ominous signs by strategists in Washington. Unless he was stopped, Nasser would move into the area, these strategists calculated—with the Soviets close behind. Such a development was unacceptable to Washington, not only because the area contains substantial amounts of oil, but also because it is strategically located in relation to Saudi Arabia, Kuwait, the Red Sea, and the Indian Ocean.[9]

Finally, in late May, 1967, the Egyptian president succeeded in surrounding two important members of the conservative group: Saudi Arabia and Kuwait. To the north, Jordan, Iraq, and Syria had become his allies. To the west, in addition to Egypt, was Sudan—then a politically unstable country with substantial support for Nasser; to the south were Yemen, with Egyptian soldiers, and the rest of the peninsula soon to be dominated by Nasser or his supporters. Libya, the fourth member of the conservative group, was considered by the Americans, to be vulnerable to Nasser's influence unless it was checked. The discovery of great quantities of oil there led some voices to demand radical internal changes. In conjunction with the internal pressure was Nasser's pressure. It was a matter of time before the archaic and inefficient regime of King Idris was overthrown.[10]

[9] See Miles Copeland, *The Game of Nations* (New York: Simon & Schuster, 1969), pp. 265-66.
[10] Even with Nasser's defeat, the regime could not withstand the pressure and was overthrown on September 1, 1969.

From the American viewpoint, the future of these conservative regimes in late May, 1967, looked dim. Jordan had capitulated; Saudi Arabia, Kuwait, and Libya were in danger of being drawn into the conflict; only Morocco, whose importance to the U.S. was negligible, remained relatively undisturbed by this chain of events. As far as the U.S. was concerned, its interests in the Arab world lay with the conservative camp. The key to the future of this camp and, behind it, America's future in the Arab world, was Nasser. To the U.S., the Middle East crisis was not confined to Nasser and Israel; it was Nasser versus America.[11]

Washington had two choices: to placate the Egyptian president *or* preserve American interests in the Arab world. It did not require any great degree of imagination or realism for the White House to decide that Nasser had to go. Again there were two alternatives for America: to do the job itself or "unleash Israel" for that purpose.[12] For the U.S. to have done the job, it would have meant sending American warships through the Gulf under the pretext of opening the gulf to Israeli shipping. Such a move would have led to a confrontation with Nasser which, regardless of the military outcome, would have been a psychological and political victory for Nasser.

It is important to recall that the British-French invasion of Egypt in 1956, although successful, made Nasser a hero of the Arab masses and a major statesman in the Third World. Similarly, an American confrontation in 1967 would have been counterproductive for the U.S. and would have defeated its purpose. A further and perhaps more important consideration was the Russian response to such a move and the prospect of a super-power confrontation. Such a possibility would have violated the rule of the game—no superpower confrontation—and was therefore unacceptable.[13]

The only other alternative for decision-makers in Washington was to

---

[11] While the U.S. was trying to determine his future, Nasser was not taking "the United States into consideration." In a reply to a question during his May 28 press conference, President Nasser said, "I do not take the United States into consideration in my reckoning. If I took into consideration the United States, the Sixth Fleet, the Seventh Fleet, and the American generals, I would not be able to do anything."

[12] Theodore Draper reported that Rusk and McNamara presented President Johnson with similar alternatives. He goes on to say that both Rusk and McNamara rejected the alternative of "unleashing" Israel. However, Draper does not indicate his source of information or why this alternative was rejected by both cabinet members. Draper, *Israel and World Politics* (New York: Viking, 1968), p. 90.

[13] James Reston suggested a further consideration one day before the outbreak of hostility: "The United States, preoccupied with Vietnam, is obviously not very enthusiastic about breaking the blockade on its own and risking a second front in the Middle East." *New York Times,* June 4, 1967, p. 12E.

"unleash" Israel.[14] Two conditions would have to be met for this alternative to be successful: first, Israel would have to be willing to be "unleashed"; second, it would have to be capable of fulfilling the mission successfully. As for the latter, both Washington and Tel Aviv were confident of Israel's capability. In Washington, President Johnson asked General Earle Wheeler, then chairman of the Joint Chiefs of Staff, to provide him with a balance sheet of Arab and Israeli forces. General Wheeler's capability estimates indicated that Israel would win a victory over the Arabs in a matter of a few days.[15]

In Tel Aviv, General Dayan, the newly appointed Israeli defense minister, held a press conference on June 3, 1967, in which he expressed doubt that diplomats would be able to settle the Middle East crisis. He went on to say that "if somehow it comes to real fighting, I would not like American or British boys to get killed here in order to secure Israel and I don't think we need it. I think we can win."[16] Therefore, in both Washington and Tel Aviv, Israel's victory in an Arab-Israeli war, especially if it were to deliver the first strike, was a foregone conclusion.

Now the question was whether Israel was willing to be "unleashed." From the Israeli point of view, there were two alternatives: either to wait for diplomatic negotiations to reopen the gulf or to go to war against the Arabs. The first alternative would have meant: (1) the indefinite closure of the gulf until (and if) there was a breakthrough in negotiations; (2) a significant diplomatic victory for Nasser who would have undone what the Israelis had accomplished eleven years earlier in the Suez War; (3) the presence of an Arab military ring around Israel under the leadership of Nasser; (4) the continuation of the state of mobilization in Israel for an indefinite period of time, which the Israeli economy could not afford; and (5) a possible decline in Israeli morale, as the crisis dragged on without any decisive development. At the same time, the pressure was building up for action, forcing Prime Minister Levi Eshkol to appoint the hawkish Moshe Dayan as defense minister on June 1.

The second alternative—going to war—in which the Israelis were assured a decisive and quick victory, would have meant: (1) opening the gulf for Israeli use immediately; (2) humiliating, or even eliminating, Nasser; (3) destroying the Arab military ring; (4) acquiring new territories; and (5) revitalizing Western sympathy for the "beleaguered" and "underdog" Israel, in the form of financial contributions and increased Jewish immigration.

From the Israeli point of view, these expectations were perhaps

---

[14] House Minority Leader Gerald Ford, in a statement favoring the lending of a destroyer to Israel to replace the one sunk by Egypt, said: "Israel had done a pretty good job of bailing U.S. interests in the area." *Detroit News,* October 30, 1967.

[15] *Life,* June 23, 1967, p. 32B.

[16] *New York Times,* June 4, 1967, p. 1.

sufficient to justify a brief war with the Arabs. However, to attribute the Israeli decision to engage in a major war against the Arabs to the above reasons is unsatisfactory. Israel's calculations during the fateful days in late May and early June, 1967, must be viewed from the larger perspective of her policy vis-à-vis the Arabs.

Since its creation, Israel's foreign policy has been based on the assumption that its neightbors are obsessed with its destruction and that, to survive, it must maintain military superiority. Furthermore, convinced of its own invincibility, it is imperative for Israel that the Arabs at no time be permitted to believe that they have become strong enough to strike.[17] The Arab challenge would not have to be military at first, for psychological overconfidence, if remained unchecked, could easily lead to a military confrontation. Nasser's action during the last days in May constituted a psychological and a diplomatic victory for the Arab people. Such a victory, the Israelis must have reasoned, would lead the Arabs to forget how invincible Israel was and how vulnerable they were.

Nasser realized his vulnerability and repeatedly declard that he was not going to attack Israel. However, the threat of an Israeli attack against Syria forced the Egyptian president to make his moves. The Israelis could not be certain that Nasser would not join the Syrians in a military counter-offensive. Armed with the pretext of having been forced to fight, and confident of their ability to defeat the Arabs, the Israelis decided to attack. It was left to the military to decide the date.[18] On Monday morning, June 5, 1967, Israel struck, rendering the Arab forces virtually impotent within hours.

As far as the Soviet Union was concerned, the 1967 crisis afforded an excellent opportunity to further advance its interests in the Middle East. Soviet interests in the region lie in removing or reducing the Western presence and influence and, simultaneously, in advancing and strengthening its own influence there. For the Russians, who for centuries tried vainly to penetrate the Middle East, Arab-Israeli relations of the last two decades have provided an ideal setting in which to pursue its objectives.

The first Soviet breakthrough came in 1955, with the Egyptian purchase of arms from Czechoslovakia. Since then the Soviet Union has given the Arabs a substantial amount of economic, miltiary, and diplomatic assistance. By 1967, it had emerged as a major power in the Middle

[17] Isaac Deutscher suggests that Israel's policy toward the Arabs is based on the doctrine which holds "that Israel's security lies in periodic warfare which every few years must reduce the Arab states to impotence." See also Part One above.
[18] Theodore H. White reported that on Sunday afternoon, June 4, the Israeli cabinet met and decided to "let the army decide time, dimension and method of response to Egyptian attack." *Life*, June 23, 1967, pp. 24B-24C.

East, and its future prospects in the area looked bright.[19] Unlike the United States, which tried to freeze the *status quo* in the region to protect its substantial vested interests, the Soviet Union was determined to keep the area in a state of flux. The May-June crisis of 1967 presented the Soviets with a fortunate set of circumstances in which they could expand their influence with a minimum of risk. In fact, the nature of the crisis was such that, regardless of its outcome, the Soviet Union was bound to gain.

Had the crisis been settled peacefully, that is, had Nasser gotten away with his moves, it would have constituted a great threat to American interests, thus allowing the Russians an advantage. Therefore, a victory for Nasser would have meant a victory for his allies, the Russians. Yet, if Nasser's sense of victory had been so great that he felt too free of superpower—that is, Russian—pressure, such a victory would have been counterproductive for the Soviet Union; for, it is easier to manipulate a weak national leader than it is to deal with a regional hero. It may be that the Russians felt in late May, 1967, that Nasser was getting out of hand, that it was becoming increasingly difficult for them to contain him.[20] Nevertheless, their overwhelming consideration was that Nasser's moves implied, above all, a threat to Western interests in the region and thus served one of Russia's primary objectives—the reduction of Western influence in the area.

The second alternative for settling the crisis was through war. In such a case, there were two serious considerations for the Russians. First, the war should not draw the two superpowers into a direct confrontation; second, Russia's existing interest in the Middle East should be at least preserved and preferably expanded. As for the outcome of an Arab-Israeli war, there were two possibilities—an Arab victory or an Israeli victory. The Russians calculated the impact of each outcome on their interests in the region and on the possibility of a  superpower confrontation.

---

[19] In commenting on the Soviet presence in the Middle East, Walter Laquer suggests that "the Soviet position in the Middle East is stronger today than it was ten years ago. This was not the result of invasion, nor of infiltration by stealth: the Soviet Union became a Middle East power by invitation. It has seized no military bases, but was offered the facilities it wanted by the governments of Egypt and Syria, Algeria and the Yemen of their own free will" (*The Struggle for the Middle East* [New York: Macmillan, 1969]).

[20] In a report attributed to a high Soviet official which was obtained in Moscow by a reporter for the leftist French journal, *Le Nouvel Observateur*, the Russian official states that "it was with Soviet approval that Nasser massed his troops on the Sinai frontier to demonstrate to the Israelis that, if they launched an offensive against Syria, that country would not fight alone. Nasser believed this would discourage Israel from initiating the attack.

"On the other hand, Nasser made the grave decisions of demanding the withdrawal of the U.N. 'blue helmets' from the Suez Canal zone and blockading the Gulf of Aqaba on his own and then informed the U.S.S.R. about them." See Part Four above.

The first possibility—an Arab victory—would have posed a serious threat to the survival of the Zionist state. Lester Velie expressed sentiments that have prevailed in the U.S. for some time:

> Could the U.S. stand aside while the Soviets helped the Arabs annihilate two million Jewish victims? Morally it was inconceivable; practically, too, it was inconceivable. Israel is one of the few democracies in all Asia and the Middle East. Since the world regards the U.S. as Israel's protector, whether the U.S. wishes to be or not, Israel's destruction would send tremors of fear throughout the non-communist world. Further, if Israel went down no other pro-western nation in the Middle East would be safe from Nasser and the Russians.[21]

Even though this is a naive and biased appraisal of the situation, nevertheless an Arab victory would have most likely led to American intervention on the Israeli side. If this were to happen, the Russians would have two alternatives: (1) to intervene on behalf of the Arabs and risk a confrontation with the United States, or (2) to avoid intervention with the sure consequence of forfeiting whatever influence they had developed during the preceding two decades.[22] Neither of these alternatives was acceptable to the Russians, for an Arab victory over Israel would have meant a setback for them. However, they realized, as did the Americans and the Israelis, that under the prevailing circumstances, especially with an Israeli surprise attack, an Arab victory would be impossible.

The other possible outcome of an Arab-Israeli war was an Israeli victory. In this event, there would be no need for American intervention, thereby avoiding a superpower confrontation. Having ruled out such a confrontation, the Soviets had to assess the impact of an Arab defeat on their interests in the region. They predicted that in case of an Arab defeat, the Arabs would first find a scapegoat (i.e., the U.S.) and then would seek outside assistance in rebuilding their armies and economies. Clearly, then, they would have no alternative but to turn to the Soviet Union, thus enhancing the latter's influence in the region. One Soviet diplomat, in confirming the preceding analysis, stated several weeks after the war that

---

[21] See *Reader's Digest*, August, 1967, pp. 39-40. The *Wall Street Journal*, June 6, 1967, had the following headline: "'Neutral' to a point; U.S. hinges its policy on hopes that Israel will win—and quickly; Washington fears it will be forced to intervene alone if Arabs get upper hand."

[22] In a speech to the National Assembly delivered on May 29, 1967, Nasser referred to "a message from the Soviet Premier Kosygin saying that the U.S.S.R. supported us in this battle and would not allow any power to intervene until matters were restored to what they were in 1956." Also, in the previously cited report, the high Soviet official is reported to have said, "At that point [May 22, 1967] the U.S.S.R. advised Nasser that it was only committed to neutralizing the United States—that is, it would respond with an escalation equal to any escalation Washington might undertake."

"our position is stronger not weaker. True, the Arabs have suffered a defeat, but this defeat has brought them closer to us—not driven them farther away."[23]

In retrospect, then, there was no way for the Russians to lose—war or peace. They could afford to remain calm and unperturbed, waiting for others to make the moves and take the risks while they reaped the benefits.

## Conclusion

The Arab-Israeli crisis of May-June, 1967, appeared to be a very ominous and dangerous one. However, the three players—the U.S., Israel, and the U.S.S.R.—were busy making calculated moves to determine the fate of Nasser and the future of the Middle East.

Nasser had made moves which, he declared, were not negotiable. The moves in themselves were unacceptable to either the Americans or the Israelis. But more important to both was the impact of these moves on the future of the region and their implications for Israel's survival and the preservation of American economic and political interests. The direct short-range impact and the expected indirect long-range consequences of Nasser's moves made it imperative for both Washington and Tel Aviv to see to it that he be humiliated at least.[24] As for the Russians, they would profit with either a heroic or humiliated Nasser.

For Nasser to be humiliated, he would have to be defeated; and since the main rule of the game was to prevent a superpower confrontation, the only alternative open to the players was to "unleash" Israel in such a way that it would achieve a quick and decisive victory. Defeating Nasser, and in the process humiliating him, with a decisive Israeli blow was in the interests of all three players.[25] These players must have been aware of the situation and the degree to which their interests coincided. The question is whether or not they preplanned everything. Did they preplan anything? The secrets of the Suez conspiracy did not become public until a decade after the Suez War.[26] Similarly, the secrets of the June 1967 War may take longer to be unveiled. These secrets might prove, as Charles Yost has maintained, that "it seems unlikely . . . that any of them plotted and

---

[23] *New York Times*, July 23, 1967, p. 23.

[24] One wonders why the U.S.S. *Liberty*, a CIA-employed ship, was stationed just a few miles off the coast of Egypt during the war and why it was attacked by the Israelis, an attack which resulted in the loss of thirty-four American lives.

[25] This is perhaps why both the U.S. and the U.S.S.R. warned Nasser on May 26 not to be the first to strike, thus leaving Israel in a position to determine the date, time, and extent of the strike. See Nasser's speech, June 9, 1967.

[26] See Anthony Nutting, *No End of a Lesson* (New York: C.N. Potter, 1967); Hugh Thomas, *Suez* (New York: Harper & Row, 1967); and Kenneth Love, *Suez: The Twice-Fought War* (New York: McGraw-Hill, 1969).

planned war for 1967. It seems more likely that they blundered into it."[27] Or it could be, as suggested by Raymond Aron, that "from May 22 onwards, as after the Austrian ultimatum to Serbia in July 1914, the diplomatic crisis developed in accordance with the merciless logic of power politics: threats and counter-threats, an escalation of security measures and an upping of the stakes, a mobilitzation without war."[28]

Nevertheless, conceptually there was a non-zero-sum game played by three players—the U.S., Israel, and the U.S.S.R.—in which cooperation among them would have maximized their gains. The cooperation could have been explicit or implicit. All that can be said is that the setting in which the Arab-Israeli crisis of 1967 took place was ideal for the three players to have conspired against Nasser. It could have happened. It might have happened.[29]

[27] See Charles W. Yost's article in Part Two above.
[28] Raymond Aron, *DeGaulle, Israel, and the Jews* (New York: Praeger, 1968), p. 114.
[29] See G.H. Jansen, *Whose Suez? Aspects of Collusion*, Monograph Series No. 13 (Beirut: The Institute for Palestine Studies, 1968).

# Resolution 242 and Beyond

Elias Sam'o and Cyrus Elahi

## Introduction

The June, 1967, war and its aftermath initiated a new era in the Arab-Israeli conflict, characterized by two developments with far-reaching implications. First, the two superpowers have recognized that both have vital interests in the Middle East and major stakes in the outcome of the conflict. Second, there has been a radical change in the perception of the Arabs and the Israelis, both toward the conflict and toward each other.[1]

The first key event during this new era was the adoption of resolution 242 by the Security Council on November 22, 1967.[2] Presumably, this resolution was to provide a general framework for a peaceful settlement of the conflict. The second key event was the United Arab Republic's—and Jordan's—recent declarations that under certain conditions,. the most important of which is total Israeli withdrawal from occupied territories, they would sign a peace agreement with Israel. This declaration was included in the reply of the United Arab Republic to Dr. Gunnar Jarring's letter of February 8, 1971. In this letter, the United Arab Republic stated that, "When Israel gives these commitments, the United Arab Republic will be ready to enter into a peaceful agreement with Israel containing all the aforementioned obligations as provided for in Security Council resolution

---

[1] It is recognized that there are differences of views among the Arab states vis-à-vis Israel. However, throughout this paper, the term "Arabs" refers to those states which are parties to the Jarring talks, namely the United Arab Republic and Jordan.
[2] See appendix for the complete text of the resolution.

*163*

242."[3] Egyptian readiness to sign a peace agreement with the Israelis ended a twenty-three-year-old Arab refusal to accept the reality of Israel, thus allowing for the present peace initiatives.

In its reply to the United Arab Republic's proposals—notably ignoring Dr. Jarring's mediatory role—Israel stated that it "views favorably the expression by the United Arab Republic of its readiness to enter into peace agreement with Israel and reiterates that it is prepared for meaningful negotiations on all subjects relevant to a peace agreement between the two countries."[4] Both the Egyptian and the Israeli replies were conditional. The key condition for both sides centered around the issue of withdrawal. While the Egyptians insist on total Israeli withdrawal to pre-June 5, 1967, lines, the Israelis refuse to withdraw to those lines. Even though the willingness of both sides to sign a peace agreement has given rise to some optimism, Israel's conditions with respect to the question of withdrawal have brought the indirect negotiations to an impasse. As the present impasse is an expression of interpretations of the withdrawal clause in resolution 242, it is our intention in this essay to explore the various meanings given to that particular clause.[5]

## The "Meanings" of Withdrawal

As the outcome of the military confrontation during the June 1967 war, became clear, a diplomatic search for ways to cope with the newly created problems was initiated on many levels. There were debates and consultations, proposals and resolutions seeking to transform the theater of war in the Middle East into a state of "peace." It was not until November 16, 1967, however, that Lord Caradon, the Permanent Representative of the United Kingdom to the United Nations, came forth with a compromise draft resolution.

On November 22, Lord Caradon's draft resolution was adopted unanimously by the Security Council and has been referred to ever since as resolution 242. Since then, this resolution has been described as a "balanced whole," and "a realistic document." Former United States Ambassador to the United Nations, Arthur Goldberg, noted that resolution 242 "is the product not only of recent discussions but, in fact, of more than five months of intensive consultations among the members of the Assembly, this Council and the parties concerned." Mr. Goldberg added that the resolution "draws inspiration and guidance from all of those and from the various suggestions and draft resolutions which have been

---

[3] For the full text of Dr. Jarring's letter and the Egyptian reply see *The New York Times*, March 10, 1971.
[4] For the full text of the Israeli reply see *The New York Times*, March 8, 1971.
[5] Although resolution 242 includes numerous important clauses, this article focuses on the withdrawal clause only.

proposed, but particularly, as its balance shows, from the ideas and concepts put forward by the Latin American countries."[6]

To date, more than three years have elapsed since the adoption of the resolution. Yet, it not only has remained unimplemented, but there is still no agreement on the meaning of its key provision—namely, the clause dealing with Israel's withdrawal from occupied territories.

In this resolution, the Security Council affirms the principle of "withdrawal of Israeli armed forces from territories occupied in the recent conflict." Despite the apparent clarity of language, the issue of withdrawal remains at the heart of the current controversy.

Following the submission of the resolution, Lord Caradon stated: "The draft resolution speaks for itself and I need not attempt any detailed explanation."[7] Later, he stressed: "In our resolution we stated the principle of the '[w]ithdrawal of Israeli armed forces from territories occupied in the recent conflict' and in the preamble we emphasized 'the inadmissibility of the acquisition of territory by war'. In our view, the wording of those provisions is clear."[8]

Even though the British Ambassador seemed quite certain in his exposition, various spokesmen have given the withdrawal clause conflicting interpretations, in fact, these interpretations began to take shape shortly before the adoption of the resolution. The Indian Representative, Mr. Parthasarathi, stated:

It is our understanding that the draft resolution, if approved by the Council, will commit it to the application of the principle of total withdrawal of Israeli forces from all territories—I repeat, all the territories—occupied by Israel as a result of the conflict which began on 5 June 1967.[9]

Challenging this interpretation, the Foreign Minister of Israel, Mr. Eban, declared: "The Representative of lIndia has now sought to interpret the resolution in the image of his own wishes. For us, the resolution says what it says. It does not say that which it has specifically and consciously avoided saying."[10] Furthermore, added Mr. Eban, "The important words in most languages are short words, and every word, long or short, which is not in the text, is not there because it was deliberately concluded that it should not be there."[11] He stressed his disagreement with the premise that a solution to the conflict could be formulated on the basis of a return to

[6] Security Council (S.C.), 22nd yr., mtg. 1381, Nov. 20, 1967, p. 27.
[7] S.C., 22nd yr., mtg. 1379, Nov. 16, 1967, p. 11.
[8] S.C., 22nd yr., mtg. 1381, Nov. 20, 1967, p. 21.
[9] S.C., 22nd yr., mtg. 1382, Nov. 22, 1967, p. 28.
[10] *Ibid.*, p. 51.
[11] *Ibid.*

the situation of June 4, 1967: "We hold that that premise has no logical or moral international basis."[12]

Anxious to avoid a controversy, yet eager to see the draft resolution adopted, Lord Caradon took the floor:

> I would say that the draft resolution is a balanced whole. To add to it or to detract from it would destroy the balance and also destroy the wide measure of agreement we achieved together. It must be considered as a whole and as it stands. I suggest that we have reached the stage when most, if not all, of us want the draft resolution, the whole draft resolution and nothing but the draft resolution.[13]

He continued noting, on the one hand, "we regard its wording as clear," and, on the other, "All of us, no doubt, have our own views and interpretations and understandings."[14]

It was not only that various states had given conflicting interpretations to the withdrawal clause, but also that highly placed officials of the same state—the United States—presented conflicting interpretations of the clause. On December 9, 1969, in a public address, Secretary of State William Rogers presented an American interpretation of the resolution. Regarding the withdrawal clause, Secretary Rogers stated:

> The Security Council resolution endorses the principle of the non-acquisition of territory by war and calls for the withdrawal of Israeli armed forces from territories occupied in the 1967 war. We support this part of the resolution, including withdrawal, just as we do its other elements.[15]

A few months later, Mr. Joseph J. Sisco, Assistant Secretary of State for Near Eastern and South Asian Affairs, presented a different interpretation of the withdrawal clause. He stated:

> That resolution did not say 'total withdrawal'. That resolution did not say 'withdrawal to the pre-June 5 lines'. That resolution said that the parties must negotiate to achieve agreement on the so-called final secure and recognized borders.[16]

---

[12] *Ibid.*, pp. 48-50.
[13] S.C., 22nd yr., mtg. 1382, Nov. 22, 1967, p. 31.
[14] *Ibid.*, p. 32.
[15] *Department of State Bulletin*, Vol. LXII, No. 1593, January 5, 1970, p. 9. Secretary Rogers has also stated that withdrawal as understood by the United States does not necessarily preclude the possibility of insubstantial border adjustments.
[16] See the National Boradcasting Comapany's television and radio program "Meet the Press" of July 12, 1970. Contrary to Mr. Sisco's assertion, the word "negotiate" does not appear in the text of the resolution. See appendix.

Today, the controversy which Lord Caradon anticipated and whose effects he tried to minimize has become the central issue. This controversy, as noted earlier, revolves around the question of whether the word "withdrawal" means "total" or "partial" withdrawal. Total withdrawal means pulling back to June 4, 1967, armistice lines; and partial withdrawal means the creation of new boundries yet to be determined.

There are several grounds upon which one may argue that the withdrawal clause in the resolution means total withdrawal. First, the Security Council, in the preamble to the resolution, emphasized "the inadmissibility of the acquisition of territory by war. . . ." Obviously, all the territories dealt with in resolution 242 were acquired by Israel as a result of the June, 1967, war. Therefore, according to the above-stated preamble, this acquisition is by definition "inadmissible." Also, the Security Council, in operative paragraph 1 (ii) of the resolution, affirms the principle of "respect for and acknowledgement of the sovereignty . . . territorial integrity and . . . political independence of every state in the area. . . ." No state could possibly consider her territorial integrity acknowledged and respected if another state forcibly occupied her territories and refused to withdraw from them. Thus, the permanent loss of any territory by any state as a consequence of the June, 1967, war constitutes a violation of resolution 242.

Second, the policy of the United Kingdom, the state which submitted the resolution, was based on the premise that withdrawal should be total. Foreign Secretary George Brown, less than two months before the adoption of the resolution, stated:

> Britain does not accept war as a means of settling disputes, nor that a State should be allowed to extend its frontiers as a result of a war. This means that Israel must withdraw. But equally, Israel's neighbors must recognize its right to exist, and it must enjoy security within its frontiers.[17]

Third, to quote from a commentary in *The London Times* by Sir Harold Beeley, an eminent Englishman:

> The resolution does not call for the withdrawal from 'part of the territories' or 'some of the territories'. It says, to quote the phrase in full, that there should be withdrawal of Israeli armed forces 'from territories occupied in the recent conflict'. The intention is perfectly clear.[18]

Fourth, since French is an official language in the United Nations, reference to the French text of the resolution may be helpful. According

---

[17] General Assembly Official Records, mtg. 1567, September 26, 1967, p. 47.
[18] *The London Times*, October 3, 1970.

to the French Representative to the United Nations, Mr. Berard, the French text "leaves no room for any ambiguity since it speaks of withdrawal *'des territoires occupés'*, thus giving a precise interpretation to the expression 'territories occupied'."[19]

The above points support the interpretation that the withdrawal clause means *total* Israeli withdrawal from territories occupied during the 1967, war. However, the current impasse attests to the fact that there is no consensus on the above interpretation. The basis upon which the withdrawal clause has been interpreted to mean partial withdrawal is essentially an attempt by Israel and the United States to add vagueness to the resolution, and in particular to exploit the absence of the definite article before the word "territories" in the English text.

If one accepts the interpretation of the clause to mean partial withdrawal, two interrelated questions emerge: How partial is partial withdrawal, and who will determine its extent?

## Definitions of Security

Whatever the extent of withdrawal, it cannot be binding unless the parties directly involved in the conflict agree to it. The Arabs have repeatedly stated that Israeli withdrawal from their territories must be total withdrawal. For example, President Anwar el-Sadat recently stated:

> We want peace, but we want peace based on justice. . . . First and foremost, there must be a complete liberation of all the Arab territories occupied by Israel in '67. No one in our country would ever agree that only part of our territories should be liberated. This would be surrender.[20]

Regardless of the Arab understanding of the withdrawal clause, at present the Arab states lack the necessary power to implement it. Therefore, Israel's interpretation of the clause may be a crucial factor in determining the extent of its withdrawal.

What are the general principles upon which Israel would be likely to formulate her withdrawal policy? As early as November, 1967, Mr. Eban summed up the policy which has been repeatedly stated by his government:

> Our policy is to insure that the cease-fire be totally maintained until and unless it is succeeded by peace treaties between Israel and the Arab states ending the state of war, establishing agreed recognized and secured territorial boundaries, guaranteeing free navigation for all shipping, including that of Israel, in international waterways, and

[19] S.C., 22nd yr., mtg. 1382, Nov. 22, 1967, pp. 58-60.
[20] *The New York Times*, November 20, 1970.

insuring a stable and mutually guaranteed security. This is our policy. It has not changed. It will not change.[21]

The central point in Mr. Eban's statement is the question of security for Israel. The same concern was also expressed by Prime Minister Golda Meir in a speech delivered recently in the Knesset. She emphasized: "A central subject in peace negotiations is that of borders. Israel desires and is entitled to defensible, agreed, and recognized borders, and she will not return to the lines of June 4, 1967."[22]

It goes without saying that the primary objective of a state is to maintain her security. However, as with the concept of national interest, the concept of security does not lend itself to a rational definition. Those who presuppose that security is synonymous with "the will to maximize power are not even aware of the ambiguity of the term they use."[23] As a prominent political scientist points out, one cannot automatically assume:

(1) that security is a concept endowed with objective meaning;
(2) that nation-states acting through their authorized decision makers, are actually engaged in a rational pursuit of an objectively definable condition of security.[24]

The concept of security has two dimensions: objective conditions and subjective feelings. The objective conditions of security refer to physical, tangible, and circumstantial factors, which would insure the minimum requirements of a state's survival. The subjective feeling of security is a psychological phenomenon which may not exist even though the objective conditions for the physical survival of the state are met.[25]

A careful analysis of Israel's security should take into account two interrelated questions: the relationship between the objective conditions and the subjective feeling of security; and the relationship between her visions of security and the territorial integrity of the Arab states.

In their attempt to maximize their security, the Israelis have come face-to-face with a dilemma. Israel's pronouncements vis-à-vis the Arab states, are based on the premise that they are committed to her destruction. The wide acceptance and constant reinforcement of this premise by the Israelis has made it extremely difficult for them to attain the feeling of being secure. Consequently, Israel has concentrated her efforts on maximizing the objective conditions of security (e.g., the preservation of

[21] S.C., 22nd yr., mtg. 1381, Nov. 20, 1967, p. 31.
[22] Jerusalem Post Weekly, March 23, 1971.
[23] Raymond Aron, "What Is a Theory of International Relations?" Journal of International Affairs: Vol. XXI, No. 2, p. 195.
[24] Samuel L. Sharp, "Security and Threatmanship," America's World Role in the 70's, ed. Abdul A. Said (Englewood Cliffs, New Jersey: Prentice-Hall, 1970), p. 30.
[25] Ibid., p. 31.

military superiority, extending her frontiers to more "defensible" positions, and tightening her "control" within occupied Arab territories). But it is a myth, as the former United States Ambassador to the United Nations, Mr. Charles Yost, points out, for the Israelis to believe that "strategic boundaries and military strength can provide [Israel] more permanent security than could an agreed settlement and international guarantees."[26] A corollary to this statement was provided by David Ben Gurion in a recent interview: "As for security, militarily defensible borders, while desirable, cannot by themselves guarantee our future. *Real* peace with our Arab neighbors—mutual trust and friendship—that is the only true security."[27]

Israel's obsession with the physical and circumstantial factors of security has made a travesty of the concept of territorial integrity for her neighboring states and has induced her to rob them of all semblance of security. In order for Israel to enjoy the feeling of being "secure," her neighbors would have to accept a position of insecurity and the violation of their own territorial integrity. Since these terms are unacceptable to the Arab states, Israel will continue to perceive them as a threat. Thus, security for Israel remains precarious and lacerated by contradictions.

According to the above analysis, Israel would obviously interpret the withdrawal clause to mean "partial," the extent of which remains to be determined. If the extent of withdrawal is to be determined either through the process of negotiations or through coercion, then we must ask whether resolution 242 was really needed to settle the conflict. For, if the relationship between the Arab states and Israel reaches the stage where their conflict could be settled through negotiations, then resolution 242 would be superfluous as the basis for a mutually acceptable settlement. Likewise, if a settlement is to be imposed through coercion, then the resolution would be irrelevant. Therefore, for resolution 242 to be *relevant* and *consistent* as the basis for a viable settlement of the Arab-Israeli conflict, the withdrawal clause would have to mean total withdrawal.[28]

## Real Estate

In a recent speech to the Knesset, Prime Minister Meir, without specifically referring to resolution 242, reaffirmed Israeli intransigence, maintaining that Sharm el-Sheikh with a territorial access to Elath,

[26] *Atlantic Monthly*, (January 1969), pp. 83-84.
[27] *The Saturday Review*, April 3, 1971, p. 14.
[28] For further analysis of resolution 242, see Cherif Bassiouni "The Middle-East in Transition: From War to War—The Ill-fated Resolution 242 of 1967." *The Arab World*, September, 1969, and Eugene V. Rostow, "Legal Aspects of the Search for Peace in the Middle East." *American Journal of International Law*, September, 1970.

Jerusalem, and the Golan Heights will remain in Israeli hands.[29] Israel's insistence on a unilaterial interpretation of the withdrawal clause to mean partial withdrawal has given rise to three crucial debates.

First, the Israelis are engaged in an all-important debate among themselves. It is evident that there are deep divisions and serious differences of views within some circles—including those at the highest levels of the government—regarding Israel's future map and her relations with the Arab states. Underlying, as well as complicating, the outcome of this domestic debate is the presence of differing attitudes with regard to peace, security, and territorial expansion.

There are in Israel a few lone voices which seem to regard peace with their neighbors as the paramount objective. This position was expressed succinctly by former Prime Minister David Ben Gurion in a recent interview in *The Saturday Review:* "Peace, *real* peace, is now the great necessity for us," he said. "It is worth almost any sacrifice. To get it, we must return to the borders before 1967." The Israeli elder statesman continued, "Sinai; Sharm el-Sheikh? Gaza? The West Bank? Let them go. Peace is more important than real estate. We don't need the territory."[30]

This view, however, is clearly overshadowed by those who contend that there is no substitute for so-called "secure" and "defensible" boundaries for Israel. This position has been expressed frequently by high-level Israeli officials. For example, in a recent address to the governing Labor Party's youth organization, Deputy Premier Yigal Allon stated:

All the modern developments in military technology cannot negate the importance of geographically defensible positions. . . . We must be sure that we have borders that will prevent a surprise attack. There is no alternative to a peace treaty and secure borders which we can defend with our own forces.[31]

A third group participating in Israel's domestic debate, which includes the Gahal Party and the National Religious Party (N.R.P.), insists on the retention of most, if not all; of the occupied Arab territories. In a recent heated debate in the Knesset, in response to the publication of an interview with Prime Minister Meir in *The London Times,* Mr. Menachem Begin—a leader of Gahal Party whose motto is 'al Shaal', meaning literally, 'not one footstep'—stated, "You are handing back our homeland to the foreign conqueror."[32] In response to the same interview, Yitzhak Raphael, Knesset Whip of the N.R.P., reiterated the Party's election program concerning retention of the occupied territories: "The Party's Ministers can

[29] *Jerusalem Post Weekly*, March 23, 1971.
[30] *The Saturday Review, op. cit.*
[31] *The New York Times*, March 20, 1971.
[32] *Newsweek*, March 29, 1971, p. 37.

never be party to any border plan that would exclude Judea and Samaria. . . ."[33]

## Peace or Sharm el-Sheikh?

Thus, while the government of Israel publicly cries for peace, it is, at best reluctant to commit itself to relinquishing its hold over the Arab territories occupied in 1967, a prerequisite for peace in the Middle East. This ambivalence has been illustrated on a number of occasions by Israeli Defense Minister Moshe Dayan, who stated recently that, if confronted with the choice between peace and Sharm el-Sheikh, he would choose the latter. With respect to territorial expansion, Mr. Dayan is quoted on an earlier occasion:

> Our fathers had reached the frontiers which were recognized in the Partition Plan. Our generation reached the frontiers of 1949. Now the Six-Day Generation has managed to reach Suez, Jordan, and the Golan Heights. This is not the end. After the present cease-fire lines, there will be new ones. They will extend beyond Jordan—perhaps to Lebanon and perhaps to Central Syria as well.[34]

The Rogers Plan, which was first presented in a speech by the Secretary of State on December 9, 1969, has given rise to the second debate. This debate, which is continuing between the United States and Israel, concerns the extent of Israeli withdrawal from the occupied territories. Needless to say, Israeli leaders—bent on territorial expansion—have repeatedly expressed their explicit and firm opposition to the Rogers Plan.

During Abba Eban's "dialogue with the American government" last November, "Israel was reported to have asked the Nixon administration to keep silent on the territorial issues . . . in other words, to abandon the position voiced by Secretary Rogers last December advocating Israel's withdrawal to frontiers virtually the same as those before the Six-Day War of 1967."[35] Ever since Egypt indicated its willingness to sign a peace agreement with Israel, the previously submerged differences between Israel and the United States with regard to final settlement of the conflict have become exposed to public view.

This divergence of views between the United States, a superpower whose interests are broader than the national interest of any single state in the Middle East, and Israel, which is concerned with its own national interests was inevitable. In other words, as Moshe Dayan recently stated in

---

[33] *Jerusalem Post Weekly*, March 16, 1971.
[34] Quoted by Ian Gilmour in *The London Times*, June 25, 1969, p. 13. For more recent statements by Mr. Dayan with regard to territorial expansion, see *The New York Times*, April 6, 1971.
[35] *The New York Times*, November 20, 1970.

a speech at the Weizmann Institute, although the United States hopes to put an end to the conflict and is interested in Israel's security, nevertheless it has its own interests in the region and would like to improve its strained relations with the Arab states.[36] As it stands today, the Americans are telling the Israelis "trust us." The Israelis reply, "We will trust no one but ourselves again."

Following his recent meeting with American officials, Mr. Eban noted that despite their divergent views, "the United States and Israel still share certain values, and I still believe that they are of greater weight than the divergences which we discussed."[37] However, the important question is whether these "shared values" between the two states are strong enough to contain their disagreements and carry them through the present crisis, or whether American decision-makers will come to view Israel as an obstacle toward the settlement of the dispute and to American interests in the area.

The third debate is taking place in the United States between those individuals and groups who generally support the Israeli position and others, who support the Rogers Plan. A microcosm of this debate took place in the United States Senate during a recent discussion of the situation in the Middle East. During the course of the debate, a group of pro-Israeli senators attacked the Rogers Plan—calling for withdrawal from occupied Arab lands—and expressed support for Israeli intransigence on that point.[38] Senator Jacob Javits referred to the Rogers Plan as concepts "drawn from formal 19th century European diplomacy. . . ." The Senator from New York continued: "What is needed now—and what Israel so rightly emphasizes—are secure and recognized boundaries based, indeed, on geography which reinforces, rather than undermines, the terms and pledges of a peace treaty."[39] Senator Henry Jackson, who also opposed the Rogers Plan, stated: "I believe the Israeli Government has properly rejected the view that external guarantees can substitute for defensible borders. They cannot be expected to relinquish a geographical position on which their survival depends."[40]

However, in support of the Rogers Plan, Senator William Fulbright of Arkansas noted:

The principal reason there has been no progress on negotiations for the settlement of this question is the belief on the part of Israel that the United States and the Senate will back it, no matter what position it takes. I believe that attitude is most unfortunate, because

[36] *Jerusalem Post Weekly*, March 23, 1971.
[37] *The New York Times*, March 20, 1971.
[38] For the text of the proceedings, see *Congressional Record—Senate*, Tuesday, March 23, 1971, vol. 117, No. 41, pages 53518-53526.
[39] *Congressional Record. op. cit.*, p. 53521.
[40] *Ibid.*, p. 53519.

I do not see any possibility of negotiation so long as Israel believes we are completely at its disposal. [41]

The American-Israeli debate is not confined to the floor of the Senate. Various Zionist organizations in the United States continue to engage in an effort to tailor American foreign policy to suit Israel's interests. Underscoring the influence of this lobby, Dr. William Wexler, chairman of the Conference of Presidents of Major American Jewish Organizations and president of B'nai B'rith, stated in a recent interview, "I cannot see the U.S. making any basic policy changes to Israel's disadvantage.... Now that elections are coming up, I cannot visualize any kind of policy change in the cards." Dr. Wexler further noted, "Above all, I thank the Almighty that six million American Jews who are very effective politically, will do what we have to do." [42]

## Allies in Conflict

Yet, Israel today finds herself isolated and under increasing pressure—ironically, from its closest ally, the United States. The Israelis fear that further pressure from the United States may leave them no alternative but to submit to the Rogers Plan. However, increased United States diplomatic pressure on Israel is not expected in the near future. For, even though the presidential election is more than a year and a half away, President Nixon is unlikely to provide his opponents with further opportunity to challenge him. Instead, diplomatic maneuvers between Israel and the United States will continue quietly in the form of a debate between two allies who find themselves in conflict.

The view which propounds that every state has an identical interest in the maintenance of peace and that the disturbance of peace is both irrational and immoral has been frequently expressed in the context of the Arab-Israeli conflict. Such a veiw suggests that if the Arabs and the Israelis were to behave rationally they would realize that war serves neither, whereas peace would serve both.

This sentiment has been expressed by President Nixon: "Each nation concerned must be prepared to subordinate its special interests to the general interest in peace. In the Middle East, especially, everyone must participate in making the peace so all will have an interest in maintaining it." [43] On another occasion, the President stated: "We are neither pro-Arab nor pro-Israel. We are pro-peace. We are for security for all the nations in

[41] *Ibid.*, p. 53522.
[42] *Jerusalem Post Weekly*, March 9, 1971.
[43] *Dept. of State Bulletin*, Vol. LXII, No. 1602, March 9, 1970. "U.S. Foreign Policy For the 1970's. A New Strategy For Peace." A report to the Congress by Richard Nixon, Feb. 18, 1970.

that area."[44]  However, as Lenin noted in 1915, peace in itself is a meaningless aim: "Absolutely everybody is in favor of peace in general including Kitchener, Joffre, Hindenburg and Nicholas the Bloody, for everyone of them wishes to end the war." [45]

One can easily cite specific gains made by Israel in her three wars against the Arab states. Israel owes its creation, continuous territorial expansion, and uninterrupted proliferation of arms to these wars. The war of 1948 transformed the certificate for Israel's creation into a historic fact and significantly expanded her territorial limits. The tripartite aggression of 1956 opened the Gulf of Aqaba to Israeli shipping. Finally the June, 1967, war—in addition to providing further testimony of Israel's military might—clearly unveiled Israel's territorial aspirations. Thus, the utopian assumption of a general desire for peace is a platitude which disguises the reality of the Arab-Israeli conflict: war has been inseparable from the creation and the continued expansion of Israel.

Until the Israelis agree to abandon their expansionist policies and begin to comply with international exhortations—based not on the illusion of omnipotence, but on what is feasible—the conflict will continue to be an "irresistible force colliding with an immovable object;" for, as it stands, the maximum offers of one side are less than, the minimum demands of the other. David Ben Gurion warns:

> In every conflict, there comes a time when to settle is more important than to get everything you want . . . and the time has come to settle. [46]

Concepts with global values such as peace, security, and stability are respected, due to their moral and ideological appeal. However, what passes for a rational definition of security in actuality often goes beyond mere self-preservation. "The quest for security," in the words of Arnold Wolfers, "points beyond mere maintenance and defense. It can become so ambitious as to transform itself into a goal of unlimited self-extension." [47] Thus, in the name of "security," Israel has gradually reinforced her image as *the enemy* to her neighbors.

[44] *Dept. of State Bulletin*, Vol. LXII, No. 1598, February 9, 1970.
[45] Lenin, *Collected Works* (English translation), XVIII, p. 264.
[46] *The Saturday Review, op. cit.*, p. 16.
[47] Quoted in Samuel Sharp, *op. cit.*, p.32.

## APPENDIX
## TEXT OF RESOLUTION*

The Security Council,

Expressing its continuing concern with the grave situation in the Middle East,

Emphasizing the inadmissibility of the acquisition of territory by war and the need to work for a just and lasting peace in which every State in the area can live in security,

Emphasizing further that all Member States in their acceptance of the Charter of the United Nations have undertaken a commitment to act in accordance with Article 2 of the Charter,

1. Affirms that the fulfillment of Charter principles requires the establishment of a just and lasting peace in the Middle East which should include the application of both the following principles:

    (i) Withdrawal of Israeli armed forces from territories occupied in the recent conflict:

    (ii) Termination of all claims or states of belligerence and respect for and acknowledgement of the sovereignty, territorial integrity and political independence of every State in the area and their right to live in peace within secure and recognized boundaries free from threats or acts of force;

2. Affirms further the necessity

    (a) For guaranteeing freedom of navigation through international waterways in the area;

    (b) For achieving a just settlement of the refugee problem;

    (c) For guaranteeing the territorial inviolability and political independence of every State in the area, through measures including the establishment of demilitarized zones;

3. Requests the Secretary-General to designate a Special Representative to proceed to the Middle East to establish and maintain contacts with the States concerned in order to promote agreement and assist efforts to achieve a peaceful and accepted settlement in accordance with the provisions and principles in this resolution;**

4. Requests the Secretary-General to report to the Security Council on the progress of the efforts of the Special Representative as soon as possible.

---

*U.N. doc. S/RES/242 (1967) (S/8247), adopted unanimously on Nov. 22.
**On Nov. 23 the Secretary-General announced the designation of Gunnar Jarring, Swedish Ambassàdor to the Soviet Union, as his special representative.

# Selected Bibliography

Abdulla, Ahmed. *The Middle East Crisis: Causes and Consequences: A Study in Retrospect.* Karachi: Tanzeem Publications, 1967.

Abu-Lughod, Ibrahim. *The Arab-Israeli Confrontation of June 1967: An Arab Perspective.* Evanston, Ill.: Northwestern University Press, 1970

al-Sayegh, Anis. *The Struggle Goes On.* Beirut: The Palestine Research Center, 1969.

Anner, Ze'ev, and Alkone, Yoseph, eds. *The War 1967.* Tel Aviv, 1967.

Aron, Raymond. *DeGaulle, Israel and the Jews.* Translated by John Sturrock. New York: Praeger, 1969.

Aruri, Naseer, ed. *The Palestinian Resistance to Israeli Occupation.* Wilmette, Ill.: The Medina University Press International, 1970.

Associated Press. *Lightning Out of Israel: The Six-Day War in the Middle East.* New York: The Associated Press, 1967.

Avnery, Uri. *Israel Without Zionists.* New York: Macmillan, 1968.

Bashan, Raphael. *The Victory: The Six-Day War of 1967.* Edited by O. Zmora. Chicago: Quadrangle, 1968.

Bell, J. Bowyer. *The Long War: Israel and the Arabs since 1946.* Englewood Cliffs, N.J.: Prentice-Hall, 1969.

Belyayev, I., Kolesnichenko, T., and Primakov, Y. *The "Dove" Has Been Released.* Washington: Joint Publication Research Service, 1968.

Benson, Alex, ed. *The 48-Hour War: The Arab-Israeli Conflict.* New York: 1967.

Bovis, H. Eugene. *The Jerusalem Question: 1917-1968.* Stanford: Hoover Institution Press, 1971.

Boyd, James. *United Nations Peace-Keeping Operations: A Military and Political Appraisal.* New York: Praeger, 1971.

Brown, Neville, et al. *Has Israel Really Won?* London: Fabian Society, 1967.

Byford-Jones, W. *The Lightning War: The Israeli-Arab Conflict.* Indianapolis: Bobbs-Merrill, 1968.

Cattan, Henry. *Palestine, The Arabs and Israel.* London: Longmans, 1969.

Chace, James, ed. *Conflict in the Middle East.* New York: H. W. Wilson, 1968.

Chesnoff, Richard; Klein, Edward; and Littell, Robert. *If Israel Lost the War.* New York: Coward-McCann, 1969.

Churchill, Randolph S., and Churchill, Winston S. *The Six-Day War.* Boston: Hoguhton Miflin, 1967.

Copeland, Miles. *The Game of Nations.* New York: Simon & Schuster, 1969.

Dagan, Avigdor. *Moscow and Jerusalem.* New York: Abelard-Schuman, 1970.

Dayan, David. *Strike First!* Translated by Dov Ben-Abba. New York: Pitman, 1968.

Dayan, Major-General Moshe. *Diary of the Sinai Campaign.* New York: Harper & Row, 1969.

Dayan, Yael. *Israel Journal: June 1967.* New York: McGraw-Hill, 1967.

———. *A Soldier's Diary: Sinai, 1967.* London: Weidenfeld & Nicholson, 1967.

Dodd, Peter, and Barakat, Halim. *River Without Bridges: A Study of the Exodus of the 1967 Palestinian Arab Refugees.* Beirut: Institute for Palestine Studies, 1968.

Donovan, Robert J. *Six Days in June (June 5-10, 1967): Israel's Fight for Survival.* New York: New American Library, 1967.

Douglas-Home, Charles. *The Arabs and Israel.* London: Bodley Head, 1968.

Draper, Theodore. *Israel and World Politics: Roots of the Third Arab-Israeli War.* New York: Viking, 1968.

Elon, Amos. *The Israelis: Founders and Sons.* New York: Holt, Rinehart & Winston, 1971.

Ered, E., *et al. Israel at War.* New York: Valentine, 1967.

Fuldheim, Dorothy. *Where Were the Arabs?* Cleveland: World Publishing Company, 1967.

Gervasi, Frank. *The Case for Israel.* New York: Viking, 1967.

Glubb, Sir John Bagot. *The Middle East Crisis: A Personal Interpretation.* London: Hodder & Stoughton, 1967.

Gruber, Ruth. *Israel on the Seventh Day.* New York: Hill & Wang, 1968.

Hadawi, Sami. *The Arab-Israeli Conflict (Cause and Effect).* Beirut: Institute for Palestine Studies, 1967.

———. *Bitter Harvest: Palestine Between 1914-1967.* New York: New World Press, 1967.

———. *Palestine in Focus*. Beirut: Institute for Plaestine Studies, 1968.

Howard, Michael, and Hunter, Robert. *Israel and the Arab World: The Crisis of 1967*. Adelphi Papers, no. 41. London: Institute for Strategic Studies, October, 1967.

Kanovsky, Eliyahu. *The Economic Impact of the Six-Day War: Israel, the Occupied Territories, Egypt, Jordan*. New York: Praeger, 1970.

Katz, Samuel. *Days of Fire*. New York: Doubleday, 1968.

Keesing's Research Report. *The Arab-Israeli Conflict: The 1967 Campaign*. New York: Scribner's, 1968.

Khadduri, Majdia, ed. *The Arab-Israeli Impasse: Expressions of Moderate Viewpoints on the Arab-Israeli Conflict by Well-Known Western Writers*. Washington: Robert D. Luce, 1969.

Khouri, Fred J. *The Arab-Israeli Dilemma*. Syracuse, N.Y.: Syracuse University Press, 1968.

Kimche, David, and Bawley, Dan. *The Sandstorm: The Arab-Israeli War of June, 1967: Prelude and Aftermath*. New York: Stein & Day, 1968.

Kishon, Ephraim, and Dosh, K. *So Sorry We Won*. New York: Bloch, 1968.

Kosut, Hal, ed. *Israel and the Arabs: The June 1967 War*. New York: Facts on File, Interim History, 1968.

Lall, Arthur. *The UN and the Middle-East Crisis, 1967*. New York: Columbia University Press, 1968.

Landau, Jacob M. *The Arabs in Israel, A Political Study*. New York: Oxford Unitversity Press, 1969.

Laqueur, Walter Z. *The Road to Jerusalem: The Origins of the Arab-Israeli Conflict, 1967*. New York: Macmillan, 1968.

Love, Kenneth. *Suez: The Twice-Fought War*. New York: McGraw-Hill, 1969.

MacLeish, Roderick. *The Sun Stood Still*. London: Macdonald, 1967.

Marshall, S. L. A. *Swift Sword: The Historical Record of Israel's Victory, June, 1967*. New York: American Heritage, 1967.

Nutting, Anthony. *No End of a Lesson: The Inside Story of the Suez Crisis*. New York: Potter, 1967.

*Palestine War 1967*. New York: New World Press, 1967.

Peretz, Don; Wilson, Evan; and Ward, Richard J. *A Palestine Entity?* Washington, D.C.: The Middle East Institute, 1970.

Reich, Bernard. *Background of the June War.* McLean, Va.: Research Analysis Corp., 1968.

Reisman, Michael. *The Art of the Possible.* Princeton, N.J.: Princeton University Press, 1970.

Rodinson, Maxime. *Israel and the Arabs.* Translated by Michael Perl. London: Pequin, 1968.

Safran, Nadav. *From War to War: The Arab-Israeli Confrontation, 1948-1967.* New York: Pegasus, 1969.

Saleeby, Samir S. *The Palestine Problem.* London: Institute of International Studies, 1970.

Shapira, Abraham. *The Seventh Day: Soldiers' Talk about the Six-Day War.* New York: Scribner's, 1971.

Sharabi, Hisham B. *Palestine and Israel: The Lethal Dilemma.* New York: Pegasus, 1969.

Skousen, Willard C. *Fantastic Victory: Israel's Rendezvous with Victory.* Salt Lake City: Bookcraft, 1967.

Stock, Ernest. *Israel on the Road to Sinai, 1949-1956, with a Sequel on the Six-Day War, 1967.* Ithaca, N.Y.: Cornell University Press, 1967.

Sykes, Christopher. *Crossroads to Israel.* London: Collins, 1965.

Teveth, Shabtai. *The Tanks of Tammuz.* New York: Viking, 1969.

Thomas, Hugh. *Suez.* New York: Harper & Row, 1967.

Vance, Vick, and Laver, Pierre. *Hussein of Jordan: My War With Israel.* New York: Morrow, 1969.

Velie, Lester. *Countdown in the Holy Land.* New York: Funk & Wagnalls, 1969.

Weinstock, Nathan. *Le Sionisme Contre Israel.* Paris: Maspero, 1969.

Werstein, Irving. *All the Furious Battles: The Saga of Israel's Army.* New York: Meredith Press, 1969.

Young, Peter. *The Israel Campaign 1967.* London: Kimber, 1967.

Elias Sam'o
is assistant professor of political science
Central Michigan University


This book provides
what every other book lacks — a balanced perspective
on the Middle East Conflict.


Contributors include
  Sharabi, Yost, Flapan, Kosygin, Deutscher and U Thant


Foreword by Eqbal Ahmad


Other publications:
The Arab-Americans: Studies in Assimilation
Palestinian Resistance to Israeli Occupation
The Unholy War: Israel and Palestine
The Arab World: From Nationalism to Revolution


cover design by L